SPRING,
HEAT, RAINS

SPRING, HEAT, RAINS

A South Indian Diary

David Shulman

THE UNIVERSITY OF CHICAGO PRESS

Chicago and London

DAVID SHULMAN is the Renée Lang Professor of Humanistic Studies in the Departments of Comparative Religion and Indian Studies at the Hebrew University of Jerusalem. He is the author, coauthor, or translator of nineteen books, including *The Hungry God: Hindu Tales of Filicide and Devotion* (1993) and *Dark Hope: Working for Peace in Israel and Palestine* (2007), both published by the University of Chicago Press.

THE UNIVERSITY OF CHICAGO PRESS, Chicago 60637
THE UNIVERSITY OF CHICAGO PRESS, Ltd., London

Printed in the United States of America

18 17 16 15 14 13 12 11 10 09   1 2 3 4 5

ISBN-13: 978-0-226-75576-2 (cloth)

ISBN-10: 0-226-75576-2 (cloth)

Library of Congress Cataloging-in-Publication Data

Shulman, David Dean, 1949–
Spring, heat, rains : a South Indian diary / David Shulman.
p. cm.
Includes bibliographical references.
ISBN-13: 978-0-226-75576-2 (hardcover : alk. paper)
ISBN-10: 0-226-75576-2 (hardcover : alk. paper)
1. Andhra Pradesh (India)—Description and travel.
2. Andhra Pradesh (India)—Civilization. 3. Shulman, David Dean, 1949–
—Travel—India—Andhra Pradesh. I. Title.
DS485.A552S58 2009
915.4'8404532—dc22

2008012647

⊗ The paper used in this publication meets the minimum requirements of the American National Standard for Information Sciences—Permanence of Paper for Printed Library Materials, ANSI Z39.48-1992.

For Patanjali Sastry and Smile

ŏkka tallik' ŏppan udayambu bŏndina
bāndhavambukaṇṭe bahuguṇamula
vasudhan ĕnni cūḍa vāg-jāta-bāndhavamb'
adhikam' aṇḍru cūvey āryul' ĕlla

Contents

Preface

Private, raw, and fragmentary, with the disorder of daily thought and feeling rampant throughout, a diary, by its very nature, seems an unlikely candidate for public distribution. It is also inevitably marked by the arbitrary nature of time itself. Why these particular seven months? Why these days or hours? A ragtag potpourri of the unfinished: is there any reason to inflict it on a reader other than the writer him- or herself? And who am I to inflict it anyway, half-baked scholar that I am, on a short sabbatical in Andhra Pradesh, with nothing very gripping to report beyond my endless struggle with the language and a few startling texts I happened upon? 2006 was a year like other years: first it was hot in Rajahmundry, then hotter; then it rained, the Godavari flooded, many dozens of villages were submerged; then the rains subsided. I was there only for three seasons of about two months each: spring, hot season, monsoon. Too short a time, alas.

Yet fragments have their own odd integrity, and sometimes a raw thought is more alive than a polished one. "One strong thought is enough / if you think it through," the early twentieth-century Telugu poet Dasu Sriramulu believed; but there are other modes of thinking, too, such as the incipient or potential insight that might or might not have a future. I'm not sure I don't prefer these, at least at certain moments when the quality of the light and the taste of the air and the sounds from the street rightly demand attention. Friends who saw some of the entries urged me to set them down in a book, an almost-book, and at some point during my stay in India I began to see and feel as if I were sharing it all with someone, telling them, as I tell myself, what has turned up on the immediate horizon, and singing the poems. I came to enjoy the rare, isolated moments of writing—usually in early morning, before dawn, as I would try to recall the intensities of the previous day. The caprice of memory intrigued me; the sheer physicality of daily experience overwhelmed the words I was reading and hearing; thought itself turned creamy and dusty, and night after night there were many vivid and elusive dreams. I tried to capture some of this, and find the links, as I wrote to myself in the half-light before sunrise.

Looking back, I see this diary records the restlessness that rules me, so the landscapes shift like the languages and the texts; I will do my best to explain (scattered pages, set in italics, offer background information and attempt to frame several of the journeys). Still, there was a sort of center. I was happy there; at many moments, I felt that I, too, could rest. Something unexpected happened: the gnawing sense that the real, or the true, or the truly intense and satisfying, lie elsewhere, always elsewhere, somewhere over the horizon, in yet another language or location or set of relations—this familiar hunger abated. I was, you might say, "healed" for a while, probably by Telugu poetry, the strongest potion known to human beings. In some ways, it felt like living out a sustained meditation, a reflection on the everyday textures of life in one corner—not a minor one—of Andhra today, partly in the light of the textures of life in Andhra five hundred years ago, as the poems describe them. These two tracks ran together in my mind, and so they run together in these pages, too. In particular, two great texts are woven into the diary entries, for I, in a sense, inhabited these poems more or less continuously throughout the months in Rajahmundry: Pĕddana's sixteenth-century *Story of Man*, perhaps the acme of classical Telugu poetry; and Śrīharsha's Sanskrit *Naishadhīya*, which tells the story of the bewildered lover Nala and his ever-lucid bride, Damayanti (and the Telugu and Tamil reworkings of Śrīharsha's original). These poems provided a mythic framing for my nights and days.

How did I happen to find myself in Rajahmundry in the early spring of 2006? It's a good question. The easiest answer would be: the river called me. She—the Godavari—is imperious, also infinitely seductive; Rajahmundry is her town. When I last saw her, in the year 2000, she exacted a promise that I would return. There are, of course, more external answers. I teach Sanskrit and other South Asian matters at the Hebrew University in Jerusalem. I come to India often. I was first trained in Tamil (by John Marr, at the School of Oriental and African Languages in London, in the early 1970s), and for years I would go to the Tamil country for longer or shorter stays—mostly in Madras and Tanjavur. Tamil was, and is, one of the active centers of my life. But then I had wanted to learn another South Indian language, and in 1982 I accepted Velcheru Narayana Rao's vigorous invitation to come to Wisconsin to study Telugu with him. Little by little, charmed by the spell cast by Narayana Rao and by the glimpses I got of classical Telugu poetry, I drifted northward toward Andhra and its mysteries. I lived in Hyderabad and Visakhapatnam, and my tongue began, clumsily, to trickle and tumble in the Telugu way. Now it was time to find my way into the Telugu heartland, the vast delta where the Godavari and the Krishna rivers reach toward the sea. One could go farther back, searching for the karmic traces, back to the small town in northeastern Iowa where I was born and grew up, to my early years in Israel, to my first love—Persian poetry—and Iran, to the golden Mittenwald violin I used to play. . . . Most of that is now as distant as a former life. I was alone in Rajahmundry, but my wife, Eileen; our three sons, Tari, Misha, and Edan; and our two grandsons, Nahar and Inbal, turn up in the diary from time to time.

On Andhra and Telugu

Some 80 million people speak Telugu, the language of the Indian state of Andhra Pradesh, situated to the south of the Vindhya Mountains and south of the states of Madhya Pradesh, Chhattisgarh, and Orissa. Historically, the name *Andhra* referred primarily to the deltaic coastland where the two great rivers, Godavari and Krishna, both goddesses in their own right, pour into the Bay of Bengal. With the creation of the modern Indian states after Independence, Andhra lent its name to the vast new political unit that took Hyderabad as its capital and that reached south to the borders of the Tamil country, toward the major city of Madras or Chennai.

Andhra is very much a part of South India, its language a sister to

Tamil, Kannada, and Malayalam, its customs, kinship system, caste structure, culinary ethos, and traditional institutions all recognizably part of the South Indian cultural complex. At the same time, there is a distinctiveness about Andhra history and a highly specific flavor to Telugu, in all its expressive modes—also a mystery of sorts, for this classical tradition has been little studied outside Andhra. One stable feature evident throughout the last thousand years of Andhra history—and relevant to the diary that follows—is the astonishing organization of an entire civilization around poetry and the highly charged poetic word as the primary vehicles for shared meaning and praxis.

Modern Andhra Pradesh is conventionally divided into three parts. There is the fertile delta of the two great rivers to the east in East and West Godavari and Krishna districts—the breadbasket of Andhra (and beyond). Yet a mere century and a half ago, much of this region was still entirely wild and uncultivated; it was only with the creation of the great Godavari Anicut and Barrage by Sir Arthur Thomas Cotton (1803–1899) that the settlement patterns we see today became possible.

To the west we find the dry, elevated, rocky plateau known as Telangana, with Hyderabad as its historical center. Before Independence, most of Telangana was ruled by the Nizam, in theory subordinate to the Mughal sultan in Delhi, from Hyderabad; the Asaf Jahi dynasty produced seven Nizams (the full title is Nizam al-Mulk) beginning in 1720 and coming to an end with the assimilation of the Asaf Jahi state into independent India (1948). The absorption by Andhra Pradesh of Hyderabad as its new capital (1956) marked the final fusion of dry land and delta into a single political framework. Telangana Telugu, in its various dialects, is distinct lexically and to some extent morphologically from the language of the coast.

Finally, to the south of Telangana, on the borders of modern Tamil Nadu and Karnataka, we find the "King's Domain," Rayalasima, a mixed ecological zone that is relatively desiccated today but was far more fertile and apparently densely populated during the sixteenth and seventeenth centuries. Ralayasima offers, among other cultural treasures, the famous boundary shrines of Tirupati, Kalahasti, and Lepakshi.

Telugu poetry as we know it begins, traditionally, with Nannayya, the court poet of the Eastern Chalukya king Rājarājanarendra, who ruled in Rajahmundry from 1018 to 1061. So the starting moment of classical Telugu culture belongs to the Godavari Delta and the Eastern Chalukya state system. Historically, however, it was the continuous interchange between Telangana and the fertile coast that held the key to cultural evolution. One particularly creative moment in terms of institutional innovation is associated with the Telangana-based Kākatiya dynasty (1000–1326), with their capital at Warrangal, some 150 kilometers northeast of Hyderabad. These rugged warriors pioneered an extensive system of tank-based irrigation; they also seem to have been the first to bind their widely scattered subordinates into a dense network based on personal loyalty to the king—what was later referred to as the *nāyankāra* model of state building. The Kākatiya example of a warrior state built on strong personal ties to the ruler was consolidated in the mature imperial structure of Vijayanagara (today's Hampi in Karnataka), which by the first half of the sixteenth century brought nearly all of South India, with the exception of Kerala, into a single political system. Vijayanagara was the last of the large-scale precolonial South Indian states.

The imperial moment at Vijayanagara is always associated with the name of the poet-king Krishṇarāya or Krishṇadevarāya (r. 1509–29), author of a major work known as the *Āmukta-mālyada* (which tells the story of the Tamil poetess and devotee Andal, among other topics). This brief period is usually seen as the golden age of Telugu poetry. A series of major poets—Krishṇadevarāya, Allasāni Pĕddana, Mukku Timmanna, Tenāli Rāmakrishṇa, Bhaṭṭumūrtti, and others—produced massive works, in profound conversation with one another, at the royal capital or, after the fall of Vijayanagara in 1565 to an alliance of Muslim sultanates, in various regional centers that continued the imperial tradition on a smaller scale. Such works are now called *prabandha*s, and all of them are *kāvya* or *mahā-kāvya*—long narrative poems in an elevated, complex, courtly style. At least one of the major *prabandha*s, Allasāni Pĕddana's *Manu-caritramu* (Story of Man), which figures in this diary, is arguably a kind of protonovel, perhaps the first such work in South India.

A final word on the miraculous properties of the Telugu language. Telugu is classified as Dravidian, a family of so-called agglutinative languages that work mainly by the cumulative addition of suffixes to nominal and verbal roots. Like all Indian languages, it has an amazingly complex and precise modal and aspectual system carried by the verb. It is spoken with remarkable speed—linguists have shown that South Indians utter, on average, more syllables per second than any other attested speakers of known human languages—and sometimes gives the impression of a bubbling or cascading stream. Many have remarked on the natural musicality of Telugu speech; perhaps not by chance, Telugu is the main language of classical South Indian musical compositions and has been so at least since the eleventh century (when a Tamil poet, Cayankŏṇṭār, noted the stable link between music and the language of Andhra). Classical Telugu poets have exploited this inherently mellifluous quality of the language beautifully, a beauty they enhanced and intensified by the complex metrical and other phono-aesthetic techniques available to them, as codified by the medieval grammarians and poeticians. Often the semantic and syntactic properties of a verse cut across the fixed metrical scheme that contains them; the result is a strangely hypnotic, contrapuntal complexity of tremendous aural power—a musical experience unlike any other, perhaps transcending *meaning* in any of the usual senses of the word. Such effects defy translation, yet I have spent no small part of my life, together with Velcheru Narayana Rao, in the quixotic attempt to translate Telugu poems into English and Hebrew. The following pages offer a somewhat random sample. One should bear in mind that Telugu poetry is never recited, as in English, but almost invariably sung—sometimes in a traditional melodic scale, at other times in a raga or musical mode of the singer's choice.

On Transliteration

In the interests of aesthetic economy, diacritics have been kept to a minimum. Names of texts and characters in classical Telugu, Sanskrit, or Tamil are marked with diacritics on their first appearance only—and again in the glossary. The palatal sibilant appears as *ś* throughout. The retroflex sibilant appears as *sh*, and vocalic *ṛ* as *ri*. Feminine names ending in long *ā* or *ī* in Sanskrit are regularly shortened in Telugu. Homorganic nasals are unmarked. Modern Telugu names appear as the individuals in question spelled them or in standard transliteration, without diacritics. Place-names follow the standard map forms, although at times I have retained the older names, with their implicit ontologies: Madras, Bombay, Rajahmundry.

Acknowledgments

I am grateful to the following individuals and publishers for their permission to reprint portions of text that first appeared in their pages: Martha Ann Selby, for her translation of *Gāthasaptasatī* 1.49, in Selby, *The Circle of Six Seasons* (New Delhi: Penguin Books, 2003), 22; University of California Press, for an excerpt from Yehuda Amichai, "Yerushalayim 1967," in *The Selected Poetry of Yehuda Amichai*, edited by Chana Bloch and Stephen Mitchell (Berkeley and Los Angeles: University of California Press, 1996), © 1996 The Regents of the University of California, and for excerpts from *Classical Telugu Poetry: An Anthology*, translated and edited and with an introduction by Velcheru Narayana Rao and David Shulman (Berkeley and Los Angeles: University of California Press, 2002), © 2002 The Regents of the University of California; Oxford University Press, for an excerpt from Annamayya. *God on the Hill: Temple Poems from Tirupati*, translated by Velcheru Narayana Rao and David Shulman (New York: Oxford University Press, 2005), by permission of Oxford University Press Inc.; Namadi Sridhar, for his poem "Purāgānam," self-published by the author 1997, translated for the present text by David Shulman and Sashi Shekhar; Gaali Nasara Reddi, for two poems, "Untitled" and "Dinântam," originally published in the local journals *Santakaalu* and *Vaarta Adivaram* ca. 2005, translated for the present text by David Shulman and Sashi Shekhar; K. Siva Reddi, for *Varsham Varsham* (Hyderabad: published by the author, 2004); Smile, for excerpts from his book of poetry, *Okhade* (Vijayawada: Kavitvam Pracuranalu, 1990); the heirs of Ismayil, for *Kavitalu* (Kakinada: Twinkle Publishers, 1989); and Sugambabu, for two poems from *Rekhalu*, self-published by the author 2006. Unless otherwise specified, translations are my own.

Let me thank my dear Rajahmundry friends: Talavajjhala Patanjali Sastri, Jaya and Aparna; Smile and Yasmin; M. C. Kanakaiah; Rentala Sri Venkatesvara Rao; Endluri Sudhakar; Satish, Nirmala and Satyanarayana. Velcheru Narayana Rao put in place this dense web of affection. My love and gratitude to Sashi, Sumalini, Jyotirmaya, Akundy Anand, Vimala, Shyam, Jitendra and Jhansi, in Hyderabad; Tataji, Hema, Teja, Krishnayya, Kamesvari, Cidananda Rao, and Mitravinda in Vizag; Bairagi Nayudu and Satyanarayana in Vizianagaram; and the hundreds of others who graciously put up with my Telugu and, day after day, unstintingly shared their world.

My debt to Elizabeth Branch Dyson, who knew how to make this diary into a book, and to Sandra Hazel, both at the University of Chicago Press, is beyond measure.

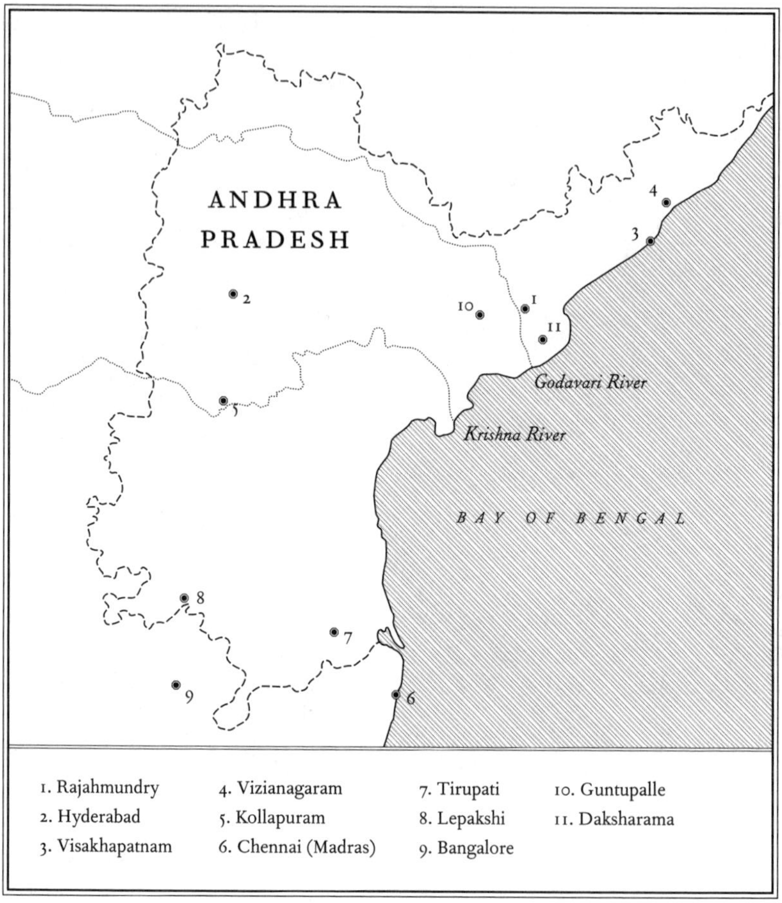
ANDHRA
PRADESH
Godavari River
Krishna River
BAY OF BENGAL
1. Rajahmundry
2. Hyderabad
3. Visakhapatnam
4. Vizianagaram
5. Kollapuram
6. Chennai (Madras)
7. Tirupati
8. Lepakshi
9. Bangalore
10. Guntupalle
11. Daksharama

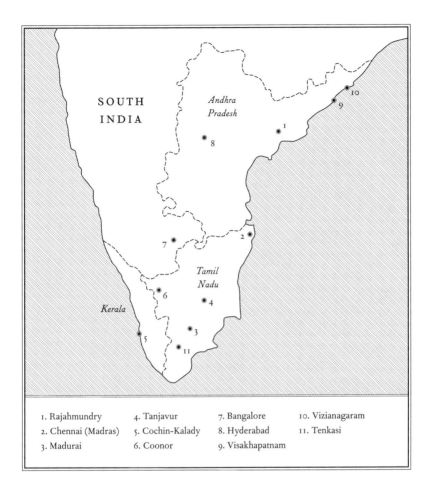

1. Rajahmundry
2. Chennai (Madras)
3. Madurai
4. Tanjavur
5. Cochin-Kalady
6. Coonor
7. Bangalore
8. Hyderabad
9. Visakhapatnam
10. Vizianagaram
11. Tenkasi

VASANTA, SPRING

February 5, 2006: East Coast Express

Rocks. Goats. Dry shrubs. Buffaloes. Thorns. A fallen tamarind tree. Tents. Red bricks in heaps. White graves, flashes in a brown-yellow universe. A motorbike on an earthen path. An auto rickshaw, yellow and black. Palm trees. Bicycles. Orange saris. A white flower in her hair. Eyes.

Mahbubabad. The morning ride across Telangana, the high plateau east of Hyderabad, seems synchronized with my need for a slow reentry. "Time" again presents itself as a question: does it exist, all of it, all past-future, as a dusty, viscous elastic casing for the mind, twisted into the mind? Each of us gets to see a small segment buried in one of the twists. For example, I have been offered the second half of the so-called twentieth century—an arbitrary boundary, after all—and on for some ways into the twenty-first. One could also run the segment backward. There is even knowledge, however uncertain, of the part that supposedly lies ahead. In fact, one can see it from the train window. Yellow and brown, flashes of white, a grave.

Nampalli station in central Hyderabad was chaotic, and no one could tell me what platform to look for. I fought my way with heavy bags, and the inevitable clumsy bottle of mineral water, up the steps and over the bridge through a vast crowd of disembarking passengers. On the coach, miraculously, pasted beside the window: David Dean Sul, age 57, berth 38.

It is early February, I am back in India. As always, being free, utterly free, feels oppressive, even sad. I can barely speak. Language is stuck in some recess of my mind, mostly inaccessible, a congealed form of forgetting, or of resistance. There is the huge effort ahead.

Slowly the landscape changes. Winter rice. Green shoots. More black rocks. The endless sky. Herons wade gingerly in a shallow pond. White over gray-blue. Lotus pads. Thorns. Boulders. Threshers. Winnowers. Brown haystacks. A river, clinging to existence. A bridge. A ridge. Two women sit, sifting grain in the sun, on the parallel track. A huge yellow sign reads Papatapalli. A boy, naked but for his shirt. The wind in the grass. Five more buffaloes. Thatched, round huts in the field. A serrated line of distant hills, orange-red as they come closer. The subtle taste of happiness. To celebrate, I take out the *Naishadhiya*, to make a beginning. I will be living for these months with, or maybe in, this book, Śrīharsha's Sanskrit masterpiece on the life of Nala, an Indian Everyman (*nara*). Nala is chosen by the beautiful Damayanti, only to abandon her as he wanders, transformed into an alien self. Like Nala, I am, perhaps, disguised, or lost; but I am heading, maybe backward, to some known home.

Rajahmundry, Anand Regency Hotel

8:45 PM

The first sight of the town, as we cross the vast bridge into East Godavari district, is only partly astonishing: a jumble of uneven houses, fading pastels, grime-laced facades, alleys, spilling up from the riverbank. It is the magic hour when the light turns molten. Dust and gold. Of course it is the river itself that takes away one's breath; probably the river, this wide sluggish sweep of brown and green, is the real Rajahmundry, the buildings and streets no more than an appendage. Arrival is the usual flurry, the usual question—why am I here, of all possible "heres"? The rickshaw drivers outside the station, well aware of their advantage, extort the ridiculous fee of fifty rupees to the hotel. I clamber in, suddenly exhausted, quizzical, a little raw. I remember these streets from the last time, in 2000, when I came to the Gautami Library, one of the major collections in Andhra Pradesh, in search of a rare Telugu book. I was lucky that time: hidden in the Gautami's dusty shelves amid other rare, nineteenth-century editions was the arcane text I needed. And a few weeks before, there was a weekend here with Eileen and Edan at the Mahalakshmi Hotel, on the riverbank, smothered in the stench of the Andhra Pradesh Paper Mills upstream.

I check in to the Anand Regency. Six years ago it was polished, slick, and new; proud to be "the only star hotel" in Rajahmundry. The new millennium had brought this self-conscious fragment of the outside world to the city of Nannayya, the first Telugu poet. A turbaned doorman in white and green still stands at the entrance. But six years have taken their toll, or perhaps it is only the clammy air of the delta; in any case, the polish is largely gone, though the pretense is still in place. I unpack and peer out the window at the white roofs of Danavayipeta as the sun sets, a pale red halo traced through the dust. The roof closest to me has a vast carpet of red chilies that have been set out to dry.

Before dark there is time for my first walk. But why here? It is hard to shake the strange sense of an arbitrary fate, or was it merely a romantic choice that came out of a fantasy of poets and scholars on the bank of the Godavari? The dense stacked alleys remind me of Bashir Bagh, where I lived (happily) in Hyderabad in 1998–99. It is hot and sticky and I am deeply alone, even alone to myself, lost, murky, unstuck.

Dinner at the hotel brings some new friends. A tall, contemplative waiter named Sharif says he reads philosophy every afternoon in the Gautami Library. What is my philosophy? I tell him it is too early to say. I am fifty-seven years old, struggling with simple Telugu sentences. Give me some time, I say, I will come back and we will discuss the great questions. Bitter-gourd curry, *kākara-kāya*, my favorite, picks up my spirits; or perhaps it is the subtle, only partly conscious sense of coming to rest. I have been telling my friends in Israel, who ask me what I am planning on doing in Rajahmundry for seven months, that I need to reinvent myself. Last week Yair reminded me that when, some years ago, before my last long trip, he asked me what I was planning to do in India, I answered that one should never go to India with a plan.

February 6

Is it possible that I came to India only five days ago? Opening this page, I record the date and suddenly cannot remember the year. Each hour has its specific gravity, its physical intensity. My eyes, my hands, my ears, my memory: all are furiously at work. I try to think it through: by now, it seems to me, it must be at least 2008. Some shred of the Mediterranean world surfaces; no, it is, at least in theory, somewhere, elsewhere, still 2006.

First things first. I want to see the town, the Godavari River, the *revus* or ghats on the riverbank leading down to the water. The morning is cool, gray-green-white. I take an auto rickshaw to Pushkaraa Revu, walk along the river, watch the pilgrims climb down the stone steps to bathe, watch the Godavari receive them with gentle attentiveness, a liquid caress, as a regal goddess should. I revisit the Mahalakshmi Hotel—now strikingly reborn, almost glowing under a new management. They take me to meet the manager, Ravisundar, who, like most people I encounter, wants to know all about the Jewish god, before all else. I try to explain. He is, I say, *nirguṇa*—without qualities, without form; in other words, a philosophical abstraction. This is about as close as I can get. The word, vaguely philosophical in Telugu or Sanskrit, means something to Ravisundar, who nonetheless appears skeptical. With the river, a living goddess, at once beneficent and capricious, flowing outside his office, he probably thinks that only a madman would bother to worship an abstraction. In fact, I completely agree. This theological excursus now concluded, Ravisundar offers to let me stay at the hotel at a reasonable rate for all these coming months. It seems possible to me, one conceivable solution, and of course there is the ravishing river always visible from the window; but first I will look for a flat somewhere in town.

In mild ecstasy, I walk uphill at Kotagummam, the old "passage into the fort" leading away from the riverbank, toward town. Nothing is left of the fort, or of the passage, but Rajahmundry tradition thinks that all the great medieval kings, Rajarajanarendra and his many successors, sat in state right here. Near the tacky white statue of Śiva-Dakshiṇāmūrti, the god in meditation, which occasionally has water—the Ganges—pouring through his hair, I turn into the small streets off the main pedestrian thoroughfare. I am roaming, fancy free. There is a cramped, densely stacked bookstore, I go in for a quick look; the old Kāśi-majjili stories, hair-raising tales of pilgrims to Benares in centuries past, have come out in a new, many-volume edition. When I have a flat, I'll come back to buy them. The owner, somewhat taken aback by the strange apparition that has descended upon him this morning—a Telugu-reading, Telugu-speaking white man—asks me in Telugu what place is my home. I don't hesitate: "Rajahmundry!"

February 7

My body seems to be seeking a new rhythm; I wake at five thirty, sleep again, dream of the toothache that tormented me before coming here, a lover who is concerned that I have to face it alone.

Heavy, I wake, wash, perform the morning ritual: a few minutes on the roof, taking in the city from this high vantage point, shortly after sunrise. The rooftops, white, gray, streaked with grime, partly hidden by the thick green clusters of palm, seem to be humming a barely audible morning *rāga*. Birdcalls, the bells on the bicycles, the constant backdrop of horns from the cars and rickshaws, the cries of the fruit vendors, the distant ring of a radio broadcasting a Sanskrit prayer to the waking god, mothers shouting at their children: all this is the *rāga* as it breaks through the surface to audibility. Fragments held by an unfamiliar *mūrcchanā* scale, rising, descending, binding these pieces together into something whole, with a few uncanny musical embellishments, *alankāra*s, added for good measure.

I call Smile, Narayana Rao's good friend; Narayana Rao has given me the number and told me to make the contact. I introduce myself, awkwardly, in my halting, bookish Telugu, which Smile naturally doesn't understand; suddenly he remembers: Narayana Rao has prepared him for my arrival. "I'm coming to your hotel now," he says. By eleven he is with me, a jocular, energized presence, a balding bon vivant, and every inch a poet. He speaks of Eluru and his student days, when Narayana Rao was his teacher at Eluru College—a young, charismatic, visionary teacher—and of other friends (the beloved Penmetsa Suryanarayana Raju), now gone. Smile's Telugu gives no quarter: it explodes into space like a geyser, and at this early moment I understand only some of it, marveling at the speed and richness. He is warm, welcoming, full of plans, excited. We will go, he says, to Daksharama, Bikkavolu,

Amaravati, Guntur, the famous sites of the delta within easy reach of Rajahmundry.

Hints of possible flats are filtering in. Anand, my good friend from Tirupati Gangamma days (1992–93), is now in Rajahmundry with a Yale project on AIDS in the Godavari Delta. He and his office manager, Satish, are starting to search for me. In the afternoon they take me to see two possible choices. The first, on Anam Venkatappa Rao Road, is in a large pink-orange complex, very reminiscent of our Vizag days six years ago. The apartment is clean, spacious, and characterless, and I can see at once that I don't want it. The second is a smaller place in a house on the edge of town, opening up to cashew groves and fields, rather isolated, as in a village. I like it.

After dark, Smile returns with Patanjali Sastry and Endluri Sudhakar. Patanjali Sastry—ravishing name—has a trim gray beard, a soft manner, dignified self-possession, deep eyes; he is a writer of short stories, a famous environmental activist, a cultivated man of letters; also the grandson of Talavajjhala Sivasankara Sastry, one of the luminaries of early twentieth-century Andhra, translator into Telugu of the Buddhist *Jātaka*s and the Sanskrit *Ocean of Story*, composer of Telugu operas. The family proudly traces its lineage to Talavajjhala Narayana Tirtha, the famous eighteenth-century author of *Śrīkrishṇa-līlā-taranginī*, a dance-drama sung entirely in Sanskrit. Narayana Tirtha traveled south from Andhra to the Tamil country, to a place called Varahur or Bhupatirajapuram; his tomb, or *samādhi*, is at Tiruppunturutti on the banks of the Kaveri, still a popular site of pilgrimage. Sanskrit and Telugu erudition were Patanjali Sastry's birthright, but he is also a Renaissance man, fully at home in European cultures—one of those Godavari Brahmins for whom the world has no boundaries, and nothing human is alien.

Sudhakar has brought two volumes of his poetry, one of them a beautiful bilingual edition; a well-known Dalit poet, he is a lecturer at the branch of Telugu University in Bommur. Full of vigor, with a forceful, lucid way of speaking. Hours pass in literary conversation, smoothed along by rather a lot of beer. I recite the opening to the Song of Songs in Hebrew and translate, certain that I am flattening out the magical words. Richness ebbs ands flows around me, too much for me, though I am eager, ready to learn, ready to plunge in. In the middle of it all Narayana Rao calls on my new cell phone. Language fails me; I manage only to say: "I'm happy."

February 8

I dream, oddly, of the Greek poem inscribed on the wall of the burial cave at Beit Guvrin, south of Jerusalem:

> Nothing else remains that I can do for you,
> or that will pleasure you.
> I am sleeping with someone else, but it is you
> I love, dearest to me of all.
> In the name of Aphrodite, I am happy about one thing,
> that your cloak has been left to me as a pledge.
> But I flee, I permit you
> expanses of freedom.
> Do anything you desire, do not strike the wall,
> it only makes noise.
> We will motion to each other, this will be
> the sign between us.

A woman, apparently, speaks to her dead lover. I carry this poem with me in my wallet. Often, when I read it out loud, people refuse to believe it was written two thousand years ago. Amiel sent me the original last year; the translation is faithful, even the "expanses of freedom."

In the dream I insist that my eyes are not yet awake. This seems accurate enough, and widely applicable, an image of my life. Then I am in class, the last meeting of our seminar; the students leave, one by one, like in the Haydn Farewell Symphony—before I can sum up and say goodbye. Another precise metaphor.

The flat by the paddy fields has vanished; various insuperable technicalities preclude this choice. Instead, I will move into a flat directly under Patanjali Sastry's office, in Vadrevunagar. I like the address: Door Number 86-6-3/4. It's a beautiful street at the edge of town, close to the National Highway, far from the Old Quarter and the river, with the scent and colors of Mylapore in the heart of old Madras, the one fixed, enduring point in my inner map. Rajahmundry is full of new flats, it is truly no problem to find one; a wave of new building has swept over the city. Mine has a bedroom, a kitchen (with three dabs of red-brown paint in one corner, an indication that the goddess is present), a small sitting space next to the kitchen, a *pūjā* room with somewhat ragged stickers showing various gods and gurus, a narrow entrance porch fenced in by an iron grill (to keep out the monkeys?), two bathrooms—one Western style, one Indian—and a spare room for guests. There are bookshelves carved into the wall, with Hyderabadi arches and medallions nonchalantly crowning the top level. This is India: light traces of beauty are routine. Plain surfaces are uninteresting, almost inhuman. I will, of course, have to buy furniture, cooking utensils, sheets. . . .

Anand joins me for a light dinner. We speak of East Godavari poets and scholars, of schools and literary salons, *sabhā*s, of Kakinada, near here, where he grew up—a place he loves. In the summer, a sea breeze flares up in the evening, and the city pours onto the promenade. As always, there are sudden vistas of vibrant intellectual production. The literary journals and presses of Kakinada were the arena of fierce battles among Telugu poets at the turn of the century. What does it mean to be "modern" in Telugu? To write free verse, to read T. S. Eliot, to reimagine Telugu prose? Must the past be slain to make way for the new? Is there such a thing as pure poetry, or is the poet, by nature, engaged in changing his world? Issues still largely unsettled. I must go to Kakinada soon.

February 9

Charles Malamoud has arrived from Paris, via Madras. It is his first trip to Andhra; he knows parts of South India well, but his special love is for the high mountains in the north, in Garhwal. Like nearly all genuine scholars, he is genuinely modest; a gentle man of exquisite taste and understated insight. Over a lunch of fiery Andhra curries, we speak of Russian writers—Platonov, Zamyatin—whom he knows deeply, in Russian. We walk the town, up and down, reach the river. Smile joins us, and we take a boat out to the nearest *tippa*, sand island. Many such islands crop up, often with simple huts of fishermen who live there, in the midst of the stream. Smile is full of happy memories: New Year's Eve, years ago, feasting with friends on the *tippa*; he can still taste the rum they drank. Godavari seems to welcome us, bearing us gently in the creamy light of this cloudy morning. "They say a sip of Godavari water cures all ills," Smile says, bemused, a modern man, a skeptic; he stretches out his cupped palm, dips into the brown stream, and slowly sips the water, grinning. The *revu*, with its steps leading down to the river, is full of pilgrims, pious Brahmins coming for their daily bath, hangers-on, impoverished priests from the tiny shrines to a mixed assortment of deities who rule, impassive, on a high ledge overlooking the water. Charles says: In India you need a multiplicity of hearts.

In the evening, an assembly of poets, *kavi-goshṭhi*, convenes at Smile's and Yasmine's to introduce me to some of the town's writers and scholars. (As far as I can see, nearly everyone in Rajahmundry, from the rickshaw drivers to the buffalo herders, has published at least one volume of poems and is only too eager to recite them to a receptive listener; those who don't write poetry have published collections of short stories.) I meet Salaka Raghunatha Sarma, who recites *Mahābhārata*—rich bass voice; measured, modulated speech; immense natural dignity. Rentala Sri Venkatesvara Rao, scholar and critic, a lecturer at the Arts College. M. C. Kanakaiah, a poet-scholar, also at the Arts College. Muppidi Prabhakara Ravu, a short-story writer. Anand, Patanjali Sastry, and a few more friends. All of them give me copies of their books, with florid signatures and dedications. I have a lot to read. I do my best to introduce Charles and explain his work on ancient sacrifice, though somehow the notion of a specialist in Vedic ritual seems exotic here among men who live the literary life with such exclusive passion. Eventually, exhausted, I lapse into frustrated silence. My tongue refuses to turn and twirl, as a Telugu tongue must. But I have found a teacher. I tell Kanakaiah that I want to read *Manu-caritramu*, the *Story of Man*, the classic sixteenth-century poem by Allasāni Pĕddana—would he come for a short lesson each day? He agrees at once. Classes will start in three days' time.

February 10

With Smile and Charles, by car, to Daksharama, stopping for sweets at the village of Kaja-Tapesvaram on the way. Kaja sweets, sticky and crisp, looped like bright orange pretzels, are known all over Andhra. I have visited Daksharama once before, in 1985, with Narayana Rao. Since then I have read Śrīnātha's *Bhīma-khaṇḍamu*, which tells the story of this shrine and its god, and written half a book about the temple. It will, perhaps, become part of the larger work on Śrīnātha that we have begun, Narayana Rao and I, if only we can find the time to meet and write.

We arrive at eleven, just before the temple closes for the midday break. We have to hurry. Will I ever get used to these Andhra temples, so utterly remote from the Tamil, Kaveri-delta mode? Tamil temples are generally well ordered, symmetrical, with clear progressions built into the pilgrim's route from the outer gates via the inner courtyards toward the god deep inside; and the stones are mostly light—flecked gray, pinkish beige, or a rich, fluid red-to-orange, as at Tanjavur. Daksharama is black, unbalanced, like a layer cake that has collapsed at some points. Hardly beautiful. Like many other Andhra temples, it is mostly uncanny, eerie, strange—hence its compelling strength. Another sort of beauty rests on asymmetry. An empty chair sits to the right of the main shrine to Bhīma-Nāyaka, the Fierce God, Śiva. Charles asks me: Is it a Buddhist chair? At Sanchi and elsewhere in the north, there are no direct depictions of the Buddha; in his place one finds his sandals or, at times, an empty throne. There is no doubt that this temple was originally a Buddhist site. The huge, two-story *linga*, Bhīma-Nāyaka—once a tall beige *āyaka* pillar such as one finds in many Buddhist sanctuaries—is wide open on every side; one could easily reach in to touch him. A mirror faces him; he can, he *must* see himself. If god fails to know himself, we fail with him.

These Andhra gods are strangely accessible, almost too close, like an overbearing uncle or a local village king; he may be king, but he belongs, like us, to the village. We know his family as well as the gossip lavished on it by generations: in a sense, this is what the *Bhīma-khaṇḍamu*, his canonical story, is all about. The great Śiva, "lord of the world," Viśvanātha, came down south from Benares and merged himself into this huge *linga* at Daksharama. If you have any doubt which is primary—the abstract and universal "lord of the world," whoever he may be, or the sheer physical reality of this tall local *linga* whom they call the Fierce God—then a quick circumambulation will resolve it. We circle around him twice, peeking through the rough stone windows that open directly onto the *linga* shrine. He seems glad to have us nearby. Might he even be a little lonely (or bored)? Is this, in any case, the fate of the fierce? The upper story of the sanctuary, like the rest of the temple, like so many old Andhra shrines, feels somehow unfinished, a little tacky, a disorderly confabulation of stone and tile. Outside, the god's wife Māṇikyâmba, Ruby Lady, stares at us from her pedestal with her silver eyes. Within the walled enclosure surrounding these gods there is a miniature stone model of the whole temple, another mirrorlike touch, as if the larger, expansive complex had sought to encapsulate itself in some small corner of itself where, complete and self-contained, it could come to rest.

The Saptagodavari Tank outside the walls—supposedly condensing within it all seven tributaries of the Godavari—looks much better this time than last, almost clean. Boys are splashing in the green-brown water. Simple slabs carved with images of snakes rest at the base of the huge temple tree; its branches are laden with wisps of thread, tied by pilgrims who have fulfilled their vows. A ferocious black Kāla-Bhairava, the boundary god of Benares who has followed the "lord of the world" all the way to this remote outpost, stands guard in his own shrine at the edge of the courtyard.

It is a frontier temple, I say to Charles; and Andhra, all of it, is frontier. Full of wilderness, a wild place, raw. A country of manly men and sturdy, active women. The dry uplands of Telangana impact on the greener world of the coast, with its great rivers; the interaction of these two ecosystems, together with the mixed zone of Rayalasima to the south, determined the history of Andhra as a whole. That much is simple. Historically, cultural innovation tended to come from Telangana, to be domesticated in the delta, then reexported to Telangana. But wilderness infuses all three regions, unlike the Tamil heartland. Like any frontier, Andhra toys with *objets trouvés*, whatever happened by, the flotsam and jetsam of ancient civilizations come to rest in this remote spot: so here, at Daksharama, we have the Buddhist memories, an overlay of Old Benares (the "lord of the world," the Black Bhairava, the beloved Ḍhuṇḍhi Vināyaka standing at the gate, and more), the clear remains of a solar cult, the snakes, the water, a proud line of courtesans, and the village goddesses whom Śrīnātha mentions—and Śrīnātha himself, the Daksharama poet, was the one who put all this together into a whole, who thus sang the temple into existence. In some sense the poet made this god. There was magic on his tongue. Things like that happen on the frontier.

* * *

At sunset we walk to Kambala Ceruvu, the "Pillars' Pond" in the heart of residential Rajahmundry, with its massive water fountain. Hundreds come in the evening to circumambulate the lake, and I assume I will often join them. It all reminds me, another uncanny moment, of childhood summers in Iowa—the cloying, humid heat, the miniaturization of life, all of life, with a few loose ends, the open horizon stretching in all directions from this one minute point. We speak of Ladakh, of the old road up from Srinagar; from the windows of the bus you can see the wrecks of earlier buses at the bottom of the ravines, an unsettling vision, to say the least. In Leh, the one real city in those high mountains, Charles tells me, he had the only true religious experience of his life. I am too shy to ask him what it was. Leh: a cold wind from Central Asia brushes the edges of my mind. I loved it there, the clogged alleys, the crystal light, the giddiness of height; as usual in a new place, I wanted to settle down, learn the language, enter deeply in. And here I am in sticky Rajahmundry with its palm trees and bubbling Telugu and meltdown gods. We circle the lake over and over, and it is as if there were ample space, a benevolent space, in this watery center of a small town in the Andhra Delta, for all the worlds Charles invokes—Leh, Garhwal, St. Petersburg, Paris, Jerusalem, the Vedic sacrificers whom he, more than anyone in this generation, has understood.

Already he admires the Andhra toughness, resuming my morning "lecture." Andhra, he says, is "rough but not harsh." An irresistible fascination—especially for someone familiar with the deep south. I was drawn to it, into it, without fully realizing the compulsion. Now it is too late. Large parts of me belong here, and I may even, I hope, be turning a little rougher myself.

But other parts remain incongruous. A comic ending to the day: at seven Anne Guion, a journalist at *La Vie*, calls from Paris to talk about my book on Ta'ayush[1] and the Israeli peace movement. Two minutes before the phone rings, a portly Telugu gentleman knocks at the door. I don't know him and at first assume he's made a mistake, but it soon transpires that he is my landlord, come to the hotel to meet me. He lives in Prakasham district, and he has a wonderful long name: Paluri Venkata Gopalakrishna Visvanatha, a name that covers all bases. I would like one like that. He is a devotee of a living goddess incarnate, Nirmala Devi, whose picture—a plump, pinkish lady with piercing eyes—hangs in the flat; who is, he says, the mother of us all. He is deeply interested in Kundalini Yoga. If only I could wake my Kundalini, he tells me, my creativity would be enhanced. Each of us contains this sleeping, serpentine female within us, coiled around the base of the spine; if we knew what was good for us, we would direct all our efforts toward rousing her and forcing her upward through the series of hidden *cakra* circles stacked vertically within our bodies. PVGV is a mild-mannered, courteous man, and he waits patiently, for the most part, while I try to answer Anne's questions over the phone: what do I think of the Hamas victory in Palestine? Is there still scope for Ta'ayush, for joint Israeli-Palestinian peace groups? How will the book be received in Israel? Do I expect to be widely attacked? I talk to her about conditions on the ground, in South Hebron. In the middle of all this, PVGV suddenly becomes impatient and resumes his discourse on the Kundalini, with occasional questions to me to be sure I'm following. What language are you speaking? Anne asks, left dangling awkwardly on the line. Telugu, I say, and explain: it is one of the classical languages of South India, with a long tradition of delightful poetry. She now wants to know if I have doubts about the future, about the wisdom of Israelis acting together with Palestinians under current conditions. Good question. Before I can answer, she asks: what exactly am I doing in India? She may well be more interested in that than in the peace work, and I wouldn't blame her. One must not neglect the *anāhata-cakra*, the energy center in the vicinity of the heart, says PVGV—do I agree? Soon the two conversations intertwine. I am not at all sure that I have kept the Yogic *cakra*s and the *sūkshma-śarīra*, the subtle body that contains them, out of the political discussion with Paris. Maybe peace will come when the Kundalini at last awakes. Soon I feel dizzy, spinning between worlds I usually manage to keep separate. Suddenly I can't remember what language I am supposed to be speaking, and on what subject. Worse, I can't remember who I am supposed to be, to say nothing of who I am.

February 11

Satish takes me shopping for the flat: I buy a heavy wooden table with round, carved legs; chairs, refrigerator, plates, tumblers, buckets, Godavari-style cotton mattresses, doormats, disinfectant, mosquito repellent. In the afternoon, sheets, pillowcases, towels. It happens fast. I am now ready to move in on Tuesday, when the current will be restored. We stop by at the flat; it looks clean, welcoming. Bhūloka-svargaloka: heaven on earth. We sit with Patanjali Sastry in his office upstairs and talk as the afternoon softens and grows dark. Patanjali Sastry is happy that I will be living just one floor below; it will make everything much easier in practical terms—there are the daily problems that crop up with any house in India, that he or his efficient assistant Raju will help me solve—but more important, we will meet each day, there will be time to talk of history and poetry and music. . . . Already, very quickly, friendship is taking root.

February 12

First lesson with Kanakaiah, in my room in the Ananda Regency. The first two verses of Pĕddana's *Manu-caritramu*. He sits facing east, pronounces the blessings. Then he begins:

> Black glistens on his chest,
> smeared with musk from Lakshmi's breasts,
> so his devotees—Sanandana and others—
> might wonder if he hasn't put Dark Earth
> in Lakshmi's place.
> May this god favor with his lotus-eyes
> Krishṇaraya, our king.

A prayer to Vishṇu, with his two wives—the golden Lakshmi, who normally lives on his breast, and the dark Earth goddess who, the poet imagines, may have taken Lakshmi's place, with far-reaching consequences. This is going to be a book about the First Man and about life lived on earth, its sorrows, displacements, and potential promise. Kanakaiah is workmanlike, straightforward, limpid in speech. The invocation has three roles: *āśīr-vāda*, blessing; *namas-kriyā*, salutation to the gods; and *vastu-nirdeśa*, defining the subject. He explains the verses at length, taking care to draw together all the strands, leaving nothing unspoken. I am to learn them by heart.

I thank him as he leaves after half an hour. He doesn't like to be thanked. He quotes his guru: "artham aite cālu" (If the meaning has been understood, that is enough).

Touching this music, as if from a great distance, I touch a vast richness; also the strangely limiting rules and erudite measures that package it, surround it, perhaps protect it. To learn like this, in the right language—for this I have come to India.

* * *

Sunday morning. Charles and I walk the length of the river, from the train station to the New Bridge, a good hour in the broiling sun. We intrude on a family of fishermen or cowherds, with their fierce dogs, living on the riverbank. Then the rotary burning ghat, Kailasabhumi, "Śiva's world" or the entrance to it. Funerals are performed daily at the ghats, bodies offered to the flames to the accompaniment of the ancient mantras. Rajahmundry is a southern Varanasi, a place pilgrims come to die; there are burning sites all along the river. One who dies on the bank of the Godavari may, so they say, escape rebirth. My Jewish greed for existence kicks in at this thought. How could one choose or hope not to be reborn into these volatile tastes and colors?

It is a quiet Sunday morning. We stop in at the Rajahmundry Museum, where I seek out the carved stone Venugopala-Krishna from Eluru (twelfth century) I have admired for years. Knee bent backward, he holds his flute to his lips as his eyes engage yours. He is bigger and better even than I remembered—lithe, off-balance, unevenly stretching toward some unseen point, like Andhra things generally. *I must change my life.*

* * *

Yonata writes from home that Ariel Sharon is dying. I feel mostly numb, even the old anger and contempt are worn away. Perhaps if they burned him on the banks of the Godavari, some of the sticky *pāpa*, decades' worth of real evil and the terrible black karma that he amassed, would be washed away.

February 13

From John Leonard's Wisconsin dissertation,[2] I learn that in 1871 the population of Rajahmundry was 19,738; by 1901 it had jumped to 36,408.[3] Greater Rajahmundry today is around half a million. What was once hardly more than a hamlet, dense with poets and scholars, is now a metropolis, though one feels none of the crowding and chaos of the bigger cities like Vizag or, needless to say, Hyderabad. But even now, Rajahmundry feels like an intellectual paradise—intellection being, in this lush setting, a certain kind of textured, tactile feeling.

I like to imagine it as it once was, not so very long ago: The Old Quarter, according to one H. C. Schmidt (1880), consisted of "one long main avenue, from which the other streets, generally narrow, run down towards the river. The houses are nearly all of one story, of clay walls, covered with tiles, and thickly shaded by large trees. . . . The houses were clustered behind the temples along the river bank, with lanes leading down to the ghats and places of access to the river. It was a crowded and not particularly healthy place."[4]

The Old Quarter has lost none of its charm. I spend happy hours roaming the alleyways like a wide-eyed boy. You can smell the river even when you don't see it; sometimes you also get a sour whiff of the Andhra Pradesh Paper Mills upstream. In between lie the bastions of colonial officialdom—the red-brick courts, the English club, some churches, the remains of a few English houses. A strong missionary presence has continued up to the present day; the modern vans of a popular American evangelist are parked in a long row just beyond Kambala Ceruvu, the Pillars' Pond. I wonder if anyone takes notice.

In the middle of the nineteenth century, the city expanded southward into Innespet, named for one Mr. Innes, a "Civil and Sessions Judge at Rajahmundry."[5] Here, far from the involute loops of the Old Quarter, various official buildings came into being: the Sub-Collector's Office, the Tahsildar's Kacceri, the Telegraph Office, and the District School. Some are still intact, though much the worse for wear. Generally, however, Innespet has been mauled by continuous demolition and construction, and there is very little left that conforms to a detailed description from 1860:

> The English Pettah [Innespeta] is a very pretty place beautifully planted and arranged—the various views of the river and the distant mountains make the scenery very pleasing. The Native town is a most important one, indeed after Bunder the most important one in the Northern Circars, the merchants are reputed to be the most wealthy, and as far as I could see there were very [many?] signs of it. Many Natives riding in buggies and other conveyances passed me, there are numbers of two-storied houses and great numbers of well-built houses—in fact I might say the great majority are large and well-built tile-roofed houses. I have seen nothing like it in Ellore or even in Bunder, the streets are level and clean and the people as far as I could judge in so short a time most respectful, for I noticed that almost every respectable person that met me salaamed as he passed.[6]

I have to say that in 2006—exactly one hundred years after the map Leonard has found in *The Foreign Missionary*, clearly showing the Northern Area, the Old Quarter, Innespet, and "Danavaipeta" to the east[7]—Rajahmundry is no less friendly. The buggies are gone, alas, and the exhaust from trucks, buses, and auto rickshaws, like everywhere in India, is wreaking havoc with every public space. But people still smile at you just like that, for no special reason, as you walk along, and a gentle, formal greeting (in Telugu) invariably produces a warm response. It is a small town, like the one I grew up in, in Iowa; even a bit like Madison, where I first studied Telugu. It is also a city of parks, rich in greenery and flowers: *campak*, jasmine, bougainvillea, flame-of-the-forest, and many more I can't easily identify, a tropical profusion much stronger, as the biblical poet would say, than wine.

February 14

MIDNIGHT

By late afternoon I am back from a quick raid on the bookstores of Vijayavada and the toy shops of Kondapalli, where I watched the toy makers, famous all over Andhra, at work. I have brought back a wobbly orange giraffe for Inbali and a glossy black head of Venkaṭeśvara, the Tirupati god, for me. On the desiccate hill high above Kondapalli there is a fifteenth-century fort, well preserved, worthy of Tagore and the other ubiquitous romantics. I suppose one can imagine, if necessary, dancing girls, poets, wrestlers going through their paces in the presence of their bored patrons.

I unpack, make some order in the flat, scrub this and that (as I remember fruitlessly scrubbing our various apartments, years ago, in Mandaiveli, Hyderabad, Vizag), attack the cobwebs, unsettle for a moment the cumulated dust. The flat is full of plastic chairs and a small plastic table, courtesy of Smile; and my overhasty purchase, a tall blue desk chair, looking ungainly and rather useless, has also turned up. Dinner, a neat pack of *chapatti*s and curries, arrives at seven thirty. I have settled the basic system with Nirmala, who lives only five minutes away, off Tilak Road: lunch each day will be a rice meal, Āndhra bhojanam, dinner a light "tiffin." Satyanarayana, her husband, asks me to choose the daily menu, but I tell him I prefer to be surprised.

My first guest, Krishnayya, long-standing friend from Vizag, arrives to offer blessings. He has brought me a pile of Telugu books about Rajahmundry, including the autobiography of the local hero and modernist crusader, Veeresalingam; also some chapbooks with the stories of several local gods and goddesses. For some reason, talk turns to Sanskrit poets and, in particular, to the greatest of them all, Kālidāsa. Krishnayya grew up in Dhavalesvaram, just a few kilometers downstream from Rajahmundry; he loves the world of village rites and the village deities of coastal Andhra, a world he knows better than anyone else in this generation. Sanskrit, to him, is always a little too removed from real life; also loaded with false pretense and privilege, a Brahminic project. I tell the story of Kālidāsa's lightninglike education: when this country bumpkin tricked a clever princess into marrying him, she refused to have anything to do with her new husband until he acquired good Sanskrit; so, at her suggestion, he locked the goddess Kali out of her shrine at the edge of the village and let her back in only when she engraved the Sanskrit syllables, *akshara*s, on his tongue. He came home singing marvelous poetry. Now the problem: since his bride was the person who sent him to gain knowledge, Kālidāsa saw her as his guru and refused to sleep with her; she, outraged, cursed him to die because of a woman. Krishnayya finds the story idiotic: even poets, he says, should have some logic. Sanskrit poetry is inimical, he thinks, to common sense. Kālidāsa should have made love to his bride.

And if he had—how different would be the story we tell of Sanskrit literature! Would there have been room in it for the thousands of poems saturated with unappeased longing?

At 10:00 PM Kanakaiah knocks at the gate. Where is east? He must face east, I should sit facing north. This settled, he sings two lovely verses and explains them in limpid, rapid-fire Telugu. At the end he asks me, "Are you satisfied?" How can I tell him how full I am? The gentle pace, the clarity, the space—these verses breathe. In me.

I look at the stars from my balcony, and then down along the length of the dark road, this perfect piece of India.

* * *

Narayana Rao has published a sharp, provocative essay in the Telugu weekly *Vārta*, which I read on the train; "Racapalem" (the nom de plume of Candrasekhara Reddy, of Anantapur) has written a bitter response. "The notion," writes Narayana Rao, "that poets should produce something useful for society has, unfortunately, taken root. It is truly a misfortune if a poet has the delusion that his poetry is meant to change society. The business of a poet is to write poetry." Sometimes tautology clears the air. He also spells out the full implication. "For a long time now, Telugu poetry has stopped being poetry. Telugu literature has departed from all the so-called literary societies, *sāhitya sanghālu*; only the *sanghālu* are left behind." He minces no words, he could hardly have been more harsh. And he has a way of delivering these broadsides a few hours before getting on the plane back to America. Naturally, people are both outraged and envious.

Historically, my role is to defend, to offer hope; each time I come back from Andhra, we argue over the current literary scene. I see promise, fragile seedlings of innovation, and I can wait; it can take a century or two for a great poet to germinate and ripen. The twentieth century produced two giants, Gurajada Appa Rao and Viswanatha Satyanarayana, and three or four near-giants—is that not a respectable harvest, almost on a par with the golden ages of the past? Such thoughts fail to comfort him; he sees mostly a scorched landscape, a withered discourse, benighted critics or pseudocritics, vast rhetorical effusions, anything but the real thing that he knew so well as a young man in Eluru. I disagree, but reading Racapalem's fatuous response I can't help but see Narayana Rao's point. "If poets have no idea of changing society, why have they been born? Who needs them if they can't envisage social change? Is it enough for them to tie flowers to their wrists and exclaim in ecstasy over the fragrance?" And so on: has Velcheru forgotten, he asks, about the women poets and the Dalits and the Telangana writers and the patriots, the usual list, all who have assumed their responsibility to bring about change? Illogical generalization, he concludes, is a sin; and it is wrong, indeed impossible, to evaluate all poetry by a single standard.

Like excellence? Like taste? Like truth?

My carefully nurtured hopefulness drains out of me in a second. I know it will be back, but for now the horrific distortion in sensibility stares me in the face and I think: Narayana Rao is right, not 80 percent right or 90 percent right but 100 percent right. That he antagonizes, deliberately no doubt, has its obvious cost. The biblical prophets also paid this kind of price. A whole generation can lose its way. And still: I know that Telugu poetry is alive, and I intend to find it. I'll probably be satisfied with a few deft exclamations of ecstasy.

February 15

Lunch comes in a tiffin thermos and three stainless steel containers stacked one on the other: carrot-coconut and cabbage curries today. The Godavari cotton mattress was perfect, I slept well, woke before dawn, slept again. Waking carries a certain sadness, as if I had misplaced something crucial but I can't remember what; and with consciousness comes the full weight of the rock of language I have to push uphill. I know it will roll downhill again tonight.

Midmorning stroll through the streets; I buy a small square mirror to hang above the sink, various soaps and scouring pads, some fruit. Well-being pervades my body—and whatever the body might contain. Or maybe it's my mind that is at peace? This savage Western thought is burned away by the morning sun. There seems to be no space left for splitting into parts. By eleven I am home, the fridge arrives—a rather archaic, turquoise relic, which cost only some two thousand rupees; I hope it has enough life left in it to carry me through to September. Narayana Rao calls from Madison: what, he asks, is the definition of a classical language? This has become a political issue in Andhra; if Tamil is granted classical status, should not Telugu have the same privilege? Is it a matter of counting up how many years have elapsed since the first poem? He is deeply skeptical of this debate, rightly so. As a working definition of the classical, he suggests: a repository of lexemes available for the creation of neologisms. Somehow I doubt this will satisfy the politicized intellectuals in Hyderabad. They want Telugu to be proclaimed classical because (a) money is involved, for example subsidies to cultural institutions of one kind or another; and (b) if Tamil got the prize, Telugu needs one just like it. But the whole debate is a shallow business. What happened to the natural self-confidence of the Telugu poets and critics of a mere century ago? They didn't need to be told they were "classical." It was more than enough for them that they could sing truth.

* * *

In the afternoon, Kandaiah takes me on his scooter to the Government Arts College (Autonomous), a venerable Rajahmundry institution. Many great names of the nineteenth and twentieth centuries sat, and later taught, in its classrooms. To my surprise, Sri Venkatesvara Rao parachutes me, unprepared, into his Telugu class. I manage, somehow, to communicate. They are curious across the board: What Telugu books have I read? What attracted me to Telugu? Did I get married out of love? They are generous and gracious, even applaud when I stumble through the Pĕddana verses I've been memorizing. Someday I'll get them right.

Rammohan Ravu from Kakinada has come to lecture on postmodernism—explaining it to the Rajahmundry academic elite. He is seventy-one years old but looks barely half that age; vigorous, forceful, eloquent, he offers a lucid Telugu exposition of Derrida that is a vast improvement, in my view, on the French original (to say nothing of Gayatri Spivak's semi-English version). There is a strangely natural quality to Derrida in Telugu paraphrase; perhaps Telugu was the unconscious substratum for his intricate, imbricate French. For one thing, the South Indian tradition had, from the start, a relatively elastic sense of its poetic texts and knew very well that these texts often produced their own author, rather than the reverse. Oral *cāṭu* verses, known to everyone, mimicking all the famous poets, did the work of deconstruction in a world that hardly privileged *écriture*.

Rammohan Ravu practices Yoga, which may explain his gift of making sense of convolution. The audience, largely students filling the ancient, uncomfortable wooden desks in the vast auditorium, seems appreciative; they know the current intellectual fashion in places like Hyderabad and Delhi. After the lecture, they perform the usual honorific ceremony, an incredible, rather tedious ritual of raucous taped wedding music, yellow flowers, the inevitable shawl. . . . If every public lecture ends like this, there will be little time left for anything of consequence. It is like the remorseless unfolding of something buried in ancient habit, maybe the Megalithic Burial Culture, who can say? Smile introduces me to Jonnalagadda Mrityunjaya Ravu, an old, highly respected scholar who has written a clean commentary on Śrīnātha's *Śiva-rātri-māhātmyamu*; I thank him, sincerely, for I have benefited from his gift.

Best of all, even better than surviving the baptism by linguistic flooding, is the afternoon ride home in the golden light through Gandhipuram and Danavayipeta on the back of Smile's scooter. This is the place I have been seeking, it is right, it is whole.

February 16: Circar Express

The water fails in the night, the taps gone dry. I have the feeling, really a kind of certain knowledge, that this will happen again, and again. At dawn I manage to fill up half a bucket from the Godavari tap on my balcony, enough more or less to wash.

My table arrives, a heavy contraption on wobbly, uneven legs that will have to be shaved and tightened. The flat is now, I think, complete except for the electric hot plate I hope to find in Madras. It is too early to leave, I would much rather stay and settle in, but I have promised my student Ophira and her teacher Scaria that I will give them a week, in Kerala, to celebrate the release of their Malayalam-Hebrew book of Cochini songs. And then, afterward, there is the hope of discovering something new, or something I may have lost, in Tenkasi, where Ativīrarāma Pāṇṭiyan—the sixteenth-century Tamil poet who has been tantalizing me—lived and wrote. From Kerala I will head north and east, through the southern Tamil country, traveling from temple to temple, like in my student days, by train and bus and foot. It has been many years since I have done this, and it is time; I feel the old joyfulness of setting out, alone, toward some distant goal, mostly unknown.

I call Smile to say goodbye: "sĕlavu puccukuṇṭunnānu" (I respectfully beg permission to take leave), one of the old-fashioned, quaint expressions for which I am fast becoming famous. He laughs. "I miss you already."

For once, I sleep well on the train, rocked by the steady drumming of the wheels; a deep, happy sleep. When I wake, I can clearly see the missing piece I was looking for, the one that gives no rest; it is, of course, the one I have set aside.

A sudden spurt of exultation: Madras ahead, the past as future, once again.

In 1975–76, Eileen and I lived for some months in Madras; to be precise, in Mandaivelipakkam, not far from the great Mylapore temple, in the south of the city. I spent those months in temples all over the Tamil country, looking for stories; Eileen was studying Carnatic singing with Ramu in Madras. They were heady days. Our oldest son, Tari, was with us, a blond, sweet boy of two. People would sometimes fall at his feet and offer worship as we walked down the street.

Mylapore will always feel like home, a fixed center in my world, more so than any other place, Jerusalem, Madison, Hyderabad, Berlin. . . . There was a time, not so long ago, when Madras was a Telugu city, the primary site for Telugu literati, the heartland of Telugu publishing. That Telugu Madras has mostly melted away. But you cannot understand anything of Andhra without gathering in your fingers the threads that lead back to Madras and to generations of Tamil poets and musicians. It is a single culture, rather artificially divided, today, by the political boundaries put in place in 1956.

So interwoven with these Andhra days were the sounds and tastes of Madras and points south—Kerala, Tanjavur, Tiruvarur. I came south again and again, as if insatiable, ghoulish memory insisted on reembodying itself inside my skin. And Tamil voices joined the internal chorus of the mind, especially the distinctive voice of G. Nagarajan, dissolute novelist of the '60s, whose novella I hope to see through the press in Abbie Ziffren's translation. Like Nagarajan himself, Abbie died very young, some ten years ago; she, too, was claimed, or mesmerized, by Madras. All who knew her, loved her.

And there was one more goal to be pursued over this time. The ancient temple of Tiruvarur, in the Kaveri Delta, some 200 kilometers south of Madras, has a set of seventeenth-century ceiling paintings telling the story of Mucukunda, the monkey-faced Chola king who is said to have brought the god Tyāgarāja to Tiruvarur. The paintings are fast disintegrating; in another few years they will be gone unless some authority intervenes. For years my friend V. K. Rajamani, doyen of art photographers in South India, had spoken of publishing a photographic record of these great paintings; we were determined to finish the work now, while I was in India. So there were two trips to Tiruvarur, with the usual hazards and adventures.

Mucukunda, they say, asked Indra, king of the gods, for the Tyāgarāja icon, which until then had rested in Indra's heaven. But Indra was reluctant to part with his god, so he asked his craftsman, Viśvakarma, to make six precise replicas of Tyāgarāja. Mucukunda was shown the complete set of seven and asked to choose the real Tyāgarāja. Apparently, the god smiled or winked at the king, so Mucukunda chose correctly. Indra then sadly handed over to him all the remaining images as well, which were put in place in six temples in the delta. But the original Tyāgarāja sits in state today in Tiruvarur.

Maharajapuram Ramacandran sings at Vani Mahal, one of the old-fashioned Madrasi concert halls, in T. Nagar. I walk the streets before the concert, aghast at the change; under the present veneer, I see Madras of 1975, the gentle, sleepy, vibrant city I loved. I am too full of feeling to sit still during the singing; riptides of nostalgia carry me far away, to some place that can only be here and now, looped back into the maddening music.

Rajamani takes me to Sudarshan Graphics in the afternoon; here we will print the Tiruvarur Mucukunda book, with state-of-the-art computerized technology. All that remains is to photograph the missing panels; and I will have to write my essay on Tyāgarāja and Mucukunda. The little office is packed with sophisticated terminals and professional designer-printers. I think back to the days when, in small towns all over Tamil Nadu, one had to typeset every letter by hand, pumping the machine with one's foot.

Madras is truly transformed; there is an energy, a verve, a somewhat ruthless confidence. Perhaps all of South India is moving in this direction. Some pieces of the city are awash in money, yet I see the ongoing struggle as well, the continuing or deepening poverty. Ramakrishnan, at Cre-A—one of the centers of Tamil publishing, lexicography, and scholarship in the city—says the threshold for economic survival is always rising, the poor are poorer, the IT money isn't trickling down. Strife sets the tone of the major cultural media.

Ramakrishnan is committed to publishing Abbie's translation of Nagarajan, and we set a schedule for future meetings to go over the draft sentence by sentence. He has many stories to tell of Nagarajan, whom he knew well—stories of his Communist politics, his womanizing, his remorseless descent into destitution. Ramakrishnan would give him money and food and clothes, but he would turn up, some weeks later, in a sordid state after sleeping for days in bus stands or in the streets. Nothing could save him. Then he died. Now even the stories and the great novella are little more than footnotes to the history of modern Tamil prose. We will do what we can to rectify this encroaching amnesia. I like the man's style, which I find almost lyrical, but Ramakrishnan disagrees. Like all Tamil prose writers, he says (ever the professional with his perfect pitch), Nagarajan could have used a good editor.

My old friend Nalini sits, like a barber, on the pavement outside her bookshop next to the Connemara Hotel—still the best in town. Inside the shop, books are piled in precarious stacks and towers, like castles built of sand. You ask for a title and she sends her gopher burrowing through the stacks, hoping he will emerge alive. I have come to buy copies of my own books for my new Rajahmundry friends; the gopher tunnels through the heavy mounds and comes back with five or six. I pay, take the packet, and head back toward the street. Suddenly I can't bear the burden of all these words, pages, ink, to say nothing of the long hours that went into writing and rewriting and correcting proofs, the hours that could have been given over to deeper and better things, to other pleasures, like singing *dhrupad* or learning the viola. I have an overpowering instinct to throw the whole parcel into the Kaum River; but, in my ambivalence, some residual investment of memory or ego or self, I resist.

In the evening I tell this story to Maya and Miriam over dinner and beer outside at the Gymkhana as the mosquitoes feast on us undisturbed. The afternoon's impulse is still alive. Maya says no—she was on the point of abandoning her studies altogether when, she says, she accidentally came across a copy of my *Hungry God* in the library of Tel Aviv University. It made a difference. Now she is writing her dissertation on the *Naishadhiya*. (But—insidious whisper in my mind—does that mean that I did have to write the book?) The two girls will join us next week in Tiruvarur to help with mapping and photographing. They have come in from Sringeri, the Sarasvati *pūjā*. They have met the goddess of poetry at close range, and she seemed to welcome them. Miriam, open-eyed, is seeing India for the first time.

Let the future books, if there are any, at least be light—light of hand and heart.

* * *

I wander into Spencer's Plaza, as if to grind my memories to a fine powder. There were the heated days when only Spencer's had ice cream—also iodine drops, mosquito nets, and other colonial necessities. One wandered through the vast red-brick rectangle, ceiling fans buzzing above, peering at the few exotic imports, sniffing formaldehyde. On Sunday afternoons we would bring Tari, two years old, for his weekly treat; occasionally, very rarely, we might even allow ourselves the luxury of a black-and-orange taxi from Mandaiveli. It was not even so long ago—but today only a piece of the original wall has been left standing, a mute testimony, inside the new mall. In the music store I buy CDs of Aruna Sairam, who sings with the exquisitely slow and careful pace of the Tanjavur line of teaching. It is not that the past is lost, it is perhaps even an illusion to believe that it recedes from us backward, as it were, and can only be seen in retrospect; the old Madras lives on, I feel it everywhere around me. And still, in this strange thick movement within time there is some newly discovered twist that is beyond thinking and almost, but only almost, beyond pain.

* * *

We go to Book Point for the release of M. Krishnan's posthumous volume of wildlife photographs. Disquieting tigers and dizzying eagles fill the screen. Theodore Baskaran, historian of Tamil cinema and the ultimate Madrasi *bricoleur*, speaks gracefully of his friend. "The goal of a photograph," Krishnan would say, "was: *every feather*."

It is, I suppose, a motto well suited to Mylapore, with its immense, careful cumulation; Mylapore, where nothing is ever lost, the one true site of what the Upanishad calls *dahara-vidyā*: the deepest, most hidden knowledge, the knowledge that matters, for me.

February 21, Kaladi, Kerala

Indu performs Pūtanā-moksha—the infant Krishna's killing of the ghoulish Putana—in the genre of Nāngiar-kūttu, a masterpiece. It is slow—and far too short at that; for two hours, moment by moment it swells and deepens to a point beyond knowing or seeing. Slowness, a deliberate subtlety, is what makes depth possible; what is slow enough might also be true. Anyway, it is, I know, my own proper rhythm, though the furious scramble of my life would seem to belie this thought. I want to bring my Sanskrit students here, to Mu̲likkulam, to see the Kudiyattam style of Sanskrit drama (of which Nangiar-kuttu is a subgenre) in its perfection—perhaps the fifth act from Śaktibhadra's play, *Āścarya-cūḍāmaṇi*, twenty-some nights, three to five hours each night. Do I have the patience? Yes, I have the patience and, more to the point, the hunger.

Kaladi, they say, is where the philosopher Śankara was born, the master of nondualism, Advaita. Life, for the Advaita, is a study in oneness gone awry. We see the world, and ourselves in it, chopped into small discrete units, a chaotic plurality rife with sorrow. Śankara tries to instruct us to experience the oneness that, he says, we in any case know as our most intimate self. But how could such diversity be truly one? And how did it happen in the first place? It never really happened. Our ignorance is what gives it this appearance. In this, at least—my ignorance—I believe. My colleague Yohanan tells me I am slowly and mostly unconsciously shifting my taste from the devotional world of Tamil temples to an idiosyncratic Advaita. Maybe I, too, could be "one."

The story they tell here in Kaladi is that the boy Śankara wanted to renounce the world, but his mother refused to allow him to do so. Only when a crocodile seized his leg while he was bathing in the river, and it seemed that death was imminent, did she agree to a renunciation in extremis. Still, the boy-renouncer, having survived the crocodile, promised his mother that he would be with her when she breathed her last. The Advaita world of oneness anyway seems to me to be a mother's religion. Tonight Ophira takes us to the Śiva temple of Trikāḷadiyappar, near the river. In the cool dark evening, we speak to the learned, patient priest. He recites Śankara's plaintive verse:

āstāṃ tāvad iyaṃ prasūti-samaye durvāra-śūla-vyathā
nairucyaṃ tanu-śoṣaṇaṃ malamayī śayyā ca sāṃvatsarī/
ekasyâpi na garbha-bhāra-bharaṇa- kleśasya yasyāḥ kṣamo
dātuṃ niṣkṛtim unnato 'pi tanayas tasyai jananyai namaḥ//

[Leave aside the pangs of giving birth,
fierce as a spear twisted into your body.
Mother: for nearly a year
you slept on a soiled cot, your skin aflame.
You carried me in your womb.
What son, even a good son,
could repay such a debt?]

Śankara speaks of oneness and of the illusion that is our world, but has an honest regard for human suffering. This priest belongs to the Kapilli mana, the family that carried the feet of Śankara's mother to the funeral pyre (another Nambudiri Brahmin family, the Talayattupilli, carried her head). The remaining eight Nambudiri families boycotted the rite, since Śankara was already a *sannyāsin*-renouncer and thus should not have been involved at all in his mother's funeral ceremony—he was supposedly beyond such earthly ties. He, however, kept his promise to be with her at her final breath. Advaita makes room for such deviation—another faint whiff of freedom.

At noon I walk the village streets, the light burning into my mind. Here one could read a verse and understand it; that is, one could become the verse.

February 25, Tenkasi

At Ernakulam station, waiting for the train to Tirunelveli, I meet a modern man: manager of a pharmaceutical company. We speak of Israel, which he knows from *Exodus* and *The Hajj*. Not, perhaps, the best foundation for an education. He is torn inside between a default hostility to Islam, hence the urge to retaliate again and again, and the Gandhian saying that if one takes an eye for an eye, soon the whole world will be blind. He invites me to his guru's ashram, where truth abides and such tormenting conflicts can, it seems, be accommodated.

The train arrives, as usual it is not so simple to identify my bogie, I prowl up and down the carriages, heavily laden with bags and books, until in the end one I find, at last, my berth, or birth. Fitful sleep; I wake to dozens of white windmills near Kanyakumari, a La Manchan touch. At Tirunelveli I check in to one of the faceless and tasteless modern Indian hotels not far from the station. The streets are dusty, crowded, noisy, a sunburned gray. But I have come here with a single clear purpose in mind. I take the morning to visit Nellaiyappar and Kāntimati, Lord Śiva and his wife in their local guises. It is my first time in this temple, one of the most elaborate and haunting in the south. Huge corridors lined with carved pillars, some of them extruding figures so fierce they are on the verge of the grotesque, connect Śiva's shrine to that of the goddess. Propped up against one of the pillars, a young woman in bright yellow, her hair heavy with jasmine, nurses her child. I wander slowly, back and forth. The Maṇi-maṇḍapa has hollow, musical pillars, a symphony in stone, visible to the eye. Here sound is, in essence, light—tangible, luminescent. What is audible to our ears is no more than an echo, seductive, once removed from the visible source. A diagram of esoteric Tamil mantra syllables is painted on the wall near the god's sanctum; if you combine the syllables correctly, singing them in sequence, you will see the god before your eyes. Sing them backward, and he will disappear. Tamil temples are made of sound—that is, light—congealed and fixed in place.

The stone carvers were playing, that is clear; and the kings who planned this vast maze, were they playing as well? A solitary clump of bamboo, the *sthala-vriksha*, or temple tree, reaches up toward some imagined heaven through a hole in the roof. No Tamil shrine is without its tree, rooted in the nether world, penetrating the sky. Such temples, I think, are a palliative—at least that—to the mind, with its tendency to split away and to abstract. Here is a moving insistence on touching and being touched; what is god is "only" an intensified mode of this sensate givenness. God is physical, not metaphysical.

After lunch I take the local bus to Tenkasi. It is packed solid, and I end up standing most of the way, crunched between sweat-soaked villagers—like the old days, thirty years ago. The same heady whiff of freedom. I have braced myself for another, smaller version of the dusty gray of Tirunelveli, but to my surprise Tenkasi is, already at first glance, blessed, open, radiant, polished clean. Purple mountains to the west hint of Kerala and the sea. It is the right place for a great poet, and that is why I have come here—to see what Ativirarama Pantiyan saw when he got up in the morning. Were the town less lovely, this romantic notion would seem absurd. But *Naitaṭam*, Ativirarama's masterpiece, a Tamil *Naishadhiya*, matters to me, I need to ground it in a landscape, so I work the streets into my feet, I go to the temple—abuzz with anticipation of Śiva's Night, Śivarātri, tomorrow. Immense stone warriors, some of them dancing, each carved from a single stone, escort the pilgrims inward to the sanctum. One sees the flourish of the sixteenth century, the confidence that something grand and new was being born. As in the poems. A tough old gentleman introduces himself as a scion of the royal Pantiyan line, thus descended from my poet. At sunset, the sky splashes purple and red. Space expands.

They say that if you die in Benares, you will achieve final liberation, *mukti*; but you get *mukti* in Tenkasi by being born here, or living here, or, if necessary, you can also do it by dying.

February 26, Sivaratri, Tenkasi

A cool morning in Tirukkurralam, its waterfall familiar from many Tamil films. Light at heart, I climb up to the temple, which is also strangely light, as if the stones might fly. It is also much simpler than I imagined: Tirikkūṭarācappar's massive *Tirukkuṟṟālattalapurāṇam*, which I read years ago in the British Museum, has prepared me for a far more monumental structure. One enters through a gate adorned with painted stucco images of the deities, who look jolly, relaxed, a little chubby, as if glad to be living in this resortlike station in the hills. (There are many more demanding postings.) Kuḻalvāymŏḻiyammai, "the goddess whose voice sings like a flute," stands at ease, blessing visitors; one receives chunks of sandal paste as her gift, *prasādam*. As is only fitting, given the proximity to his proper home on Potiyil Mountain near the southern tip of the subcontinent, the dwarf-sage Agastya is also here, a superb image in his own small shrine. At the *śakti-pīṭha*, the "goddess seat," I discover that I have no small cash to give the priest as his expected *dakshiṇā* fee; in desperation I offer him a dollar that has somehow survived in my wallet. He examines it carefully, holds it up to the light—he has never seen one before—asks how much it is worth in real *paṇam*.

By Pantiyan standards, the waterfall is a miracle (in New Zealand, it would be negligible). The rock face is carved with many *linga*s, glistening under the water. Families stand close to the cascade, soaked to the skin, receiving benediction; the washerwomen are at work; monkeys dash in and out of the spray. Mothers clean their babies in the cool, steady stream. Sunshine splatters in the mist. Somewhere nearby a Kuratti gypsy, who lives here, at Tirukkurralam, according to a famous eighteenth-century Kuṟavanci opera, must be telling fortunes—but this morning I don't need her to tell mine. A certain restlessness is needed before you seek out the diviners.

In the evening, I take the train to Madurai, traveling in the shadow of the Ghats. Past Srivilliputtur, with its white *gopuram* towers on all four sides of the immense temple, then ever more luxurious fields; the sun sets as if fusing into the depths of fiery green. I read the essays I have brought with me from Kerala; I read of Brahmins, Aryans, northern oppressors, primeval Dravidians, the standard mythography of modern South India, driven by a barren need to classify, to clarify an imaginary, brittle sequence. . . . How our ideas pale in this intense luminosity. I don't believe in any of the historians' categories. A Christian boy, "Ben Zwi," no less, attaches himself to me and, glued for hours to the seat across from me, speaks of truth, a single truth, which must, I can clearly see, by virtue of this claim alone, be untrue.

March 1, Tanjavur

7:00 AM

Wild peacocks on the road, like yesterday from the train. It is getting hotter. The bus from Madurai is Nagarjunian, a meltdown of perception: Are you distinct from the bus? Is there a subject that is not the object? Old Tamil films play at high volume—so high the words are totally incomprehensible, a continuous screeching—on a small TV propped up beside the driver.

Tiruppattur, Putukkottai, Perungalur, Tanjavur: I have crossed Tamil Nadu from the tip to the heart. In Madurai I lecture for Sam Sudhananda at the American College on matters of the imagination, on what the poeticians thought was real. A thoughtful first-year student asks in Tamil: is not the Sanskrit theory of poetry highly abstract and theoretical, while Tamil poetics focus on the concrete?

One wakes to the thickness. The air is thick, saturated, heavy with heat, dust, light, existence. Memory is thick, soaked with sadness, fear, hunger, need, hope, with the sensual imprints of color, taste, sweat, prickly skin, wrinkled self. The moment of experience is far too thick, laden with layers of added packing, laden with the physical density of knowing or unknowing, thus finally unknowable. The "mind"—does it exist?—is strained and weighted; objects merge into, cram the space that would have been available for thought. Language is thick, viscous, creamy, a mass of buffalo-milk sentences, intricate whirlpools of sound on the edge of meaning. One wakes exhausted: outside, the dawn light is already burdened with all of this, the dust, taste, cream, even the longing we drag along inside us can only be felt as an intensification, *upacaya*, *vijrimbhaṇa*, of what is already in place—the overlapping spiral segments with their gaps and their bizarre connections, as if what is missing, always, is only another kind of link, invisible but no less dense or continuous than the rest. *Kāvya*, poetry at its strongest, takes this thick bodily matter and shapes it, stretching perception like clay or resin. It is no wonder the poet can *make* something be, for what he sees is already there, in the thickness.

March 1, Tiruvarur

MIDNIGHT

Gurumurtti and his friend Abhirama, wise and knowledgeable devotees, collect us at a quarter past ten in the Land Rover and drive us through the delta to Tiruvarur. Gurumurtti is a highly successful businessman from Coimbatore, a man of great dignity and presence. He speaks Tamil as it is meant to be: with profound composure, *amaiti*, a great rarity. He has unparalleled knowledge of Tamil temples, which he visits as pilgrim-cum-connoisseur. On the road he asks me over and over: "Have you been to Temple X?" Mostly the answer is no. And I thought I had seen *many* Tamil temples.

Rajamani and Charu are waiting for us, the heavy cameras ready to go. The hotel, like much of Tiruvarur, has seen better days. Maya and Miriam shift their room three or four times; each new space has its own lush population of beetles, cockroaches, and scorpions. By early afternoon we are in the temple, wandering happily among the shrines scattered through three large enclosures. We go to pay our respects to Tyāgarāja, for whose sake we have come. It is his paintings—the story of his arrival in Tiruvarur—that we have come to photograph and preserve.

I can see why he wanted to be here. The great temple is as complete a cosmos as anyone could want: with the great fixed *linga* (Valmīka-nātha, "Lord of the Anthill"), a set of goddesses, magical bronzes, a vast array of sculpted niches, a few charming monsters, a cave (Hāṭakeśvara) leading deep into the underworld, and the huge Kamalâlaya Tank outside. Add to this the resonances from that extended moment in Carnatic music, at the end of the eighteenth century, when three master composers were born and lived in this village. With Venkatesan, Rajamani's assistant, I go to visit their houses in the Brahmin *agrahāram* streets outside the temple; Śyama Śastri's is the best preserved, a site of perfection, *siddhi-sthala*, deep with space and light. The whole town radiates outward from the temple, a rather grimy grid centered on the fact—that is what it is, incontrovertible, compelling—that God, Tyāgarāja, is living here among us, enfolded by the heavy stone walls.

Pradosha-pūjā for Tyāgarāja at 6:00 PM: it is hot, febrile, in the sanctum. The deity stands at the end of a long stone corridor, with an empty chamber at his back; pilgrims press toward him; some, especially women, seat themselves on the pavement at his feet. First the priests do the *hāratti* waving of oil lamps counterclockwise, a half circuit and down the middle—for the goddess, Ambal, and the son, Murugan—then three to four clockwise whirls. The names of Śiva's five faces are recited backward, from Aghora to Sadyojāta, the reverse of the standard order. A priest carefully, with the precision of a brain surgeon, places flower after flower on the god after applying ash to him in open space, *ākāśa*. They are thickening him, and each flower counts. Precision counts. It is the most beautiful *pūjā* I have seen in many years; beauty is fundamental to this god. But what can this mean? Is beauty a surface notion? The god has a deep need for color, fragrance, perhaps a love of symmetry (a desperate wish?), a preference for bronze, for oil lamps, dark recesses, with empty space—the locked chamber—behind him.

In the dark, as the evening cools, the temple becomes mysterious, less stark. A row of pilgrims sits on the floor eating *prasād*—the god's gift of cooked rice—off green banana leaves. A long-haired, voluble priest, standing outside the Tyāgarāja shrine, has much to tell us of the temple rituals, the Uttarakāmikâgama canonical foundation. There are some, says Gurumurtti, like this man, who are generous with knowledge; others hoard and snarl. The priests have only one copy of their main liturgical text, the *Mucukunda-sahasra-nāma*, which they bring each night to the temple for the recitation; when it gets too battered, they copy it by hand and burn the old one in the *homa* sacrificial fire.

After dinner at Vasan's, the top of the line in Tiruvarur, best undescribed, Gurumurtti draws me back to the temple to meet the Executive Officer. Opaque negotiations ensue. Rajamani's photographs are in our hands, we need only to make good a few lacunae; but the EO adamantly resists our request for permission. Only the Commissioner in Madras has the power, he says. Oblique politesse, and Gurumurtti's long-standing connection to this temple, are to no avail. We will have to start over, in Madras. A painful shiftiness on the part of the EO colors the conversation. Later, in the hotel, Gurumurtti sums up the art of political transactions in India: There is always X, who has power, who reports to Y, who knows only that 1 + 1 = 2. If you do not have 1 to give for my 1, you do not exist.

Lacking the EO's permission to enter the painted *mandapam*, and unable to get another appointment—to plead our case again—until the afternoon, we spend the morning in Vedaranyam, an hour's ride through the paddy fields to the coast. Vedaranyam is another Tyāgarāja temple: when Indra gave Mucukunda the true image of the god, destined for Tiruvarur, he also gave him the six look-alikes with which he had tried to confuse the king; Vedaranyam got one of them. I have never seen this Vedaranyam, "Forest of the Vedas," which turns out, naturally, to be another magnificent site, the sanctum clearly very old, carved in the earliest, bold Chola style. We have arrived on a festival day celebrating the famous moment when two Tamil poets, Tiruñānacampantar and Appar, authors of canonical poems to Śiva, were visiting this shrine. They found the doors to the temple locked. Campantar asked the older poet, Appar, to sing an eleven-verse *patikam* to cause them to open; Appar sang ten verses and nothing happened, but the eleventh verse (the *tirukkaṭaikkāppu*, "the closing seal") proved irresistible:

> irakkam ŏṉṟ'ilīr ĕm pĕrumāṉīre
>
> [You are utterly lacking in compassion,
> you who are our great god.]

Śiva could not bear the reproach: the gates swung open. After their vision of the god inside, Appar asked Campantar to sing a *patikam* of his own in order to release the gates and allow them to close once more.[8]

We sit on the steps of the inner portico, watching families bathing in the tank. When you have visited a god like the lord of Vedaranyam, it is not polite to leave too soon. You are meant to sit somewhere nearby, keeping him company. He likes his visitors and doesn't want them to go. Gurumurtti, a fine draftsman, sketches the intricate pillars and their carvings. A gentle priest, bare-chested, his head shaved except for the slight Brahminic tuft, serves us tea in tiny clay cups.

By four o'clock we are back with the EO, who somewhat reluctantly allows us at least to enter the *mandapam* and map the ceiling, to establish the narrative sequence. By the time they bring the key, it is already getting dark. We race against impending night, our enemy, as it was for the washerman Tirukkurripputtontanayanar who had promised the god clean, dry clothes before dark (on a rainy day).[9] Maya and Miriam furiously and meticulously sketch on loose pages a précis of all four and a half painted panels. Maya is imperious, impetuous, daring, and, in the critical moment, entirely there, capable, sharp, in control. We hop, barefoot, from one rusty metal bar to another, over piles of dry logs, old rags, dead squirrels. When it is finished, we emerge outside into a miracle of raindrops, red-orange light softening into mauve, gold-white clouds, the sweetness of revelation, the opening of the sky, as if the god were satisfied and were sending us a sign. He is glad we care for his paintings. Maya says: it is like what happened with Mucukunda—only he had the privilege of seeing Tyāgarāja's smile; probably only we can see this wonder. Though we have failed to take the photographs, the world is, for the moment, right side up.

I like the idea of a god who needs to be thickened with flowers.

March 3

Light rain in the morning—like my first time at Tiruvarur, in 1975. I stood, soaked and innocent, at the bus stand, asking the way to the temple, until a local poet, Pulavarmani Vittuvan Irattina Tecikar, took pity and guided me there. I think of the startling sculpture of Śiva's first revelation as the *linga*, the *lingodbhava*, glistening in the rain. Brahmā and Vishṇu tried to find the top and the bottom of this pillar, respectively, and failed; you can see Brahmā flying upward in the form of a goose, Vishṇu digging down as a boar. Another Chola masterpiece, casually set into the temple wall. God has no limit, and sometimes there *is* a first time.

Before we say goodbye, sitting in the car beside the tank, Abhirama sings from a *patikam* on Tiruvarur by the third Tevâram poet, Cuntaramūrtti—a pointed essay in remembering:

kārkkuṉṟa' malaiyāyp pŏḻivāṉai
    kalaikk' ĕllām pŏruḷāy uṭaṉ kūṭi
pārkkiṉṟa uyirkkup parintāṉai
    pakalun kankulum āki niṉṟāṉai
orkkiṉṟa cĕviyai cuvai taṉṉaiy
    uṇarum nāviṉaik kānkiṉṟa kaṇṇai

ārkkiṉṟa kaṭalai malai taṉṉai
 ārūrāṉai maṟakkalum āme

[He comes pouring down
 like rain over dark mountains:
substance of all sciences,
he has love
for those living beings
 who look to him
 and are with him.

He is day and night,
the attentive ear,
the tongue that knows taste
and the eye that sees,
the roaring ocean and the mountain—

how, then, could we forget him,
 the lord of Arur?]
 (59.3)

How much have we forgotten? Suddenly Abhirama remembers the lovely verse by an anonymous poet that says: if Brahmā and Vishṇu, who had tried so hard to reach the upper and lower limits of this god, had only come to Tiruvarur, to the doorstep of Paravaiyar—Cuntarar's first wife, who was reconciled to her husband only when Śiva himself came at night to her house as a love messenger (*tūtar*)—they would easily have seen him entire, from top to bottom.[10]

Miriam, before leaving for the train, gives me an old wooden Tamil ink stamp, its letters now very indistinct, illegible, which she found in Udipi—so that I will remember, she says, that I have left a mark.

March 4, Mylapore

On the night train I dream I am trapped in a lecture by a dreadful postmodern linguist; there is no escape. My wiser friends tell me, in jest, that *Derrida*, in Telugu, is Daridra (impoverished)—so *postmodernism* would, I say, be Dāridryamu, following Panini's rule on nominal abstraction.

I wash off the many-layered grime of Tiruvarur, savor Rajamani's relief at being back. Charu takes me shopping, near the temple, for an electric hot plate, a key component of the Rajahmundry survival kit. Mylapore, again and always: this miracle of gold-gray space, my space. In the evening we watch the Telugu *Annamayya* film on DVD, or as much as I can stand of it. It offers a cheap hagiography of the fifteenth-century Tirupati poet, one of the most original voices in Telugu literature, a man who revolutionized the sensibility structured into the Tirupati cult. As I have so often, I marvel how a poet so tough-minded and inventive could have been so radically sentimentalized. Even the *padam* songs themselves, interlaced with the story, become sticky and crudely pious.

March 5: Coromandel Express

Heading "home." In the train, for whatever reason—is it the breath of my Tamil memories sweeping through my mind, or the wrench of leaving Mylapore again?—a frenzy seizes me. It is one of those moments of sudden pseudoclairvoyance, when the world seems almost to make sense. The cityscapes outside give way to green paddy fields and palms, and, lulled by the gentle clicking of the wheels on the rails, I succumb.

This morning before my departure, Charu says that there is an expert in Nāḍi—divination by opening texts at random—at the Vaidīśvarankoyil temple, near Mayavaram; she wants to take me there so he can read my former lives. She'd like some confirmation of her strong hunch that in a former birth I could recite Tamil and Sanskrit poems.

But the Nāḍi readings, I suddenly realize, go far beyond such retrospective predictions. If you have a certain flaw in your birth chart, the expert will prescribe a solution: see the goddess Mayūravalli at Mayavaram, for example, offer *pūjā*, and the troublesome *dosha* flaw will be removed. Each such prescription is specific, pragmatic, and semiotically secure.

So the world is thick with signs and highly specialized modes of emergence. Planets, karma, previous births, mistakes, dreams, obscure impulses, fateful intentions—together they form an immense, crisscrossing grid within which a person can, with a little help, navigate successfully. "Sages" are capable of seeing the wider grid and articulating the connections. Gods play with the grid, but they are also part of it, nodes within it; at the same time, they seem to enjoy a measure of plasticity denied us. The grid is so dense and saturated with determinate vectors that one might want to free oneself entirely—*mukti*, the ancient goal of release. Anything, even leaving behind the world, for a few gasps of fresh air. Divine-human relations, like the links between any other two levels or entities, are heavily interdependent and interactive.

Since the whole system is continuously buzzing or vibrating, like the drone of the *tampura*, with inaudible or barely audible music, language in its varying modes may provide arteries, crossroads, a mechanics of transition. Here a notion like "beauty" is far too primitive. *Camatkāra*, the smacking of the lips in wonder, is more effective. One often wonders. What one sees or hears, in any case, is surface—momentarily visible and/or audible—emergent and de-emergent.

Within so thick a web, dying is next to impossible; but suffering is the stuff of experience. One is constantly clearing out some "inner" space—"inner" in the sense of viable and vaguely private (always in a family context), not internal to self. Self is the total permutation. Waste disposal is not much of a problem: the whole system is a remainder, *śesha*, in relation to *your* space. But taking in—food, drink, thought—inspires anxiety, to say nothing of desire, which is also not quite internal to self. Hence the endless boundary restrictions, above all those relating to oral consumption, a horror of absorbing foreign substance.

One is drawn, magnetically, to greater or higher intensities: intensity resolves obstructions. Since the whole system is present at any given point and at every moment, a new surface can be created simply *by paying attention* or, a hopeful modality, *dissolved by imagination.*

There is an irresistible urge to generate subsets in the web: seven *viṭanka-sthala*s, five Tamil temples of the elements, eight mythic achievements (*aṭṭavīraṭṭānam*), and so on. Such subsets can be superimposed to great effect. Always, however, there is a *rahasya*, some secret, a sealed chamber, like at Tiruvarur, a curtain or veil or diagram where the more generative connections are mapped. The *rahasya* is close to the point of emergence. Zero is such a point, very full but free of clutter, lying somewhere between 1 and 2. Footprints will naturally predate the foot. Dreams will often contain the future. Time condenses, thickens, stretches, tugs, extends in differentially intensified domains.

What is real? Śankara, prophet of oneness, sees only the whole, its discontinuities healed. Nāgârjuna, explaining "emptiness," sees the "interbeing," the space where our imaginations project and interweave, which renders logic barren. The poeticians think only the tensile fusion of "real" and "unreal" counts as poetry, that is, true, expressive language. *Utprekshā*, poetic fancy—the transfer of features from one domain to another, alien one—is the paradigm figure, releasing blockage in some given part of the grid. More generally, a notion like "awareness" seems to demand the superimposition or conflation of subsets that could forge paths out of or away from a surface obstruction, like in Snakes and Ladders. But a true poet has the freedom and power to take the grid apart and reconstitute it under conditions of singularity.

Rajamani says a camera sees better than the eye. Our vision is distorted by who we are, by feeling or thought. Handelman, however, has always claimed that photographs *must* lie.

* * *

Train meditations. Gradually a deep peace settles in. Kerala was good, Tenkasi superb, Tiruvarur—real work, working again. Touching Mylapore centers me: dependable *camatkāra*, the delight or wonder that, according to the Sanskrit poeticians, changes one's world.

* * *

Rajahmundry

8:00 PM

As if it could be anywhere in India, an arbitrary point, I get off the train and I am here and this is home.

Patanjali Sastry has waited up for me—the train is an hour late. "Are you walking from Vijayawada?"

Two straight hours of Telugu conversation with Ravindra, pharmaceutical engineer; he speaks beautifully but cannot read. Then reading riddles with Samhita, black-eyed, bouncy, five years old, the prototypical train moment.

The AC unit is installed in the bedroom, ready to go. The Mylapore hot plate works. The fridge is turned on, the house clean. I make Venkaṭeśvara in the *pūjā* room less lonely: Sarasvati's conch (Maya's gift) and Nellaiyappar, from my Tirunelveli excursion, join him on either side. Pictures of our grandsons, Inbal and Nahar, have arrived from Eileen. I unpack, dinner arrives. I stare awhile at the fragrant street outside.

Home.

Then a mistake. I have brought back from Madras a new CD of Subhapantuvarali *rāga*, sung by Aruna Sairam, my favorite. I put it on, late at night. Mournful and relentless, it overwhelms or possesses. I lie under the fan, consumed, every cell aflame. So *this* is what I have longed for. There will be no sleep tonight.

Composed in the early years of the sixteenth century, Allasāni Pĕddana's astonishing Telugu poem, the Manu-caritramu, *tells us how the First Man—Svārocisha Manu—came to be born. Day after day my teacher Kanakaiah would come to my flat to teach a few more verses, first reciting them melodiously, then crisply explicating them in a slightly formal modern Telugu. I was expected to learn the verses by heart—and I did try, diligently, to do so, with mixed results. I knew the text from earlier reading, but I had never studied it in this methodical way, guided by a demanding connoisseur who felt every syllable had a purpose. The pace was right for me; the verses infused my days with fragrance. Since they came to impinge upon much of what I was seeing and feeling, and since the diary passages repeatedly refer to them and to the cumulative narrative they tell—a parallel track to my own odd progression through space and time—I offer here, by way of introduction, a synopsis of the story.*

The pious Brahmin Pravara lived with his family in Arunaspada, in the plains. His greatest longing was to see the famous pilgrimage sites he had heard about, especially those in the high mountains. One day a wandering Yogi gave him an ointment that, smeared on his feet, would allow him to travel throughout the world. Pravara took off at once for the Himalayas. But after an hour or two of wandering, amazed by the novel sights and sounds, over the cold slopes, he was ready to go home for lunch. Alas, the ointment had washed off his feet in the snow; Pravara was stuck. In his distress, he came upon an apsaras, *a divine courtesan, playing the veena; thinking she could perhaps direct him southward, he ventured to speak to her. But this woman, Varūthini, at once fell in love with the radiant and handsome Brahmin. She used all her womanly arts and eloquent words to seduce him; but Pravara steadfastly refused her invitation, even pushed her away violently with his hands. He then prayed to the god of fire, begging him to take him home; and Agni agreed to this request and spirited Pravara back to Arunaspada.*

Varuthini was left aching with unrequited love and desire. Each passing moment—sunset, nightfall, moonrise, dawn—only intensified her pain. But at this critical juncture, as her life hung in the balance, a divine gandharva *magician (who had once wanted her but had been rejected) saw his opportunity. Using his surpassing skills, this* gandharva *took the shape of Pravara and presented himself to Varuthini, who was, of course, overjoyed. This Māyā-Pravara, counterfeit of the human original, declared himself ready to sacrifice his body, and his dharmic scruples, to save Varuthini's life—on condition that she fully satisfy him and that she keep her eyes tightly shut during their lovemaking. She agreed, and the couple happily made love.*

Soon Varuthini became pregnant (with the physical seed of her gandharva *lover that fruitfully combined with the burning image of the real Pravara in her mind), and Māyā-Pravara was bored and restless—also afraid that she would somehow discover his deception and curse him. So he took his leave with disingenuous, brutal phrases: "Neither union nor separation are permanent states. Don't lovers come and go? If I go, will my devotion to you diminish?" Once our debts to the past are paid—this is the poet speaking—even a love as dear as life itself will fall away. [This is as far as I got in my lessons with Kanakaiah.]*

Varuthini, doubly abandoned, gave birth to a boy, Svarocis. Hunting in the mountains, Svarocis saved a young woman, Manorama, from a demon who had been pursuing her for three days. This demon turned out to be Manorama's own father, originally a gandharva *named Indīvarāksha, who had wanted to study medicine, Āyurveda, but was rejected by the teacher; when this teacher discovered that Indīvarāksha had managed to listen in on his lectures after all, he cursed him to pursue his own daughter. Svarocis married Manorama and learned the arts of healing from her father. He used this new wisdom to heal two of Manorama's girlfriends, who were afflicted with leprosy.*

Svarocis lived happily with these three beautiful women in the forest. One day he was hunting a wild boar when suddenly he was addressed by a doe; she begged him to kill her instead of the boar, for, she explained, death was preferable to the agony of watching one's beloved playing with other women. "Who is your beloved?" asked Svarocis; and the doe answered, "You." Svarocis embraced her and, thus held in his arms, she turned into a beautiful young woman, an embodiment of the Wilderness Goddess, sent by the gods to produce a human son, Manu, for Svarocis.

Soon the Wilderness Goddess gave birth to this boy, Svārocisha Manu, the First Man of his cosmic age.

March 6

Light on the green palm fronds, the yellow-gold house across the street, the mauve bougainvillea: like a king bathing his poets in gold, each dawn transfigures the view from my balcony.

Kanakaiah turns up early; we are now entering the story proper after the invocations and encomia to the poet's patron-king. The innocent Brahmin Pravara, living on the sultry plains, suffers from wanderlust; with the help of the Siddha-Yogi's magic ointment, he is able to fly off to the Himalayas. Dazzling landscapes inhabit these early verses. Clearly, our hero has never felt real cold before; he naturally links it to his notion of doomsday, the fiery end of the world and its periodic cooling and rebirth:

> When all that exists
> loses its shape and melts down
> in the fires that burn away creation
> in age after age,
> would things ever solidify again,
> could plants germinate and sprout
> without the cold touch of this
> frozen mountain?
> (2.10)

But soon it is noon and he is hungry and eager to go home. Alas, he discovers that the ointment has washed off his feet in the snow. Disconsolate, in increasing panic, Pravara roams the menacing slopes. . . .

In seems a long way from Rajahmundry to the Himalayas; reading the verses, remembering my days in Garhwal, I feel a certain kinship to Pravara and his naïve amazement. More to the point, Pĕddana's magic is far more potent than the Siddha's ointment. This poet never leaves you stranded. The verses, strangely intimate, weave themselves into my thoughts, popping up unpredictably in the course of my meanderings through town, or late at night when I sing them to myself as lullabies. Sometimes I think I am seeing East Godavari through Pĕddana's piercing eyes.

At seven Krishnayya drives me on his scooter through Old Rajahmundry, where he grew up—the sinuous streets of the Fishermen and the Herders and the Pleasure-Women. One piece of life is tucked inside another, folded together with the dust and sweat. The dingy, dorky facades nurture recesses where life happens, cumulates, centuries are stored. A shattering beauty. He leaves me on the riverbank for the first of the evening *kacceri*s (concerts)—a Rajahmundry tradition in the month of March. An ensemble from Tirupati is playing, flute, violin, *mridangam*. When it is over Kanakaiah walks me all the way to Danavayipeta, first half an hour along the river, then through the town. At every step there is memory. Here is the Markandeya temple, mentioned by Śrīnātha in the fourteenth century. Nannayya, the first Telugu poet, must have walked here, along the river, near the Mahalakshmi Hotel. Kotagummam: the old palace or fort. Kandakam Road: here Veeresalingam gave a famous lecture. Here is Ratnam Pens, sought after by anyone who wrote things down in South India over the last century. Subrahmanya Maidan. At Devi Chowk there were once open-air theatre performances all night long, in the street. He would sit on the fence or the steps and listen. *"Appaṭlo"—then*—the phrase keeps coming to the surface, an utterly substantial nostalgia; suddenly Rajahmundry is like Jerusalem, or Athens, the staggering richness of continuous, intensive cultural production for a thousand years.

This nighttime walk was the irreplaceable moment of the day. Kanakaiah knows his city. A nagging doubt arrives, on schedule: have I given anything to these people? What do I have to give?

March 7

Dust, there is no end to dust, infiltrating every porous place. One could wash the floors several times a day and still they would never be clean. It is a task beyond human volition. Perhaps the constant flood of light, from the hint of rose as night ends to the molten gold of noon, condenses as dust, the quivering atoms, *trasa-reṇavah*, of the poets. These same motes seem to inhabit the space of awareness, vibrating there beyond thought or meaning. Sometimes awareness, too, condenses and solidifies and shatters, leaving behind, in the mind, tiny, indivisible gobbets, like when a thermometer breaks and the mercury scatters in shimmering dots of poison—the stuff of intellection.

Some days I oscillate between elation and deflation. There is the early morning walk up Nehru Road past the "Future Kids' School" toward the National Highway that connects Calcutta with Madras. Many dozens of middle-class Rajahmundrians walk here at dawn, when the air is cool. Sometimes I struggle with the Telugu newspaper, *Āndhrajyoti*, after breakfast; it is tedious in content and sluggish, meretricious, in its language, like newspapers everywhere. Joy resides in living speech (but I don't always understand it). And I am impatient, I tire of the regression, the role of the uncomprehending child. How can their tongues turn so quickly? Years ago, in Hyderabad, Vimala taught me to say, "nālika tiragaḍam ledu" (My tongue won't revolve). It's still true. Telugu tongues seem endowed with an astonishing slippery lubrication, and what one hears is a continuous watery mixture of melodic vowels, trickling plosives, and a rapid pitter-patter of various forward and backward *l*'s and *n*'s.

There are, however, those merciful souls who speak gently and precisely. I pay a visit to Lakshmi Narasamamba, who lives off Korukonda Road, across from the Ramakrishna Mutt. We met in Mysore in 1995, at the Folklore Conference; she has written a dissertation on Muslim women's songs in Telugu, collected in the Godavari region. She plies me with *arise* sweets and milk and the ambrosia of perfect Telugu articulation. She speaks with respect, even awe, of the ancient sages of the Veda, who had visions of truth that cut through the everyday surface. I tell her I am reading Chalam's novella *Maidānam*, that it has somehow bewitched me. It tells the story of Rajesvari, a woman who escapes her dull marriage by running off to the wilderness with her Muslim lover. In its day, in the 1940s, the novella scandalized Andhra. Still, Lakshmi is not at all sure that Rajesvari, a protofeminist, offers a viable model. It is a man's feminism, I say, not a woman's; mostly a male dream of what he imagines a free-spirited woman might want or respond to, might want a man to do. No woman could have written this book, and sometimes I wonder what it is like for a woman to read it. Still, there is the spell, maybe no more than the hocus-pocus of Chalam's indisputably lush syntax. Lakshmi says she would like to reread it. We set to meet regularly in the late afternoons for Telugu conversation, after she comes back from the school where she teaches.

I step out into the fragrant dusk, the fierce roar of trucks, buses, and auto rickshaws on the Korukonda Road. I buy a few oranges and roasted peanuts from a vendor. The air is heavy and moist; a hint of jasmine jars my mind. The memory of Chalam's novel pales and dissolves; it was, I suppose, no more than a diversion, like most of the modern works. But the Pĕddana verses—that is another matter. They have a way of coming alive, focused and pressing, at any moment. In the dusty street, I think, in the thick mélange of taste and sound, how easily "all that exists / loses its shape and melts down."

March 10

Kanakaiah calls to say he is late but will come. Fine, I say, I am here. Phone conversations with him are frustrating; like many people here, he treats the phone like a potentially hostile force and tends to shout into it. That, together with the speed of his Telugu, makes it almost impossible for me to understand him. Struggling to communicate, I marshal my bookish Telugu: *mīkosam kācukuni uṇṭānu*, I say, wanting him to know that I will wait expectantly for him. But what the phrase actually means, I later discover, is something like "I am lurking in ambush for you." Kanakaiah is, hopefully, learning forbearance.

Hunting for the washerman they say lives somewhere close by, I happen upon Satyanarayana and Nirmala, the housewife who sends me my midday and evening meals. Satyanarayana has a car for hire, and I am sure I will need him. Nirmala is young, playful, pretty, witty; she teases me when she can't understand me; she plies me with tea in an eagerness to give, to offer something to this awkward guest. I see her tiny kitchen, hardly more than a corner in the cramped two-room flat. Out of this dark cell come the vast servings of fiery Āndhra-bhojanam day after day.

* * *

Smile comes at half past three to take me on his scooter to the Damerla Rama Rao Art Gallery: Narayana Rao called to say he wants to use this Rajamundry painter's magnificent *Pĕḷḷi kūturu* (Bride) on the cover of his *Kanyā-śulkamu* translation. Damerla Rama Rao is a sad story of promise unfulfilled; he died in 1925, of smallpox, at the age of twenty-eight. Had he lived, he would certainly have become a national figure. What is left of his oeuvre is stored here, in Rajahmundry. But when we arrive, we find the gallery locked: Friday holiday, *sĕlavu*. We comfort ourselves on the way back with milky *bāsuṇḍi* at Anand Sweets in Danavayipeta, a venerable Rajahmundry institution. Danavayipeta, with its pastel facades, where every second house is a doctor's clinic, glows golden brown in the late-afternoon sun—the light thicker, sweeter than the *bāsuṇḍi*.

* * *

Friday night. Next door to me, an immense Shamiyana canopy has gone up, blocking off the street. A *griha-praveśam*—ritual entry into the new home—will be celebrated tomorrow; a white cow wanders up and down, looking for food. Much fussing over benches, tables, pots. They will be serving a huge meal to a host of friends and family, and the cow, too, will get her share. She is, no doubt, slated as a gift to some worthy Brahmin at this auspicious hour. The evening cools off. Bits and pieces of me scatter and collide, aimlessly, unclearly. This limbolike lack of focus must mean something. Telugu flees from me, as from a demon.

March 11

By 5:00 AM the street is bubbling with the sounds of metal vessels—stirring, boiling, pouring, splashing. Huge tubs are being filled with water and milk. The cooks shout cheerfully at one another, as if it were midday. No point in trying to sleep. White light is filtering through the clouds along with the sloshing of the tubs, the water flowing through the taps, the morning devotionals on the radio. A little crumpled, I get up, absorb the imminent blessings from next door. I take myself out for a walk past the cashew groves and fallow fields toward the National Highway, the Kadiyam Road. Clarity and peace fall into me, or out of me, like raindrops. Smile comes for Turkish coffee at eleven; today, for some reason, maybe it's the auspicious vibrations in the street, the well-fed cow, anyway my Telugu flows—a small victory. Kanakaiah appears late in the evening, recites two exquisite verses, and departs. Does a man need more than two Telugu verses to redeem any one day?

March 12

Mornings on the balcony as the light begins to flow, the cool air heavy with sweetness; a few verses of the *Naishadhiya*, yesterday's *Manu-caritramu* poems, over and over until they congeal, thick as air, in memory. Thus the day begins with benefice. At seven Smile calls to say he has just read the introduction Narayana Rao and I wrote to Pingaḷi Sūranna's sixteenth-century novel, the *Kaḷāpūrṇodayamu*, and that it is very good.

Yesterday we tried and failed again to see the Damerla Rama Rao collection: every second Saturday it is closed (along with government offices). By now there is a ritual; this time on our way back from the locked museum we go for Badam milk at Anand Sweets. Smile likes to keep up a running commentary on Rajahmundry as he drives me past Devi Chowk, then the vegetable market, the gardens of Danavayipeta. "*cālā pāta town*, it's a very old town," he says to me, and all his love for this place is there in the simple words. He's not supposed to eat sweets, or drink alcohol, but he lives, with great verve and directness, in the defiant mode of the connoisseur poet. Life is too delicious to be held hostage to doctors' demands. I think Smile remembers in detail every good meal he has ever eaten, and he takes joy in describing them as they come to mind—not only what was ordered and served but where, when, how, the colors, the blending of tastes, the quantities of spice, the features of cook or waitress, a witty word that was spoken, the breeze that was blowing, the hour of the day or night.

March 13

After my dawn walk, as I stop to buy a paper, Endluri Sudhakar sees me and takes me home for morning tea. He has just finished composing a new poem—the ink is literally not yet dry on the pages he shows me. He is happy to recite it to me, another *cri de coeur*, his own counterclaim, as a Telugu Dalit, on the language that others, "higher," the Brahmin elite, have appropriated. At moments the personal protest turns lyrical, swerves away from the political; and there is the music of his voice. I listen intently. Sudhakar's wife serves snacks as neighbors, consumed by curiosity, peer through the window. Sudhakar's house is very close to mine, he shows me a shortcut, *dŏḍḍi dāri*, the "calf path" or "backyard way": the backyard is where they would keep the cows and calves. He asks me to come whenever I have time.

Midmorning, Patanjali Sastry comes by, full of his triumph: the Supreme Court has ruled in his favor in the matter of Kolleru Lake. He has been fighting this cause for years, with great courage, in the face of endless obstacles, verbal attacks, even threats of assassination. Industrial fishing has ruined the ecofabric of this great lake in West Godavari—one of the largest in Asia, and formerly home to many rare species of migrating birds. Now it seems industrialists will be compelled to restore it to its original, healthy state. The judges had no patience for their greed and their lawyers' endless delaying tactics and outright lies. All in all, this story has an unexpectedly happy ending. One good man can make a difference. I tell Sastrygaru that he has to tell the story, from the beginning, in a Telugu book that will read like a thriller.

* * *

It seems the day is auspicious through and through. On our fourth try, Smile and I find the Rama Rao gallery wide open. There are 34 surviving, finished oil paintings, and 129 watercolors—but the colors are fading; conditions in the museum are very far from adequate, as is generally the case in Andhra. If something is not done soon, these paintings will be lost. They speak of digitalizing the collection; at least that.

The Bride, *Pĕḷḷi kūturu*, is dazzling, and right for the cover of *Kanyā-śulkam*. Many of the works are hardly more than exercises, but some—the sketch of a young girl's face, the sitar player Abdur Rahman Khan, and the large-scale *Pushpâlankāra* (Adorning with Flowers)—are brilliant. There is an Andhra touch, as one might expect: a hint of the elongated human figure, as at the ancient Kakatiya temple sites of Palampet and Hanumakonda; and that particular rubescent glow that seems truly to inhere in this soil and this sky. He has unerringly captured this subtle tint, a defining feature of light in Andhra. There is a surviving picture of the artist, cut down so early in life: black hair with a curl falling across his forehead, a thin mustache, narrow build, delicate eyes—hardly more than a boy. I buy a postcard of his wistful sketch of the girl, to grace the wall in my flat.

On the way home, Smile stops to buy watermelon and beer, to celebrate today's successes. The watermelon, Smile says joyfully, is filled with Godavari, soaked up through the soil, like everything else we eat and drink in Rajahmundry; the river thus flows through our mouths and stomachs, nourishing and healing and caressing. Godavari is not somewhere outside us but deeply alive within.

March 14

Listening carefully to Kanakaiah's teaching, I ask myself: What comprises real understanding, *avagāhana*, for him? What is knowledge?

Part of it seems to be a way of mapping domains onto one another. There are always three of this, four of that; you find them reflected, *pratibimbita*, in the text in a nonlinear, cumulative way. The art lies in discovering the hidden connectedness (behind this drive lies a horror of disconnectedness). To know means inscribing these maps in one's memory so that they become accessible on demand.

If you peel away the opacity of surface, what you see is the individual moment embedded in the whole rich warp and woof. This moment reverberates: you learn to listen to the emergence, see the sound—the reality principle at work. Imagination is one conduit for unveiling the linkages, that is to say, for dehabituating ourselves, undoing solid surface.

Imagine a history of the French Revolution that would seek to pair each major event with a corresponding echo event in, say, the Russian Revolution or the American one. Only in the relations, the superimpositions, does the story make any sense. The historian patterns the echoes, thereby healing breaks in sequence, temporal gaps, lapses of awareness. Only rarely, cumulatively—the perspective from the guillotine?—can the whole be perceived.

We think of analysis as a means of separating out the strands. In India, analysis integrates by playful, imaginative superimposition, filling in cracks and empty spaces.

* * *

Krishnayya, visiting in the late afternoon, speaks with passion about Lord Venkaṭeśvara at Tirupati. Once, he says, this god must have been a person, very lonely, deserted by his wife, bald, given to headaches, needy, poor. In this mode he became God (a cowherders' god?).

March 15

An unidentifiable animal—dog? donkey? buffalo? child?– cries piteously through the night, a Dostoyevskian nightmare. The wailing enters into my body, I can't sleep. Shortly before six o'clock the milk girl, Ratnam, from a family of buffalo herders who live farther down the street, turns up with my first half liter of fresh buffalo milk. To my surprise, she speaks a lovely "standard" Telugu. This is to become part of my daily routine, the morning milk delivery; Ratnam is punctual and precise, almost German in her manner. Elated, I rush to boil the milk, marveling at its ability to expand, rise, and overflow, like a living being.

* * *

Last concert of the season, by the river. Tiruvaiyaru P. Sekhar, from Madras, a student of the famous Balamuralikrishna, sings in his master's familiar (too familiar) mode. We sit for these hours on the riverbank, offering our bodies to the mosquitoes in the manner of the self-sacrificing Bodhisattva, listening intently, playing at identifying the *rāga*s. Toward the end Kanakaiah hands over a note asking Sekhar to sing something in Amrita-varshiṇī *rāga*—a worthy conclusion to the evening. Afterward, Venkatesvara Rao drives me home on his scooter; on the way, traversing the Kandakam Road, I remind him of the Muttusvami Dikshitar composition, *Ānandâmrita-varshiṇī*, sung in this *rāga* to bring rain to drought-stricken Ettayapuram, in the dry land of southern Tamil Nadu—the haunting *kriti* Eileen learned so many years ago in Mandaiveli, the one that always moves me to tears. Like bringing rain. The composer started singing, and the skies opened up and then the downpour wouldn't let up, so he had to change the wording of the song—from "Rain! Rain! Rain!" to "Stop! Stop! Stop!"

These conversations from the backseat of the scooter, into the wind—a prevalent Rajahmundry genre—are not too satisfying. Parting, Venkatesvara Rao tells me I speak Telugu "very correctly." It is my driving ambition to reach a point where something like natural, idiomatic speech will obviate such unhappy compliments.

March 16, Kakinada

I have been longing to see Kakinada, Rajahmundry's twin city, an hour and a half away. I think of it, saturated with literary nostalgia, as an almost mythic landscape. So with Krishnayya I take a morning bus through the sumptuous paddy fields. It is the Holi festival of spring: children have painted their faces in bright colors, and many passersby have been stained by flying paint and powder. We are met by Krishnayya's student Moses, now a lecturer at the local college, and several of his students, our eager guides.

They show us the "downtown" with its three parallel thoroughfares: Main Street, Cinema Street, and Temple Street. Each concentrates on its own specialty. You don't have to comb the city to find a cinema hall; they stand nonchalantly together, like conscripts, in a straight line (more or less). The city has the mild, slightly sleepy aspect of a seashore resort, a place where one might dream something as phantasmagoric as the pink OM building, former home of the Brahmos, nineteenth-century reformists and modernizers: crenellated towers and squashed cupolas crown this mostly abandoned masterpiece of the absurd. Some unknown Andhra Gaudi in a former era found scope for his genius here in Kakinada. There are also the old mosques and the early churches and a plethora of striking houses that have miraculously survived the last century or two.

We drive along the coast, past Koringa Bay and its white sand, to Yanam, once a remote piece of France. Nothing much remains of the French overlay; red bougainvillea spills over the facades on the one major street, a tropical pastiche of pastels that could be Mexico or Marseilles. Cellapilla Venkata Sastry, the great extempore poet-scholar of the early twentieth century, lived here for some time, though no one can show us his house. Years ago in Paris I met several Telugu families from Yanam; they took advantage of the offer of French citizenship and set up their own small countercolony in France. What they left behind here is the passionate riverscape, a glow of blue, green, gold. The fishermen are out in their wooden boats, some flying patched gray sails with an occasional hole in the center. The boats glide and veer under the breeze. Konasima, a mass of distant trees, stretches toward the sea from the other bank of the river. An imposing black Śiva-linga, like at Puskarala Revu in Rajahmundry, clearly a recent, rather crude afterthought, stakes a claim to this side of the water. It is late afternoon, the sun peaceful, light, the boats tracing vivid arcs in the blue-brown waves; the air hints of honey, and this river, I realize, is more beautiful, more eloquent, than any I have seen before. Personally, I would never trade it for the Seine, or any other. No sooner do I think this thought than the moment is gone—incipient terminal retrospection—before I manage to take it all in.

March 17: Gautami Express

Ratnam, lanky and demure in her faded purple sari, turns up with the fresh milk at a quarter to six in the morning; each day a few minutes earlier. Her arrival at my doorstep is, I think, the only punctual event in all of South India. I am afraid to ask her to come a little later—probably the whole system will lurch into disorder, clocks will no longer run, train schedules will go awry. So my day starts at five o'clock, though it is no longer cool even at this early hour. A humid heaviness sits upon the air, waiting for sunrise to boil.

Following Krishnayya's earnest advice, I have decided to offer Kanakaiah some symbolic remuneration for his daily lessons. He gives me an hour of his time each day, and I know he takes time to prepare—this in the midst of a busy schedule at the college. So I prepare an envelope with what I optimistically call a *pāritoshikam*, an honorarium, hoping the neutral term will not put him off. But I should have followed my own instincts. He adamantly refuses to touch the envelope, even looks at it with a kind of horror or scorn. "These poems we are reading," he says to me, not angry but with definitive clarity, "are eternal, *śāsvatamulu*. What have they to do with money?" That settles that.

Leaving again—very reluctantly. There are meetings to attend in Jerusalem; I will be coming back with Eileen. Departure feels utterly unwelcome, a rip in the fabric. I have barely begun. I love the flat, the street, the river. Time, so viscous and elastic, has suddenly wrapped itself into a small knotted tangle. I cling to the hours, the grains of light; I mop the floor. Smile brings sweets and beer, to see me off; and, with Sastrygaru, we finish the watermelon. I am pensive, a little distracted: "Davidgaru is already in Jerusalem," says Sastry. There is a rush at the end, a flurry in me, the hasty rickshaw ride to the station through the alleys of Innespet, the potholes in the streets.

Anand is traveling by the same train to Hyderabad; we meet as the train arrives. In the midst of my usual harried procession inside the bogies, from the wrong end of the train to my compartment, Anand suddenly says, "You want to see Godavari?" I look out the open window: the world is a river.

March 18, Hyderabad

On the train, I immerse myself in the *Naitatam*, my beloved Tenkasi Tamil version of the *Naishadhiya*. For the last few days in Rajahmundry, after my morning coffee with Sastrygaru and some Telugu prose to put my mind in gear, I have been reading these Tamil verses, puzzling over the sense of something quite new—a strong sense of a modern sensibility at work in the minds of the main protagonists. Nala is in love with the princess Damayanti. On his way to the *svayamvara* ceremony in which she will choose her husband, he is stopped by Indra and three other gods; they, too, are in love with Damayanti, and they cruelly request Nala to argue their case before the woman whom he loves.

Other than you, who have conquered Love,
for all his power,
by your own beauty, who is there
to heal the suffering spread
by *his* honeyed arrows?
(11.26)

Indra's demand is much worse, the poet tells us, than asking Nala to give up his life. Nala at once loses his mind (*karuttu*); forgets who he is (*taṉṉaiyu' maṟakkum*). He cannot say no to the gods, cannot lie to them—though suddenly "lying" seems to him to lose its terror, and "truth" to expand its register. Uncertainty washes over him:

Is it her eyes (think of her bangles, think of her waist,
studded with jewels), is it the arrow of hostile
Desire, is it this dharmic business of lying
being classed as "bad"?
Something is eating at my life
when I'm at my weakest, most vulnerable,
like a sword twisted in my heart.
(29)

Tamil poets are fond of such inner states, but the poet Ativirarama has pushed the analysis further than usual—beyond anything in the parent text of Śrīharsha. He seems to see directly into Nala's mind and to listen carefully to the words that this mind produces in an emergency. Nala wavers, protests, debates with himself, briefly turns against conventional morality and its hollow categories, hesitates again, makes silly pronouncements, and ends up complying with external constraints—like me.

He could almost be *der Mann ohne Eigenschaften*, though Tenkasi, with its paddy fields and palm trees, hardly conjures up prewar Vienna. (I like the juxtaposition. Every once in a while two or three of the incompatible worlds inside me collide and shatter; I hear the crunch of broken glass.) In any case, introspection of this order—the inner gaze ripe with self-doubt and unnerving honesty—is a new departure in Tamil, a sixteenth-century invention: the unmistakable mark of modern man.

In the morning, before arrival, thinking back over these verses, I wonder if the defining feature of the "novel" might not be the imaginative autonomy of the characters. The author can never fully control them once they have come into existence as fictive entities. Add to this the dependable thematization of "reality" in relation to something else, perhaps "fantasy" or "fiction"; and a certain loosely integrated totality, a total statement, always singular in tone and texture. *Naitatam* qualifies on all three counts—the first Tamil novel? Or perhaps it would be better to say: the first Tamil work of fiction, in the fullest sense. What kind of metaphysical order is needed for such works to emerge?

Dawn on the outskirts of Secunderabad is white and granular, a clairvoyant prelude to arrival and immediate immersion in waves of dust, fumes, clatter.

March 19

Vimala plies me with riddles. "ciṭāru kŏmmuna, miṭhāyi pŏṭlam" (On the top of a tree, a packet of sweets). The answer, slow in coming (I have to remember what *pŏṭlam* means): *tenĕ paṭṭu* (honeycomb). She says, to my vast relief: this is the first time she is hearing me speak Telugu, not some bookish concoction of my own. Perhaps, after all, I have come some way from the time I studied with her in Hyderabad, almost ten years ago. Those days in Bashir Bagh were intoxicating, my first immersion in living Telugu speech. I remember going with Vimala to see Cecil B. DeMille's *Ten Commandments*—playing in Hyderabad as if it had just been released—and doing my best to explain to her the niceties of the biblical story, in Telugu, in whispers. The reel they were showing was very old and had been spliced in dozens of places, leaving many unintelligible gaps. When we left the theater, Vimala pronounced her verdict: *manci sīnima*, a good film, with a not uninteresting narrative. Echoes of Mandelstam, who was fond of saying that a person needs only one good book in life; when his friend said, "You must mean the Bible," Mandelstam answered: "Yes, why not?"

At the Salar Jang Museum, amid the clutter, the bric-a-brac of centuries, I find a wonderful thirteenth-century Chola Śiva and a very fine Kulu painting of Śiva meditating in a circle of ice.

The air is so dry that chunks of it could break off, fall to the ground like clods of gold. My eyes itch with dust and sun. I stop at Kalanjali for gifts, some taste of Andhra for friends at home. Pochampalli carpet; Kondapalli toys for the boys; a shirt for Edan. It is a little hard to conjure up the reality of Jerusalem, the meetings that await me, university, students, my old world. Has it been only six weeks?

Late afternoon, sun-drunk, to the airport. From the plane I survey the baked city below, white roofs, the Tank Bund hugging the Husain Sagar lake, the tacky statue of the Buddha wading through the water, a furious beehive of scooters and auto rickshaws, the eloquent rocks. I think, suddenly struck breathless by the idea, defenseless, as with a woman: I am in love. With Andhra. This place, this language, these people, this air, this light.

April 6

North Indian intermezzo, with Achyut Bhai and Suchitra. We see lions in the wild at Sasan Gir, the Ashokan inscription at Girnar, Gandhi's childhood home in Por Bandar. We travel the coast, the western edge of India, soaked in light and delicate spice. Like Andhra, Gujarat feels to me like a frontier world—beckoning. I want to live here some day, I want to learn, again, to speak. In Ahmedabad I talk of the Israeli peace movement to an audience of Gandhians, students, writers. They are receptive to what I have to say, but many of them are at pains to convince me that Gandhi is truly dead in Gujarat. "Perhaps," I say, "but he has surfaced again in Palestine, in the village of Bil'in."

At Prabhas, on the coast, Ashok Bhai tells us a Gujarati version of Krishna's death. After the *Mahābhārata* war, Krishna was sitting under a tree, thinking back, "as a politician might," about his career—of this mistake and that one. He grew more and more tired, lost in his mind. "I'll sort it out in the morning," he thought, before falling asleep. That is when Jarā, the Hunter Old Age, struck with his arrow. "Hey Ram!" cried the god, and then, coming fully awake, "but *I* am Ram." Before dying he said, "This comes of not doing what needs to be done instead of just thinking about it." That is why he says to Arjuna at the end of the *Bhagavadgītā*, "Do what must be done, never thinking of the fruits."

* * *

And now home. Hyderabad seems harsh, dense with noise and heat. The sun has turned the lever higher, yet another turn. On the cusp of the hot season. Lonely. Lost. Still absorbed in the tactile images of Gujarat. Where have the lions gone? Airdeccan has cancelled the Rajahmundry flight tomorrow, we have another day in the big city. We try a film, *Being Cyrus*, at Hyderabad Central, a futuristic implant in the savory city I knew; and the film, too, is mostly a horror, we walk out after an excruciating hour.

Walking along the Tank Bund in the early evening, opposite the bewildered white Buddha incongruously floating in the reeking water of the Husain Sagar lake, Eileen says, shouting above the immense racket of the road: "You have to live without knowing."

April 7, Rajahmundry

From the air, Godavari spins and pirouettes, a liquid dance very welcome after an hour of staring at baked Telangana browns. We fly over the high peak of Korukonda with its shrine to the Man-Lion, Narasimha, before landing at Madhurapudi. Within minutes of reaching home, Sri Subrahmanyesvara Sarma knocks at the gate, sent to us by Anand. He teaches Carnatic music, has given over a thousand *kacceri*s; he is young, full of energy, very confident and eager. Eileen wants him to teach her Tyāgarāja's famous composition, *Nagu momu*, in the haunting Ābheri *rāga*. She spreads a mat, and at once lessons begin.

> Don't you know what comes over me
> when I can't see your smiling face?
> Won't you come to take care of me?

Later we walk along the riverbank, in sight of Dhavalesvaram, the Godavari flowing peacefully, gold-green-brown, on our right. To the left, the crowded, century-old neighborhood abutting the train station. Always there is the miracle of the streets, the winding cement staircases, peeling paint, flat roofs, white *muggulu* designs at the threshold, bougainvillea and guava and lemon trees outside. People stand and stare at us, as if we had fallen from the moon. "Summer" is clearly coming closer, we feel the breath of his vanguard in the fiery breeze.

In the evening Smile visits, excited to have found several small bottles of an oversweet, red Pondicherry wine, vaguely reminiscent of the wine the Jews use for Shabbat blessings; he has brought a bottle for each of us. Anyway, it isn't the taste that matters. The main thing is the happy adventure, and someone to share it. Already he and Yasmine have "adopted" Eileen; tomorrow she will be taken to the tailor to be fitted with new Andhra clothes. Smile's bonhomie is a gift of nature, bountiful as the delta and the river.

April 13, Bikkavolu

It takes some time to locate the temples. We wander the village, an hour's drive from Rajahmundry; dogs bark, roosters crow, housewives still in their long nightdresses stare at us from the doorsteps of the old wooden homes. Eventually Dillesvara Ravu, a college student, turns up with a key to the first of the Chalukya masterworks, dated between the ninth and the eleventh centuries. All three temples are unfinished. The villagers say that the gods laid down a condition—that they be completed in a single night—and dawn came too soon. "Why did it have to be a single night?" I ask Dillesvara Ravu, and he says: "Gods! Don't you know the gods?"

Some ten or twelve village children cluster noisily around us, as if we were Pied Pipers, while we walk round the first temple several times, stopping now and then to photograph. They of course want their pictures taken, too; truth be told, they are far more beautiful than the decaying sculptures. The second temple stands intact, a lonely witness, in the midst of the paddy fields, soaking up the sun. The peasants direct us over footpaths beside the canals. Here, in the heart of the delta, you are always liable to run across some broken, silent fragment of the early kings, an Ozymandias stone hemmed in by growing rice. And then there is the name of this village, the "monk's place," an even earlier (Buddhist) fragment?

We find our way through the fields to Golingeśvara, still a living temple with ongoing daily worship of the god, where we meet Gandhiji, a local poet and culture critic, an expert on the Bikkavolu temples; and we are introduced to the manager of the Andhra Bank, the only bank in this village. We pay the mandatory ritual visit to his office. No, it is not entirely a ritual: this man, too, is very lonely, eager for contact with someone from outside, someone who reads poetry. He explains the life of a bank manager here: he works from dawn to dark, day after day, without rest. Politicians are continuously pestering him, pressuring him, for favors, most of them on a very large scale. Most of his life is devoted to resisting this pressure. It is hard work, and boring. He gives us coffee and cold drinks and very reluctantly allows us to depart.

In the Vināyaka temple—the immense stone image with the elephant's head that emerged naturally one day, they say, from where it was buried under the mud of the paddy fields—one whispers one's request into the god's huge ears.

At Dvarapudi, in blazing noon, we see a grotesque, huge Naṭarāja, Śiva as Dancer; as if sheer size were the key to something (when everything else is lost).

April 16, Visakhapatnam

M. Adinarayana appears at four o'clock, unmistakably himself—I have been reading his walking journal, *Bhramaṇa kānksha* (Wanderlust), which Smile gave me, with the author's picture on the back cover; Adinarayana says Smile is his best friend. The book, illustrated by the author, is a best seller in Andhra. It is, in fact, very engaging reading, this record of weeks on the roads. This man has walked from Vizag to Darjeeling, among other adventures. He is gaunt, lithe, fast, too fast, a loner, unmarried, unencumbered; a barber's son from Ongole in the south who taught himself to paint and sculpt. Now he is a professor in the Department of Fine Arts of Andhra University, and a walker. He gives me his card: "Enjoyed Walking for 15,000 kms, published 4 Books on Travel, Exhibited Art 5 Times." I like a man whose card tells you what he enjoys. At the bottom is written: "Walking Is A Prayer With Feet."

It all began when he was riding the train somewhere in Madhya Pradesh, years ago. He caught sight of a hill he wanted to climb. Unable to bear for another second the insufferable fact that trains go on fixed tracks, he disembarked at the next station, tore up his ticket, and began to walk. He's never stopped. He wants to come to Jerusalem, by foot of course, perhaps from Basra, the nearest walkable point. How far is it? he asks. I don't know, I guess it must be a good fifteen hundred kilometers or more. "Oh, that is nothing at all"—the smallest unit he thinks of is a thousand kilometers.

He wants me to come visit him in Ongole: he defines himself, he tells me, as an Ongole bull. (Ongole, far to the south of Andhra, is famous for its powerful bulls.) An eccentric, through and through; likeable, innocent, mad. He reminds me of my friend Danny Sperber, who walked from Istanbul to Calcutta three times, in the early '60s; who played a critical role in moving me toward studying something Indian when I was more than hesitant. Adinarayana is a passionate devotee of Rahul Sankrityayana, my student Boaz's great hero, early twentieth-century explorer, redeemer of manuscripts from Tibet. If one must have a hero or guru, Rahulji might be a good choice.

Smile sends us in the evening to visit Attaluri Padmini in CBM compound, not far from the main road. A small group is waiting for us on the roof of their flat (her husband, Narasimha Ravu, a well-known specialist in modern Telugu literature, is out of town). I meet Vasireddi Navin, anthologist of Telugu short stories, a close friend of Narayana Rao's. In a room choked with Bobbili *veena*s—Bobbili, north of Vizag, is famed for its exquisitely crafted *veena*s—Padmini, an accomplished musician, plays an Annamayya *padam*: *Emŏkŏ ciguraṭadharamuna*.

Those marks of black musk
on her lips, red as buds,
what are they but letters of love
sent by our lady to her lord?

In exchange, Eileen sings the Tyāgarāja *Nagu momu* that she has been practicing all week. As always, as in Madras long ago, she has the gift of learning these songs on first or second hearing, with the exotic Telugu words (that she doesn't understand) and the intricate rhythms to which they are sung. I used to wish she would give herself completely to Carnatic music (rather than to dance and dance therapy), since listening to her sing is as close as I can get to what is real.

Another moment of flooding, I will go mad with this richness.

As we are walking back late at night, Venkat, the Tiger Dancer, rickshaw driver, my old friend from Chinna Waltair, spots us on the road. I have been meaning to call him, or the neighbors; he has no phone of his own. We have been here for two days, and I keep putting off the call. I haven't seen him for some years, and he doesn't know we're back. How could he pick us out of the thousands winding their way through the black streets? Eileen says: how could he not?

April 17, Hyderabad

Balai Ramachandran sings a *kacceri* in the open courtyard at Key's High School in Secunderabad. After an hour, the skies open up with rain. He goes on singing. Much of the audience joins him on the stage, trying to escape the downpour; the singer embraces them with his song, they enter into the song. When it is over, we try in vain to find an auto rickshaw to take us back to the hotel. The streets are soaked, gleaming in the dark; there are muddy puddles at every step. Like walking home in London, years ago, when I was struggling with first-year Tamil, the dream of Madras still undreamt—and Hyderabad no more than a distant name.

Midday is devoted to buying Andhra earrings at Tanishq. Layers of gold enfold a jet-black stone: the primary colors of Andhra; the subtle, red glow of the soil inheres in the gold. In the afternoon I see Eileen off at the airport, return deflated to the hotel room, now stark and monkish: where are all the *things* that a woman brings? The room has reverted to absurdly straight lines, fragranceless.

At Navin's invitation, I join the poets' circle at the Ganga Restaurant in Dwaraka Hotel, in Lakdi-ka-Phul. Navin is precise, self-possessed, humane. He introduces K. Siva Reddy, entirely and evidently a poet, a white-haired hawk. He is immersed in reading through his old published books, which he has brought to give me; he likes those poems. They look to me like Mayakovsky, though more highly charged with verbal sorcery. Much rhetorical excess: I think revolutions, aside from being wrong, are mostly boring. When did the old instinct for *prīti*, the sheer pleasure of poetry, disappear? It always was, it still is, a higher goal. One volume has been done into a kind of pseudo-English, which exacerbates the strident harangue. But there are some fine poems, too, manly and bold. Mayakovsky, they say, once gave some new poems he had written to Roman Jakobson; when they met a few days later and Mayakovsky asked, a little nervously, for his friend's opinion, Jakobson said: "They're good, but not as good as Mayakovsky."

An older poet, Sugambabu, is here for the traditional afternoon sitting, which sometimes goes on for hours; he is eager to take charge of drilling me in spoken Telugu. I am speaking too fast, slurring, stumbling; it won't do.

So this is the poet's life in Hyderabad: manifestos, tea, collected volumes, residual incantations—very like Jerusalem or Berlin, with the intensity I would recognize anywhere, but perhaps a little sweeter in the midst of this endless, dusty heat and chaos. At night, again, clouds suddenly appear: *akālapu varsham*, untimely rain. It clears the air, but they say the mango crop will be ruined. This seems to be a law of nature in South India. There is lack, or need, in one place, and eventually it is filled, overfilled, in some extreme, erratic burst that causes vast distress somewhere else, close by. No even textures.

April 18, Rajahmundry

It rained here, too. The flat is clean. I unpack. At sunset I sit by the door watching the son et lumière in the sky. Incandescent orange ripens into mauve and dark blue. The builders across the street are spraying water over the day's tentative confabulation of brick and wood. Peace falls into place, into a waiting, ready space. For a moment, for now, I am at home, with my Kutch goddess on the wall. Sastrygaru, as always deliberate and solicitous, stops by to say hello. It is cool under the fan. Kanakaiah will come, poetry will happen, I can learn, I am speaking, the bougainvillea burns on the branch. A slow burning in me.

April 24

The electric power fails in the middle of the morning; the whole street is out. Hours expand, stretch, a boiling mass of unusable time. By mid-afternoon I am demoralized. Without the ceiling fan or running water, life is mostly a matter of simple survival from one moment to the next. It is quite impossible to read, or even sit in a chair. Smile's plastic white chairs are on the point of meltdown. Inside the flat, one breathes in the wet air of a stagnant swamp. Outside, walking anywhere is like swimming through a caldron simmering over a slow flame. All that is missing is the mad dance of cannibals somewhere near.

At such moments—and perhaps more generally, now, as the heat intensifies—time is a sticky, undifferentiated mass: what the Brāhmaṇa texts called *jāmi*. To name the day of the week is an effort; it even feels a little foolish, since chopping up time into such conventional fragments has become wholly artificial. One might stick labels on the burning exterior of a fiery furnace: this segment, let us say, is something called Wednesday, and a similar one will, perhaps, turn up sometime next week—a dubious fiction.

At six, the ceiling fan groans reluctantly, back to life.

* * *

A man walks from South India to the Himalayas in order to see a famous guru. The teacher allows him one question. The questioner wants it to be very precise, so he says: "Can I ask in Telugu?"

"Yes," says the teacher, "and that was your one question. The rest you must ask your heart."

April 25

The days get remorselessly hotter. At 5:50 in the morning, it is already far from "cool." The cloud cover helps; I try to make it to the highway and back before the sun pierces the veil. When it does emerge, it is red, threatening, and hazy, nothing akin to the Mediterranean sun that balances its fire with the sea. Nehru road is full of early morning walkers who seem to me to be hoarding shreds of coolness, as if they could keep them alive, somewhere in the mind, at the very least as a memory, for use when they will need them in the evening.

Last night the *purugulu* attack again, this time in the bedroom. Millions of tiny winged antlike creatures come to rest on my bed; I spend an hour, Sisyphus-style, picking them off my neck, stomach, arms, hair. Again my friends assure me that these bugs know when it will rain—their arrival is a sign. The future exists as a mark, or rather, millions of minute, irksome marks.

* * *

Venkatesvara, lanky bachelor in the flat downstairs, greets me when I come back from the morning walk. Each day at dawn he sits in the courtyard, reading the morning paper. He is a farmer, a devotee of Sai

Baba. The Swami, he tells me, has already announced his future avatar as Premababu, who will be born in a small village in Rayalasima. A male devotee will be reborn as his mother. He knows. What about the father? I ask. "There's no need for a father. Rāma, after all, God Himself, was born from *pāyasam*, sweet milk pudding."

* * *

I have come to love the *tampura*-like foundation of reality in Rajahmundry, the ceaseless hum of the ceiling fans—the subtle and dependable *brahma-nāda*, the buzz of God, that fills the world (that *is* the world?). Everywhere one goes, if the electric current happens to be working, you hear this faintly metallic whirl. Although it sometimes makes it hard to hear what people are saying, there is a gentle comfort in the drone. The heat continuously intensifies, but you are not alone.

* * *

The woman who runs the store that sells soft drinks, betel, cigarettes, and snacks on JN Road—monolingual, very articulate, and happy to talk—asks me the name of my Jewish god. As usual in such circumstances, driven back to the monotony of Mediterranean monotheism, I say: "He is nameless and formless." I am not about to attempt to explain the niceties of the Abulafian Kabbalah with its hypertrophy of divine names. But my friend is shocked (as often happens when I provide some answer to her questions). "What use is a god who has no name?"

* * *

Sugambabu's poems arrive at noon, I find one I like:

> Above this
> paper flower
> how long can the bee
> be—
>
> O true
> illusion!

Eileen says, when I send her the poem on the e-mail, that we are all of us true illusions.

In this vein, in Kanakaiah's melodic recitation, Pravara has now met Varuthini.

> She was sitting on a raised platform
> at the foot of a young mango tree
> in the courtyard of her house, which was built
> of precious gems.
> And, as a cool wind blew against her face,
>
> the red skirt inside the white half-sari
> that veiled her thighs
> turned the gleaming moonstone beneath her
> red, and the gourds of the veena
> rubbed against her firm breasts
> as her delicate fingers seemed to caress
> sweet music from the strings,
> and she was languid with longing,
> her eyes half-closed as if,
> flowing with the song, she was slowly
> making love with expert skill,
> beyond herself with pleasure,
> while the bracelets on her hands
> chimed the rhythm of the song
> and there was joy, brilliant joy,
> as she played on.

An unsettling apparition for a naïve Brahmin from the plains. For Kanakaiah, Pravara is always lucid, aware, and controlled. It is inconceivable to Kanakaiah that the pious Brahmin might actually want her. Perish the thought. Kanakaiah thinks desire, *kāma*, is external to the self, now no less than then. Here, perhaps, is another unexpected continuity with the present, one worth contemplating. So much classical poetry is about pure, mad desire, a distinctive mode of possession; so little deals in love. As for me, I have the role of the un-innocent wayfarer who has wandered into the story and decides to stay.

GRĪSHMA, HEAT

April 28, Rajahmundry

Smile comes very early, laden with *chinna rasālu*, a lush variety of mango that you have to suck through a small hole you make on the tip. Mango season has begun. I try one: a revelation, a golden electrocution. I have never, all my life, tasted something so full of goodness, so richly condensed. Taste intensified and overdetermined to the limit of the tongue's experience, or the mind's ability to process sensation: perhaps this is what Freud meant when he wrote of condensation in dreams.

We speak, as everyone does, of the heat. A great sensitivity to minor variations, a sort of thermal connoisseurship, comes through. It was 41 degrees yesterday, and the humidity is horrible, especially in the late afternoon. Sometimes heat, *veḍi*, seems to me the name of an animal, a living, menacing being, roused, relentless, driven by its own autonomous moods and needs. Smile says he can't stand it now and doesn't leave the house until evening, when he goes to his air-conditioned club to play cards and chat.

But, as ever, it is his delight that comes through most clearly—and once again we speak of the Eluru student days, the Rajavilasam Hotel, quail curry, discovering Sartre and Camus, and making a living by the American translation projects (Thomas Jefferson must be done into Telugu). Smile had a clear handwriting, so he would make the clean copies to be sent to the press—Narayana Rao dictating. I wonder how Thomas Jefferson sounds in Telugu. In those days, Narayana Rao wrote stories, even published a collection. The book has disappeared; few, if any, copies have survived. When Sartre refused to accept the Nobel Prize, Narayana Rao, Smile, and Raju sent him a congratulatory telegram from Eluru. Such was the life of the mind in Eluru, and other small towns in South India, fifty years ago: intense, universal in scope, curious, engaged.

Smile has presented me with a copy of his volume of poems; also of *Khāli sīsālu* (Empty Bottles), his prose collection. The poems are strong, clear in feeling, often capable of surprising. There is a New Year's poem that, says Smile, he wrote very quickly as a gift to a friend:

> Her embrace, children's flowering smiles,
> cigarettes, whiskey bottles, packs of cards, silken threads of secret
> pleasure,
> good poems written on paper,
> friends' loving fingertips,
> piteous eyes, eaves of eyes, of the unlucky—
> holding on to all this, again
> I
> must swim across 365
> rough seas.[1]

Kanakaiah has sent his wife to visit her mother, so he has to take care of his sons, bring food from outside, do the chores. His mornings are busy; he comes at two, just as the heat crouches down in ambush. Today we will finish the second canto. Aroused and frustrated, Varuthini makes her move. Words are not working, despite her elegant formulation of love as ultimacy:

> Now her face showed disappointment
> as she said:
> "Handsome man,
> if you let your youth go by

in these dreadful rites,
when will you enjoy your life?
Isn't the point of all these rituals
to go to heaven
to make love to us?
When the heart unfolds
in love, when it finds release from within
in undivided oneness, like a steady flame
glowing in a pot, when the senses attain
unwavering delight—
only that joy
is ultimately real.
Think about the ancient words:
ānando brahma, God
is ecstasy."[2]

But this, says Kanakaiah, is only *bhautikânanda*, material ecstasy, the lesser kind; Pravara wants a *mānasikânanda*, mental ecstasy, or better still a fusion of mental and material. Kanakaiah sounds almost like Diotima; the soul is split, and Pravara has set his sights high, on release and self-transcendence, a transempirical metaphysical state. Kanakaiah is on his side, no doubt about that.

It is enough to drive any woman to desperation, and indeed Varuthini, utterly frustrated by Pravara's fastidious, clipped phrases of distaste, leaps at him, tries to kiss him; he turns his face away, shakes her shoulders. She pretends he has hurt her with his fingernails—one last try, says Kanakaiah. It doesn't work. Ritual tasks and the householder's life carry the day. Pravara prays to the *gārhapatyâgni*, the household fire, a form of the Fire-God Agni, to take him home, addressing him with the pregnant vocative *svāhā-vadhū-vallabhā*: "beloved husband of Svāhā." Agni is married to Svāhā, the oblation; Fire, too, is a bourgeois. Pravara's inner fire blazes forth with the presence of Agni, which suffices to carry him back home and out of our story. Intense heat, I think to myself, may indeed burn away extraneous desire.

So the Brahmin's Brahminhood is safe; the poet offers us some relief. Two cantos are accomplished. Kanakaiah, a genuinely modest, lucid man, asks forgiveness for any mistakes he may have made in interpreting the verses. He doesn't think his commentary is anything very special.

I tell him it is perfect, my satisfaction greater than even Pravara could imagine. We speak of going together to Mahanandi, Nandyala, and Ahobilam sometime in July.

Toward sunset I venture out to visit Lakshmi. I tell her I'm thinking of keeping the Rajahmundry flat indefinitely, a place to come back to; this, she says, is not a good idea, a waste of much money, and there will be perpetual problems of maintenance—water, power lines, insects. Yes, I say somewhat ruefully, already I have *cedalu*, white ants, in the kitchen and the bathroom. How do I get rid of them? It's a fairly complex process, she says; you call the exterminators, then you have to vacate the flat for a week, remove all items, they bring in powerful and dangerous poisons, etc. etc. No way, I say: the white ants and I will live together very comfortably for a while more.

She takes me up to the roof. A lush world of palms, guavas, and grasses spreads itself below. The Godavari is just beyond the range of vision. Or maybe it has climbed into the sky, which is flowing around us in maddening waves of orange and red. I cannot believe my eyes; cannot believe such dense color can exist, and in such gentleness. I can hardly speak. It is, she says, like the Gāyatri mantra, the essence of the Veda, materialized before us; or that hour when the Man-Lion god, Narasimha, can act, neither day nor night but an in-between, godly moment of far-reaching change. I am on my way, as she knows, to Simhacalam, just outside Vizag, where the Man-Lion incarnation of Vishṇu lives on after he performed his gory task; at just such an hour, in the interstice of ocean and land, he killed his skeptical enemy, Hiraṇyakaśipu. Lakshmi has offered me a graphic prelude to my visit. Dripping red light, awash inside, I say goodbye and climb down to the street.

I walk home meditating on Varuthini's loss and the poet's empathy for her. Pĕddana had the boldness to articulate her hunger. Will I ever be able to say this, in some semi-intelligible way, in a Telugu essay? Would it communicate to anyone? Danavayipeta swirls around me in the dark. In the Shirdi Saibaba temple, the evening *pūjā* is in full swing, bells ringing, flowers flowing toward the deity, all of this open to the street. I fold my hands as I pass. Writing the essay is not so important. Living in Andhra is important. Again and again, more and more. Anyway, why should I struggle to write something in India? Life itself is too interesting. I'm not sure I could create a space conducive to that kind of work. It can wait.

The papers have been talking about an emergent storm in the Bay of Bengal, moving north toward coastal Andhra. Suddenly I realize that the night has cooled. A strong wind is rocking the palm trees. Within a few minutes, the vast heaviness of the day's heat has been blown away. The monster retires, for the moment, to its lair. At home, I open all the windows, drink in the cool air. Perhaps it will rain.

April 30, Akshaya-tritīya, Simhacalam

Why did the god not want to see us on this day when he stands revealed in his true self, his *nija-rūpam*? No doubt it is my flawed heart; I am obstinate, intensely impatient, utterly at the mercy of my fierce desires. Unsteady. Uneven. Ignorant. Diffuse. I constantly make mistakes in Telugu. Again and again, the same mistakes. For that matter, in Sanskrit, too. No wonder he wouldn't let me in.

We leave at seven, the morning cool, in Ravi's car: me in front, Krishnayya, Kamesvari, Cidananda Rao, and Mitravinda squashed together in the back, at their insistence. The back road to Simhacalam takes us past the Vizag Golf Club, a colonial relic, then Mudasa Lova, its small lake glowing green in the sun, and the Vizag jail; then it is forest all the way—the deeply satisfying, temperate forest of the Eastern Ghats. A long, sleek brown cobra—the goddess Ellamma, possibly pregnant—slips across the road. At Simhacalam, at the foot of the mountain, the village is abuzz with pilgrims. We stop for *idli*s and tea. The police—a strong presence—tell us there's no taking the car uphill to the temple. Not today, with the huge crowds. We stand in the sun pondering this problem, which eventually sorts itself out in the usual way. Perhaps Ravi tells them we are driving on, not stopping at the temple, and they accept this fiction. Perhaps, having made their point, they are now prepared to wave us on. It is, as ever, a mystery. On the loudspeakers at the bus stand, we can hear the prayers being sung in the temple. Special buses for the *candana-yātra*, this day when the priests peel away the sandal paste that normally covers up the image of Lord Appanna, are pouring into the village, packed with pilgrims on their way uphill.

Halfway up the mountain, the queue begins. People are standing in the sun, still miles away from the temple. Many have small books or texts to recite during the long hours ahead. The mountain is flooded with color: bright orange and purple saris, white shirts and dhotis, a golden flash of wings in the glowing green foliage of the forest. We drive past. At the general entrance to the temple enclosure, thousands are milling around. The atmosphere is carnivalesque, expectant. A vast space has been set apart for depositing one's sandals. Tens of thousands of pairs, mostly black, lie together on the ground. Peons offer chits as you hand over your shoes. A long queue has formed to reach this first station.

On the right, before the entrance, several booths are selling tickets at differential rates. There is the simple, free line, the one that stretches far down the mountain. Then there is a 30-rupee and a 100-rupee ticket, and a 500-rupee one, and a thousand-rupee booth next to the "Information" counter. Krishnayya fights his way through to ask at this counter whether our names are recorded, since we have been told that tickets will be waiting for us. And, a miracle, they are. Our friends have been busy for days trying to pave our way into the *darshan*. Phone calls have gone back and forth from Hyderabad, and the Endowment Minister himself has intervened. We are to go into the thousand-rupee line, the fast lane to the god. All five of our names are high on a list, and a small piece of paper is issued at once, our flimsy, unlikely, precious ticket.

I was skeptical about this from the first, but I was wrong. The "system" works, in its chaos. Somehow. Or does it? How far does the minister's influence go? The temple is a world apart. Still, so far things look promising. Maybe Appanna does want to see us after all. I had thought we would go up the mountain as simple pilgrims, in the gratis line. The endless snake of pilgrims winding its way over the road has shown me what this would mean: how many of them will actually manage to get inside, and when? So, like Krishnayya—a far more serious skeptic than I—I am relieved. Unfortunately, Cidananda Rao, normally silent and a little spacey, has disappeared at this crucial moment. We search for him in the swirling mass of human beings, the explosion of light and heat and color, outside the gateway. Anyone could easily get lost in this rich collage. We can hardly go in without him, and he is nowhere to be seen. Eventually Kamesvari spots him, a lonely island in the moving sea, quietly standing and watching, at peace.

We are ushered through the gateway, the VIP opening at the far right. Behind us, hundreds of thousands are patiently queuing. Slightly to our left is the 500-rupee line, by no means a small one. We flow into a sticky mass of pilgrims. We flow through them. It is, at first, as if we had been magically endowed with the Yogic *siddhi* of passing through hard objects. Space opens up. There is movement. We cover some two hundred meters, turn a corner. Suddenly there is a barrier, policemen behind it, monitoring and slowing the flow. From behind, there is the pressure of more and more people pushing forward; ahead of us, a solid wall of thousand-rupeed aristocrats, most of them waving their tickets in the air at the police. It is getting hot, and many are shouting now. After some minutes we wriggle through, Krishnayya manfully holding aloft our pass.

But now the ordeal begins. Ahead of us is a far more serious set of metal barriers. On the far left, there is the gratis queue, a painfully slow trickle upward toward the temple. Next, the hundred-rupee channel, equally slow. In the middle, the 500-rupee line, also more or less static. A narrow space is kept apart for emergencies, or for occasional pilgrims heading *away* from the god, downhill. And to the right is our narrow hatch to heaven, a tight opening in the metal doorway, beyond which a seemingly stable line feeds into the steps leading into the temple. Dozens of policemen man this front, struggling to keep the crowd from bursting en masse into the enclosure.

The police are in remarkably good humor. At times they descend into the flailing sea of VIPs to the right, molding them into a semiqueue, like the potters poking and slapping and shaping the soft clay image of a goddess. It is a hopeless task. They cry to the crowd, very politely: "Please form a line. Take two steps back. Please. Just two steps." Given the constant swell of urgent pilgrims and the sheer impossibility of containing them, these policemen surprise me with their gentle manner. Occasionally, they succeed for a few minutes; something approximating a line does emerge, only to curve back quickly into a mostly undifferentiated, heaving mass. Every ten or fifteen minutes, two or three lucky souls squeeze through the hatch. A brave woman who has made it through stands on a ledge waving frantically at her family, still trapped below it. We, too, have been cut off from one another, carried here and there by the waves, though I can still see Krishnayya and Mitravinda a few meters ahead of me, Kamesvari and Cidananda Rao somewhere behind.

It isn't too bad, but it's going nowhere. Long minutes pass, an hour, an hour and a half, perhaps two. We have advanced perhaps three meters. Still, it looks for a while like within another hour or so we might negotiate the hatch. Behind us, a tough line of policemen, arms intertwined, has cleared an open space, so for the moment there is no more pressure from below. A cool breeze blows down from above, a gift of the god. Volunteers are distributing water packets, *pulihora* snacks, and *majjiga*, watery buttermilk, from huge pails. But there are very angry shouts from within the crowd. "I've been standing here for three hours, we're not moving, get the Executive Officer, Sankara Reddy, down here." "We paid one thousand rupees apiece to be trampled and squeezed to death like this!" One genial policeman, standing at the edge of the crush, points to his cap and says: "You see this? This is the only difference between me and you. If I take it off, I'm just like you. What do you think I can do?" The bottleneck is corked tight, and it's getting hot. And what awaits us uphill? Another policeman, aptly named Simhacalam for this mountain and its deity, explains that at some point the four different queues all flow together toward the inner sanctum. Will it be another crush like this one, only worse? What will happen to the vast thousands still standing in the sun miles below the temple?

There are doubts: Appanna is my own personal deity, my *iṣṭa-devatā*, but perhaps I should come back to see him on a day when he's not so busy. I hate crowds. This one looks like the shore at Dunkirk or the last rooftop in Saigon when the Americans fled. I remember almost being crushed to death in Vizianagaram at the end of Paiditalli's festival in 1998. A crowd has a life of its own, as Canetti knew so well. Still, I am prepared to stick it out. It is not every year that I can be in Vizag for the Sandal-Peeling Festival, Candanotsavam. For years I have read about it and thought about it.

It is no small matter, this peeling away of layers from the god. Normally Appana is hidden under a thick layer of sandal paste. He looks something like a *śiva-lingam*, though everyone knows that, buried deep inside, is the somewhat spindly, boar-faced, lion-tailed image of his true self. There is a good reason for the sandal paste. Lord Krishna, they say, wanted to offer some living creature, whom he had killed, a chance to even the score against him. So this creature was reborn as a tribal hunter—here, at Simhacalam. Krishna, who lived under the name of Appanna in a multilayered anthill at Simhacalam, took the form of a wild boar and trampled on the growing millet crops in the hope that the hunter, who was guarding them at night, would shoot him. But for the first two nights, the hunter slept through this rampage. (Why is it we are usually asleep when God appears?) On the third night he woke, saw the boar, shot a poison-coated arrow at him, and went back to sleep. The boar, that is, God, writhing in agony, sought refuge in his anthill home that is still at the heart of this shrine. In the morning the hunter woke and saw a trail of blood; he followed it and found his victim. The god said to him: "You know the herbs that poison and the herbs that can heal; heal my wound." Said the hunter: "I can heal you, but a scar will remain." The god indignantly refused this offer: "What good is healing that leaves a scar?" That is why he is normally coated in analgesic sandal paste; each morning the priests scoop up the pus from his wound in golden cups.[3] But today the sandal is gone, the naked, aching truth revealed.

Suddenly, what we feared unfolds. Egged on by several violently angry men who have reached the limit of their endurance, the huge crowd behind the police line breaks through it. A tidal wave carries us forward toward the metal barriers. There is no way to stop it, and it seems that in a moment we will smash into the fence. The pressure grows as more and more push their way forward. Wedged into the whirlpool, barely standing, drowning, I feel myself sucked inward toward the bars. Krishnayya, in a moment of bold decision, waves to us to fight our way back, outward and away. It is not so easy, but the five of us do eventually manage to extricate ourselves from the riptides and to reach safety in the somewhat more open ground below. We will not get to see the god today.

It is a lesson, Krishnayya says as we head down, in the meaning of a word like *line*. In India, nothing so straightforward can endure. People get anxious and uncomfortable when there is not enough chaos around them. My friend Handelman might put it in slightly different terms: A line is not the shortest distance between two points. It is a tentative arc spinning or twisting through itself, devouring its own tail. That is what feels real. Linear, two-dimensional movement is boring, or wrong. If by chance you encounter it, you at once begin to stretch it and bend it, poke it and extend it, adding depth and further dimensions and some sense of thickness. If it is elastic enough, or thick enough, there will be no scar.

Disappointed, we hunt for Ravi and his car. He has parked outside the Satyavati Guesthouse of the Simhacalam Devastham, where Anand Gajapati Raju, the son of the last (beloved) king of Vizianagaram, resides when he comes to see the god. On a whim, Krishnayya suggests we go and pay our respects to Anand. We know him from our Vizianagaram days with the goddess Paidi Talli, three years ago; we met him, together with our students, right here on Simhacalam. At that time, he told us at some length that the only truth is the Advaitic oneness of being; gods and goddesses are no more than displaced fragments of that overwhelming unity. "What about Paidi Talli?" we asked him. "Oh, that is different—she is our Auntie."

Anand is at home, and we are ushered in. He remembers us well. He has had his vision of the god, *darshan*, this morning—the first of the day, still reserved for the king who is the patron and hereditary trustee of this temple—and he seems unmoved by our failure. God provides for all living beings, he says; our freedom lies in being satisfied or disgruntled. It is our choice. Once a skeptical king wanted to test this proposition of divine providence, so he had an ant sealed into a metal box; when the box was opened after some days, the ant, miraculously, had a grain of rice in its jaws. Anand tells the story with a certain detached panache, the moral meant to be perspicuous.

Ramalingesvarasvami, my old friend, the Ayurvedic doctor from Vizianagaram and a copious mine of local lore and gossip, is sitting with Anand; he asks me about Edan, whom he remembers well, as a young boy. Anand offers us water and sweet balls of *laḍḍu-prasādam* from the temple. He is a tall man, his voice commanding, his manner self-assured. We did not reach the god, but we did have *darshan* of a king who had received, directly to his own hands, the god's first gift of food. Appanna has, after all, provided us with a tangible sign of his care. The line twists back on itself again. Leaving the mountain, I am not disgruntled, after all; not very gruntled either. I feel sorry for the thousands who will stand in line all day, into the night, hungry to see god's hidden self. It is a hunger not easily appeased.

May 3, Visakhapatnam

Two days ago Naxalite "revolutionaries"—to dignify them with a term they don't deserve—hijacked a tourist boat at Nagarjunasagar, one of the great Buddhist sites of ancient Andhra. They didn't hurt anyone, but they sat the tourists down and lectured them: "Why have you come here? Is it worth coming so far to see old rocks? Why waste your money? Don't come back here, where no one can take care of you." Then they set them free. They burned the boat, but within a few hours the police caught up with them and shot them.

Since I am on the side of the old rocks, I feel I have to ask my friends, again, why the government doesn't put an end to the problem. How many Naxalites are there in Andhra? Ten thousand, twelve thousand? The central government has immense resources, enough money, more than enough soldiers. The Israelis would long ago have imposed a radical solution. The consensus at Krishnayya's is simple enough, indeed obvious if you read the papers: they don't want to end it. The Left is, of course, against physical liquidation; the rest are content with a system that serves everyone's interest. It is useful to have an enemy, especially if he is one of yours. But there is more to this, something no one speaks of; something compelling and continuous with the distant past.

* * *

Krishnayya recalls his student days in Benares with the wise T. R. V. Murti, whose book on Mādhyamika philosophy I have admired. Krishnayya was working on Buddhism and Sartre, and Murti, a scholar of the old school, a master of Sanskrit philosophical texts, had never read Sartre; so Krishnayya brought him a copy of *Being and Nothingness*, all five hundred pages of it. At their next week's session, Murti said: "I read the book, it is not uninteresting, but couldn't the author have said it all in ten or twelve pithy phrases, like the Sanskrit *sūtras*?"

Northern coastal Andhra is a world of is own. The dark mountains of the Eastern Ghats rise, as if by sudden caprice, straight out of the rich paddy fields spreading inland from the sea. There is a major town, Vizianagaram—home to perhaps the most creative moment in modern Andhra history. Indeed, it is here that a certain type of modernity was, one might say, invented by the great dramatist-poet Gurajada Appa Rao in the last decade of the nineteenth century. Gurajada's play, Kanyā-śulkam, or Girls for Sale, is the foundational text for the new sensibility, which was further defined and explored by a series of famous poets, prose writers, and performers—such as the singer of mythic tales, hari-kathā, Adibhatla Narayana Das, the short-story writer Cha. So., the poet Sri Sri, and many others. Why did this creative moment of far-reaching change take place in Vizianagaram? That is a story waiting to be told.

Twice a year, the goddess Paidi Talli, "Golden Mother," has her festival in Vizianagaram. Like other goddesses, Paidi Talli undergoes a natural, annual cycle. In May she emerges—as a spark in the hands of one of her devotees—from the turbid water of the Big Lake. She is then carried, latent, in mud drawn from the lake, to her main temple at Three-Lanterns' Junction, not far from the old fort-palace of the Vizianagaram kings. There she will incubate and ferment, infusing a series of clay and metal pots with her essence, for some three months. Afterward these pots, a full form of the goddess, will make the rounds of old Vizianagaram on Tuesday evenings—preparing the city for her arrival in yet another form. In early October she comes in a dream to her chief priest and informs him that she is "growing" as a tree in such-a-such a grove, somewhere in the vicinity of the city. After negotiations with the owner of the grove, this tree will be worshiped, recognized as Paidi Talli, and gently uprooted—to be brought into town, where the goddess lies for some ten days in the street, gathering strength, drawing love from her people.

On the Tuesday after the autumn festival of Nine Nights, the log is fastened to the Sirimanu—a cartlike, wooden contraption that allows the log to move up and down. At its tip, some fifteen feet in the air, the priest—now himself filled with goddess—dangles precariously as the Sirimanu moves three times from temple to palace and back. A vast crowd of devotees assembles, usually some half-million people who hurl bananas at the priest floating between heaven and earth. Why do they throw bananas? "What do you want us to throw, coconuts?" is the answer people give in Vizianagaram.

I had seen the October Sirimanu festival twice; with my colleagues, Don Handelman and M. V. Krishnayya, I had taken four students from Jerusalem to see it as well. But the hot-season segment, the birth of Paidi Talli *from Big Lake, was new to me. This was a chance to complete the cycle and, perhaps, to strengthen the foundation for a short book that we have planned on this remarkable goddess. I spent the early part of May with Krishnayya in Visakhapatnam, preparing for Paidi Talli's birth from the mud. We interviewed her attendants and devotees in Vizianagaram city; and we also explored the city's hinterland, the villages lying between Vizianagaram and Visakhapatnam, in the hope of penetrating the logic that binds her to the cycle of rice cultivation—for Paidi Talli, whatever else she may be, is also a goddess of the paddy fields, growing and maturing like rice. These villages also worship other goddesses, known as Peranṭāḷḷu, local women who have died (usually on the funeral pyre of the husband) and thus successfully translated themselves into divinity. Krishnayya is interested in these stories and the religious practices that go with them; and thus the Perantallu came to mingle with our study of rice and Paidi Talli. The northern Andhra coast is a region soaked in goddesses who germinate in the paddy fields and blossom in the streets.*

May 4

Krishnayya and I spend the morning in two villages, Tanavaram and Chinnapuram, relatively close to Vizianagaram. We want to learn about rice.

Tanavaram is exquisite, a village so radiant that I contemplate retiring here someday. Fields and palm trees encompass it. The old farmer we are looking for, named Paidi Talli for the goddess, is not home. What shall we do? We see a circle of hardy, weather-beaten farmers standing in the shade by a kiosk off the main road, and we walk over to ask them if they will speak to us about rice. They are happy to do so; curious about the strange descent into the village of two astronauts, but very articulate when it comes to telling their story. Rice is the *pĕdda paṇṭa*, the big crop, in this village, and the cycle begins just before the rains come, in June. We follow them through the creation of a small seedbed, the *āku-maḍi*, then sowing, transplanting, and the slow emergence of the grain within a few weeks of transplantation. First the rice shoot develops a "stomach," *pŏṭṭa*; this turns into a "big stomach," out of which a "backbone," *vĕnnu*, emerges and flowers, *pūvāram*. The critical stage in flowering is a milky self-impregnation (*pālu posu kovaḍam*); if you squeeze the shoot, a slight white liquid comes out. This stage is analogous in every way to human pregnancy (we, the astronauts, know that rice is wind fertilized; but the language the farmers use points to female self-impregnation, conception and gestation). Out of the milk pregnancy comes the soft seed, *ginja*, which eventually hardens to the point of ripeness (*pākāniki rāvaḍam*). When the stalks are heavy with ripe seed, bent under their own weight (*vangaḍam*), it is time for the harvest, in late October or early November. The farmers see these changes and know at a glance if all is going well; no need to touch the growing paddy. As rice matures, so does time itself and all that lives in time. Goddesses, too, are not givens, they have to be grown.

At Chinnapuram we go through the whole cycle again with B. Erni Nayudu, a sun-dried farmer with a lyrical turn of phrase. He speaks in dialect, beyond my understanding. When he has finished and we are about to leave, our hosts, relatives of Krishnayya's neighbors in Chinna Waltair, suddenly ignite. A village shouting match unfolds, sister-in-law screaming obscenities at her brother-in-law, among others. They seem to need Krishnayya's presence for this cathartic moment; or perhaps it is just that the cup has overflowed, or boiled in the intense heat, and there is no holding back the violent words. It goes on and on, the young sister-in-law hurling sexual insults like missiles, the elders replying with bitter scorn. When we finally escape back to our car, they all meekly stand and wave goodbye, as if nothing untoward had happened.

Kanakaiah, by happy chance in Vizag for university examinations, comes to Krishnayya's flat in Chinna Waltair in the evening to teach Pĕddana's verses. We are at the start of canto 3. Varuthini, rejected by Pravara, is burning with longing. The sun sets in a blaze of red, as if angry at the cruel man who has left the woman in this state (3.10). Kanakaiah thinks, like many others, that this verse must be interpolated; Pĕddana has been very sympathetic to Pravara up to this point. Suddenly, the poet sees the world through Varuthini's eyes. But this shift in perspective seems right to me in a book about the grandmother of the first human being. Anyway, I also think that Pravara is priggish and cruel.

Suddenly, the pages almost explode with fire. I have been waiting for this crescendo. The true magic of Telugu poetry leaps into life, and the world is changed.

Tigers sleeping in deep mountain caves
  wake to drink at blood-
  red streams.
Deer roaming the grassy slopes
  tremble at the sight of a sudden
  forest fire.
The highest branches of the trees seem to be hung
  with the ochre clothes of a million
  wise men.
The gods flying above
  these craggy peaks
  come down to land on what they think
  must be the Golden Mountain.

With gentle flames
red as *kimśuka*, as coral or *kunkam* petals,
as blossoming *kankeli*, *bandhujīva* and *japā*,
an aging sun burnt that
unmoving mountain.
  (3.11)

Red, ochre, or gold—all these are variants of the same color. As so often in Pĕddana, we are in the realm of cognitive delusion. Tigers think the water, stained red by the setting sun, is blood. Deer think the forest is on fire. The gods are lost and confused without a map. Such mistakes are the stuff of everyday perception. But as Kanakaiah points out, the fascination of this verse lies in its contrasting movement; the lower the sun sets, the higher its rays, coloring layer after layer of the landscape—starting at water level, then slowly climbing up through the slopes and the treetops to the height of the mountain peaks. It is as if language itself were pitched at this slant between incipient darkness and the incandescent summit. The movement remorselessly accelerates as the sun sinks lower, its redness ever more intense. The last line opens with a pointed contrast: the whole world is in motion, but the mountain absorbing this movement is *nagambu*, a "nongoer."

And so on, in verse after verse, each new one intensifying still further nature's unwitting correlates to Varuthini's pain, the precondition to a new birth, still blocked, locked in by fire, like the burning air outside in Chinna Waltair. It looks easy; but this kind of lucid compression is far beyond what most poets can hope to achieve. If one enters this landscape deeply, a certain dizzying spin takes over. I will follow my own principle—of always reading poetry in the language in which it was written (that is the easy part), but also absorbing it in the setting *where* it was written—and try to memorize the verse tomorrow when I walk around Chinna Waltair.

May 7

We leave early for Tanavaram, to revisit our rice informants and to search for songs or stories about Perantallu—women translated to goddess status, either by dying young, still virginal, or by something akin to *sahagamanam*, the widow's immolation on her husband's funeral pyre. Krishnayya has been wanting to complete an essay on these Vizianagaram district Perantallu. The old *District Gazetteer* mentions the small towns of Jami and Sringavarapukota as having such cults, and we learned last week that Tanavaram has one, too—also sung texts to go with it. We think a day in the village may produce some new knowledge.

Ramu is with us, in a glowing purple sari. She ran away for a few days from her drunken husband, came to Vizag, to Krishnayya's neighbors;

now she is going home with us. She usually has a bright smile and an impish eye; she is full of spirit, playful, insouciant, independent. Her lively bodily presence next to our driver, Appa Ravu, seems to unnerve him. He is perhaps unaware of the cause, but the car swerves unevenly over the road as Manmatha, god of desire, invisible as always, shoots his flower arrows. In the interests of safety, Krishnayya tries to change places with Ramu, to get her into the backseat, but she, with characteristic self-possession, refuses; we will have to take our chances.

The fields radiate a viscous wet heat already at eight o'clock. Green hills melt into the reddish soil. As always, I am moved by the sheer physical splendor of northern coastal Andhra. The road weaving among the villages is lined with palm trees and tamarind. I spot a "flame of the forest" with its glowing orange flowers. What is it called in Telugu? I assume a village girl like Ramu must know the names of all these trees, but she doesn't. Neither Krishnayya nor Appa Ravu know. I am prepared to let go of the useless query, but Appa Ravu seems to feel that if the odd *dora* white man in the car needs specific information, it must be a matter of some existential urgency. He stops the car and interrogates the villagers walking by. No one knows. The last to be questioned says, slurring, irritated, *erriki tsa*—"Who the hell cares?" To Krishnayya this is a sign that the old cultural world of the village, with its rich scientific knowledge, is dead or dying. I recognize the theme. Many of my friends are given to lamenting the loss of a remembered universe.

Still, my question does have an answer, which arrives later in an e-mail from Suchitra in Ahmedabad:

> As for the "Flame of the Forest" (*Butea monosperma*), you may have seen a Palas tree (known in Telugu by these names: Moduga, Modugu, Palasamu, Togarumoduga, Tella moduga). It's got almost fluorescent orange flowers with petals shaped like a parrot's beak. If you saw a "Gulmohar" tree (*Delonix/Poinciana regia*) it is called Peddaturayi, Erraturayi, Erra sunkesula, Seema sunkesula in Telugu. The tree has an umbrellalike silhouette; it has a five-petaled flower—four of them vermilion-orange and one a speckled white.

So much for village wisdom; in future, I'll stick to city dwellers.

It is already into May, and the heat still feels mostly bearable to me, though I notice in myself, and I think in others, a certain crankiness, short temper, as if one's nerves were both baked dry and soaked in sweat and grime. There are hours when I suddenly long for a breath of northern European air—also for the grays and greens of Europe, and other clarities. On the other hand, think what would be lost were I to be anywhere else on the globe. We pass through Jami village, and I remember our adventure here in 2002, when I was here with Handelman and four anthropology students. I had been telling them that the Vizianagaram area had a strong tradition identifying itself as Virata, from the *Mahabharata*—the land where the Pandava heroes spent the thirteenth year of their exile in disguise. The story is told in the *Virāṭa-parvan* of the epic, and all the episodes are mapped onto these villages—Alamanda is where the cattle raid took place, Vijinigiri is where Arjuna (Vijaya) hid himself, Padmanabham is where the Pandavas were cursed to hide themselves for a year. . . . And Jami, lovely Jami, sees its name as derived from the *śamī* tree where the heroes hid their weapons before moving into Virata city. So, my students asked, where is the tree? Probably here somewhere, I say. But Krishnayya, who was with us, was extremely skeptical. No way, he said; it's all some late story, there's nothing here. I had to work hard to get him to agree to ask one of the villagers, just in case. Reluctantly, he accosted a passerby: "Do you know anything about a *śamī* tree, the Pāṇḍavas, where they hid their weapons or something?" "Of course," answered the villager, "it's right over there, turn left down this lane." We spent the morning in the temple that marks the spot.

Tanavaram is welcoming, as before. Women are performing *pūjā* to Sūryanārāyaṇa, the sun god, offering him the first mango fruits. They circle a small altar, sprinkle it with water, then take a mango and throw it high into the air—to be caught by one of the village boys farther down the street. We seek out the little kiosk where we sat last week. Some of the farmers are nearby, they of course remember us; but they are impatient with our persistent questions: just how long does it take the rice shoot to germinate its seed, to develop from "stomach" to "big stomach" to "backbone" to "flower"? They have already told us, and today they offer a different, confusing order. Hot-season fatigue sets in: it is midmorning, very hot, and why are we pestering them with these details? Who are we, anyway? The ex-*sarpanch*, or headman, of the village arrives, an authoritative man, limpid in speech, eager to take charge. Soon a new crowd gathers on a cement *pyol*, where there is at least hope of an occasional breeze. A retired schoolmaster, eloquent and calm, joins us; finally we have all the details straight, and the crucial point is clear: the final stages in the rice cycle, from the *pālu posu kovaḍam*, when the flower falls away and the shoot is "pregnant with milk," to the golden ripening of the seed coincide quite precisely with Paiditalli's self-revelation as the growing tamarind tree and her consequent Sirimanu ride, between the festival days of Vijayadaśami and Dipavali. This goddess fertilizes herself, then ripens along with the pregnant paddy, her other medium, her "self."

Talk turns to the Perantalu of this village. There was such a woman, in the British time. When she learned that her husband had suddenly died, she rushed home, successfully revived him—apparently only for a moment—with her innate *śakti* power, then entered the fire together with him. Her continuous, benign presence is, they say, crucial for the village on every level. There is a song about her; someone produces a notebook and reads out the words. Many of these men know the lines, or some of them, by heart.

We have bought vegetables and other necessities in Jami, and Ramu cooks us a large meal, which we eat sitting on the cool floor of Paiditalli's house, a fan flitting beside us. The extended family filters in to watch. There is a young widow, twenty-five years old, with two children; her husband died from a brain tumor. She has a field to look after. She won't starve, but she seems to my foreign eyes to be profoundly lost, or stuck, or—to use a word utterly alien to her consciousness, I am sure—unfulfilled. But then who cares about fulfillment here? Krishnayya offers to take her to Vizag, to work for him for a while, but she refuses; she has her obligations in the village. There is no way she will extricate herself, not now, not ever. Certain things are given. The Perantalu, it seems, refused this same option and chose *sahagamanam*, death by fire, the only alternative. It is a cruel choice; but who am I to judge? A grateful, mostly silent guest, I create a small afternoon diversion by taking pictures with my digital camera—the regal grandmother, the daughters-in-law, the new baby, the white-brown goats beside the palm tree, the widow with her staring eyes, the astonishing, light-drenched street. They laugh at the static, frozen images of themselves on the tiny camera screen.

May 10, Hyderabad

For three days Sugambabu hosts me in his home outside Hyderabad, in G. D. Metla—a long ride northwest from the city. Actually, his home is a few kilometers beyond G. D. Metla, in what is now called Suraram.

These are new neighborhoods, part of the continuous urban expansion into the countryside. Suraram is perhaps the end of the world; take another step and you will find yourself falling freely past the cosmic turtles. From Sugambabu's roof you see the typical Telangana landscape of animate boulders, a small lake, crispy, baked hills. Hyderabad is growing rapidly; the paper says that by 2020 there will be 12 million people living within the urban configuration of this city. Will they have water to drink? Air to breathe?

On the first afternoon, suddenly dark clouds mass over the hills, and soon it is raining, a swift sweep of gray water soaking the parched soil. Great gusts of wind swirl over the rocks, the cement houses, the ragamuffin shops. A family of pigs in the neighboring lot, a black sow and four or five of her young, is galvanized into movement. A moment before, they were sleepily rummaging for edibles among the weeds. Suddenly, under the driving rain, they start to dance, scurrying in mad spirals, racing in twos and threes as if in ecstasy back and forth across the courtyard. I would never have believed a piglet could run so fast, a streak of dark lightning. Maybe they are afraid.

Sugambabu is in his late fifties, married to a handsome Brahmin wife, with two sons; one works in the railways, the second is a dental technician in Nizamabad. Forty years ago he was at the center of a minor literary movement, originating in Guntur, known as the Paigambara poets: Deviprasad, Olga, and Sugambabu himself. *Paigambara* means "prophet," from Persian *paighambar*, the name a deliberate echo of the so-called Digambara ("naked") poets—another radical wave of rhetorical, highly politicized writing. I can't say I like any of it. But now, decades later, Sugambabu has settled into a meditative mode, happily nonpolitical. He calls his short, Zen-like flashes *rekhalu*, "wings." I spend some hours trying to work a few of them into English. My favorite:

Even then,
whenever
I speak of my troubles
in Telugu,
life speaks
Tamil.

It sounds like my own case, but reversed: I still think, at times, in Tamil, and the world keeps addressing me in only partly intelligible Telugu.

When we are not looking at the poems, Sugambabu earnestly plies me with profound philosophical insights. It is often, like much philosophy, an intrusive habit, as when he bursts into my room at six o'clock in the morning to exclaim, with grim emphasis: "Truth is God and God is Truth!" It is not easy to disagree with this *siddhânta*, the logical conclusion to an argument, though I am not sure I can accept all its implications. And what if language speaks truth while twisting it into a lie, as the Advaitin monists might say? But Sugambabu is no Advaitin, and the *rekhalu*, vaguely reminiscent of the medieval iconoclastic poet Vemana, are surely a vast improvement over his earlier revolutionary verses that, he tells me, Naxalite prisoners used to inscribe in blood on the walls of their cells—some decades ago.

* * *

Jyotirmaya takes me to a dinner of pasta and pudding, a relief from the constant rice and curry. His grandmother, a majestic Tamil doctor, moved to Rajasthan at government invitation to set up a clinic. She quickly learned Hindi, and all that came with it. If a patient complained to her of some symptom, she would ask when the pain began. "It was six months after the coronation of Ram Singh." Or: "In the last year of the three-year drought." The doctor had to know how to map these statements onto our impoverished mode of Newtonian time. This Renaissance woman was, says Jyotirmaya, the decisive influence on his life.

Jyotirmaya is a big man, in all ways—physically towering, with the deep voice of a singer (which is what he was); experienced and savvy in all the ways of modern India, for he was the editor of the *Hindu* and the *Times of India* here in Hyderabad. A philosopher, trained in Oxford. He seems to know everyone in the city, which he chose some years ago for his home—it was, he says, love at first site. He speaks of what he calls "development corruption," a distinct genre, quite unlike simple, straightforward corruption such as one finds all over India. In Andhra, he says, if someone contracts, let us say, to build a new road at the edge of the city, he will build the very best road in the world—and at the same time, through this tender, he will make his own extra pot. Andhra is moving forward, as one can see at a glance in this city—whatever *forward* might mean. Perhaps this is how things always worked here, the medieval pattern, the middle ranges subcontracting at the expense, or at the behest, of the king. The difference is that here the work does get done.

May 11

Worn out by the "wings," I shift back to town—first to Sumalini's home in Domalaguda, then with Sashi and Jitendrababu to Dilsukhnagar, across the reeking Musi River. Sashi Shekhar is Patanjali Sastry's son, cut in the image of his father—the same deliberate movements, thoughtful manner, deep eyes. He has published a book of astonishing photographs of Buddhist remains in Andhra. They are everywhere: Andhra, he says, has the largest concentration of Buddhist ruins anywhere in the world. Once it was a Buddhist land. Jitendra, speaking a rapid, precise, richly conceptual Telugu, is a *rākshasa*, as they say here—a kind of "demon," that is, a wildly creative, productive man, advocate in the High Court for half of each week, gentleman explorer, humanist adventurer, scholar, Sanskritist, literatus for the other half. He is filled with the Telangana romance (he comes from a village in Nalgonda). Telangana, he says, is where Telugu comes from, its *fons et origo*. The delta has distorted it. (Sivanagi Reddi says that for all that Jitendra prefers women from the delta. He has collected almost two hundred mostly forgotten texts on erotics, *kāma-śāstra*.) He has a library of 150,000 volumes in the village. His edition of the *Vyavahāra-cintāmaṇi* of Vācaspati Miśra, one of the standard texts of Hindu jurisprudence, is just coming out, a brilliant work. He seems to know every rock in the Deccan, and every poetic line ever written in Telugu. I have been waiting a long time to meet such a man.

In the car, Sashi asks me about A. K. Ramanujan, whose poems he knows very well. I tell him that Raman was deeply unhappy for many of the years that I knew him, and that he died in, perhaps from, this unhappiness. No one can explain the medical catastrophe at the end, in Chicago. My friend Handelman, I tell Sashi, says that Raman was done in by his own insistent precision. Sashi responds to this at once. He knows all about Brahmin precision, especially its South Indian variant.

The paper today tells of a woman in one of the villages. She was studying black magic, sorcery. It was time to practice some exercise, prescribed as homework, so she got her husband and his brother dead drunk, cleaned them, coated them with turmeric, garlanded them, and hacked off their heads while they slept. She apparently thought she would be able to revive them soon after—the lost art of replacing the severed head. All the texts promise that it can be done; in a way, it is the whole point of the ancient ritual system. What a shock it must have been when it didn't work. Probably she mispronounced one of the mantras.

May 12, Vizag

Back in Vizag, with Krishnayya in Chinna Waltair. We are three days away from Paidi Talli's rebirth. The heat relentlessly intensifies, and here the air is heavy with fluid, in marked contrast with Hyderabad; I feel myself cooking on a high flame, and I assume the goddess, too, must be in some such state. Getting ready, coming close.

In her honor, I have my hair cut in a barbershop on the street; the barber is hardly more than a boy, maybe fourteen or fifteen years old, and he works with crude rapidity; in two or three minutes, cutting wildly, he removes thick clumps of hair, leaving others unevenly scattered over my scalp. It is the worst haircut I have ever had, but perhaps the goddess will see it as an offering, an idiosyncratic act of devotion; I can tell people that I have taken a pilgrim's vow to have my head shaven in irregular stages. Why not? Many vows are no less bizarre. If the goddess asks, you obey; and she is anyway certainly capable of caprice. I pay the boy, try my best to avoid the mirror he flashes at me, and emerge back into the dusty happiness of heat and light.

Wandering the streets of Chinna Waltair, as if held at each moment in a crisscrossing web of subtle, unforeseen connections, some stretching back centuries to Varuthini's world, I wonder again about a deep, classical culture—is it as vulnerable as everyone seems to think? There is the standard lament of the intellectuals, who always seem able to remember some organic, integrated world in which the old, seasoned words lived gracefully in the mind. Is it a fantasy of childhood? Of course, any finely honed sensibility is easily fractured. Look at the damage inflicted by the modern poet Sri Sri and his imitators, an entire generation lost, displaced in specious rhetoric. On the other hand, it is possible that a rooted culture remains mostly impervious to such wounds. It may hibernate, hide, withdraw; bide its time. It is never dependent on what people have in their minds at any one moment. The Andhra case? The longer I stay here, the more I sink into this life, the more sanguine I become.

May 13, Vizag-Vizianagaram

Krishnayya is hunting Perantallu—mostly cases that would elsewhere be called *satī*—in the villages around Vizianagaram. They are thick on the ground. Not recent cases, in general, but stories that invariably refer to the "English time." One leads to another. In Tanavaram, Sringavarapukota, Jami, Mammidipalli, Alugubilli, there are prominent Perantallu, worshiped by the villagers as the source of continuous presence and care. We spend the day collecting their stories, visiting their shrines.

By seven thirty we are on the road. I went to bed very late, rose early; Krishnayya asks me how I am feeling. I am, above all, heartily tired of always answering this question in the same simple, primitive way. Desperately searching for an alternative, I say to him, "nimpādigā unnānu." I hope this means something like "I am well, at peace, relaxed." He laughs. This is a frequent occurrence when I speak Telugu with him. Unlike other friends, who maintain a bemused, mostly silent tolerance of my highfalutin language, Krishnayya does me the welcome service of bringing my sentences down to earth. Nobody would say what I just said. Nobody would say most of the things I keep trying to say. So, I ask wearily, what *can* one say? "cāla bāg' unnānu" (I'm very well). That is all. I am beginning to think that all sentences in Telugu are slight variations on this one template.

The morning passes in Vizianagaram. I sit outside Paidi Talli's temple, watching the unbroken flow of devotees. The image of the goddess is dressed in a wide brown sash, very elegant, perhaps some intimation of the fact that in two days' time she will emerge from the muddy waters of the Big Lake. It seems the people of this town feel her incipient arrival. There is an electricity in the air around the Square Temple. My friends, Bhaskara Ravu and Satyanarayana, greet me warmly; we will meet, I say, on Monday.

There is time to wander the streets, from the psychedelic white Fort with its stubby pillars to Gurajada Appa Rao's House, then on to Maharaja College, the Music College, and back to the Clock Tower and Main Street. I have been here many times, and very often, like today, it is cloudy and sticky, the dust and grime nesting heavily on houses and shops. I want to get the city into my feet, to know it with my body. Its strange, almost eerie, yet somehow nonchalant beauty condenses into a question: Why here? Why did Gurajada—and with him a whole rich series of great poets, writers, and scholars, musicians, wrestlers, tiger dancers, and other performers—reimagine Andhra from within this particular twisting maze?

At Dharmavaram village we stumble on the famous shrine of Sannyāseśvara, the *sannyāsin*-renouncer who tamed the local Paidi Talli. She was famous for enticing young children into a tree and then devouring them. The Sannyāsin arrived innocently from the hill shrine at Punyagiri (I remember it well from a pilgrimage some years ago) and was conscripted into the struggle against this wild goddess. He spoke to her: "Look," he said, "you can't go on like this. People have to live. Let go of the children. Eat something else." She agreed in principle but still could not control her appetite. So he threatened to imprison her inside two mazelike, geometric *yantra*s, one named for Venugopāla-Krishna and the other for Bhairava-Śiva. This worked. Since then she has been tame, on a strict vegetarian diet; and the Sannyāsin's cell, where he used to sit in meditation, is a place of worship. The *pūjāri* priest says it all happened in the fifteenth century, which apparently means: long ago.

It is midafternoon, and dark clouds mass in the east; a few raindrops fall. At Sringavarapukota—the name is so long that even local people call it S-Kota—there is a shrine to another goddess, Erukalamma, who is present in two large, staggered images. She had a dream which warned that her husband should not go into the forest to look for firewood; she told him the dream, but he derided her cowardice and went off anyway, with his two younger brothers. "Women imagine all sorts of things," he said. A tiger killed him and remained atop the body. When Erukalamma heard the news, she rushed into the forest; she cursed all tigers to remain far from that hill, and she brought her husband's body home. Then she announced that she wanted to enter the fire with his body (*guṇḍam tŏkkaḍam*). First the elders, then the king tried to dissuade her; the king was struck blind by this woman in her rage. Thus punished, he relented. The wife revived her dead husband for a few minutes, just long enough to be burned to death together with her. Now the villagers worship her and perform marriages on the portico of her shrine (all except Komati merchants, whom she cursed, still in her irascible mode, never to tie the wedding necklace, *mangal-sūtra*, inside that space).

Her story as sung by the local bards was recorded and published in a small booklet by Potnuri Suryanarayana, the executive officer (*dharmakarta*) of the temple, a former schoolteacher. We find him at home, just after his afternoon nap, in an old house crammed into the corner of a lane. He is very suspicious of us at first, angry at our sudden appearance, but Krishnayya melts down his fears; soon he is happy to talk, at length, about the goddess and the poem. We sit on the roof under the cool clouds; he is bare-chested and rather slow of speech, as he is still recovering from a stroke that left him partly paralyzed. Erukalamma appeared to him after his operation, a white mass of light, and promised to protect him.

With somewhat unsettling candor, Suryanarayana tells us that he edited the bards' sung text before printing it. In particular, he deleted passages that he deemed exaggerated (*atiśayoktulu*, hyperboles, the old term used by the poeticians). Like what? For example, at one point the bards said that Erukalamma served a dinner that had nine curries, with all nine flavors, or *rasa*s. Suryanarayana regards this small narrative moment as absurd—what village woman would serve so many curries?—so he took it out. Even leaving aside all my philological instincts, my prejudice about preserving the text as a whole, as sung, I am amazed at the sensibility that objects to a nine-*rasa* dinner but accepts as perfectly plausible, indeed factual, all the rest: the dream, the tiger, the curse, the reviving of the dead spouse, and the graduation into perpetual goddesshood. Nothing hyperbolic there. Tigers, we read in the 1922 *Gazetteer*, used to be very common in this district and were quite capable of dragging people out of their houses and gardens into the forest. One sees the need for an efficient goddess.

May 15, Vizianagaram

Tonight she will come.

I know I won't sleep, there is a long night ahead. At 5:00 PM the city seems subdued. We begin by visiting Aitam Rajakumari, one of the great stage actresses of this century. She performed nearly four thousand times, most notably as Madhuravani, acerbic, quick-witted heroine of Gurajada's *Kanyā-śulkam*. Now she is seventy and lives alone in an old house off the main road, down one of the sinuous lanes. She is gracious, elegant, happy to talk to us, happy that someone has come from so far with a love for *Kanyā-śulkam*. She speaks with the limpid articulation of a seasoned performer, and her Telugu is creamy, ripe, an organic growth fed by decades of serious artistry in this city. She is a link, tenuous but still alive, to the illustrious past. As a girl, she would see the great Adibhatla Narayana Das—master of Hari-kathā storytelling—walking, each day, acolytes in tow, to the City Club. She heard stories of Gurajada himself, knows to tell us that he acted in one of the first performances of his play. I probe a little, with Krishnayya's help, hoping to reach a little further back, but memory mostly fails. Her maternal grandmother, Cinnasuramma, was a dancer in the Simhacalam temple; and *her* mother, Kannamma, performed for the Parlakimidi Raja near the Orissan border. The family itself was firmly rooted in Srikakulam; Kannamma's husband was a diamond merchant, perhaps from Gujarat. Rajakumari's father, and his father, were advisors to the Pusaparti court in Vizianagaram town. She says that when the court was disbanded, some three hundred court servants found themselves suddenly reduced to poverty. Here are the linkages, which we can still dimly perceive: king, court, temple, classical music, poetic genius, dance; a rare flowering. A trace of the old Vizianagaram world hovers in her room, hung with framed pictures and yellowed clippings, in the evening light.

Then, too, Paiditalli went through her annual process of birth, maturing, fermenting; as the Vizianagaram kings provided a foundation to arts and scholarship, so Paidi Talli kept this kingship alive and well. But tonight the court or palace has no role to play. The goddess will be born, as she has been born over long centuries, into the hands of her devotees—mostly farmers, fishermen, and low-caste Malas. The scattered pieces of her existence will coalesce. It has already begun. When we arrive at Bairagi Nayudu's house in Hukumpet, we find that the eight pots, *ghaṭālu*—one salient form of this goddess—and the festival image of Paidi Talli have already traveled from the Wilderness Temple to the *ammavāri sthānam*, the open goddess place or space that can be reached through a narrow passage between two densely stacked houses. This "goddess space" is full of movement. The pots, heavy with Paidi Talli, sit on a cement *saduru* platform in a corner of the enclosure, waiting for the moment when they will be carried through the streets to her other shrine, the Square Temple near the royal palace. For now, people from the neighborhood, mostly housewives, cluster around, bringing her food—plates or leaves laden with mangoes, rice, lentils, bananas, split coconuts. They want to feed her, they are insistent, they touch her, open the pots, pour offerings inside, touch her again. They are happy. She is here, and she is coming. A lightheartedness seems to rise up from the crowd. There are bards, *jamukulavāru*, singing her song to the accompaniment of their drums. They, too, are happy tonight. They sing with evident gusto, playfully accentuating the syncopation, swaying with the words which not even Krishnayya can understand; they are in some archaic, rustic Telugu, fossils left over from the beginning, if there was a beginning.

I am moved. God(dess) exists. If there is meaning to human life, it is something palpable like this, a mango fed to a goddess resting amid the camphor lights as she waits for the other pieces of her being to reappear. Meaning cannot be ethereal and is surely not abstract. It is a touch. Light, warm, alight. Plate after plate descends toward the pots, mothers hold their daughters tightly in hand as they make the offering, caress her, wave their fingers before the flames. Night has fallen, the connection is joyous, intimate, and easy. There is no crush, no rush, no politics, administration, police to hold back the crowds, as at the time of the Sirimanu in the fall.

Bairagi Nayudu is Paidi Talli's chief priest. Twice I have seen him mount the Sirimanu log during the fall festival; I have seen hundreds of thousands of devotees pelting him with bananas as he dangled at the end of the high pole. Tonight he sits in the "goddess space" before the pots, holding his crutch. He looks frail, though somewhat better than when I last saw him at home. Paidi Talli is his goddess, closer to him than wife or children. He greets us warmly, and soon we are enveloped by our friends from the temple. People bend down to touch his feet: he is Paidi Talli, too, filled with goddess, embodying her presence.

At ten thirty, a little later, the pots set off for the Square Temple at Three-Lanterns' Street. Sharp drumming fills the streets, which have come alive with guises, *veshālu*: tigers, Koya tribals, wrestlers (*sāmugariḍīvāḷḷu*), transvestites, and an apparently overheated Kālikā-vesham—a tall, dark man with long feminine hair, a headdress of peacock feathers, a skull, a *triśūla* trident, all slightly comical in their incongruous combination, and all very heavy in the thick heat of the night. He keeps removing the headdress to cool off. The fierce Kālikā is said to be the "true form" of this goddess, but the dancer himself seems dazed or reluctant. Other dancers are in ecstasy, leaping, bouncing through the streets. Families crowd the doorways, watching. The joy is now spilling through the public space. A tacky band—clarinet, horns, an old hurdy-gurdy mounted on a wagon—holds the middle of the procession by sheer volume, piercing our ears. The clarinetist, drunk, comes over to ask me to write my name on a scrap of paper, a treasured memento of the foreigner who came to witness and worship.

Behind, the pots move slowly, stopping frequently as the bearers adjust the weight on their heads and as householders reach out to touch, to bless. Isolated raindrops, another benefice, fall from above, and there is also a welcome, cooling breeze.

To my surprise, there is no trace of weariness in my body; I, too, am light, elated, swimming in an unfamiliar state of profound physical well-being. The procession turns left toward the town; Krishnayya and I sit for some time in the eerie lane as the drumming drifts in from the distance, the water buffaloes meander near the water pump. Gusts of wind blow dust from the street into my eyes. Soon we see lightning streaks in the sky. The air has changed; suddenly it is profoundly, sweetly cool, whatever was blocked or locked is loosening, readying for the birth. Tonight, I say, they will not have to beg and cajole the goddess to come; she is almost here, she is eager, the world is open to her and she to us. Old wooden houses, dark with grime, peer down over those who have taken their cots outside to sleep in the lane. Five dogs scurry through the empty street, silently playing. A drunk staggers home. No one, I say to Krishnayya, would believe that this little town, ripe with a living goddess, could exist—if it did not already exist.

2:45 AM: A party of women lamp bearers, who have lit the pots' path to the Square Temple, wearily heads home. We ask them what stage in the procession has been reached. "They are in the temple, soon they will leave for the lake." We drive to the Square Temple. In the dark, Three-Lanterns' Junction looks like a war zone: the daytime crust of human beings in continuous, uneven movement has been peeled away, and what one sees, the whole length of the main road, is a chaotic jumble of potholes, rubble, loose piles of bricks, collapsing facades, mounds of dust, broken steps, like pictures of Berlin in 1945. None of this diminishes the unsettling beauty of this place—sublunar, swathed in sweat, doggedly and grimly mysterious. A small group of people is milling around the temple; Bairagi Nayudu sits, exhausted, serene, on the steps leading into the shrine. From outside one can see the pots being set in place inside the sanctum, which is then locked shut. The priests' work is finished for now. One of them approaches me in the street. "Take me to Israel to worship the goddess there." I wish I could. Krishnayya, suddenly the retired professor of philosophy and religion, patiently explains to him: "All the world's religious traditions, *sampradāyam*, once had Mother Ammavāru. She was everywhere. Now, in Israel, in the West, she has been lost, she is completely gone. Only in our Bharata-deśa is she still with us." Indeed, it is clearer to me than ever what is missing in our life, and for a moment, in the unlit, dusty street, I surrender to a private lament.

A *jangiḍi* wicker basket emerges outward, tarries briefly under a tattered red cloth canopy in the street as drumming resumes. Then the procession is off to the Big Lake. We help Bairagi Nayudu clamber slowly, painfully, into the car. Left at the Clock Tower, then right, and the lake lies before us, flowing ebony, dotted with algae and lotus pods near the shore. A new white metal fence is in place along the whole length of Big Lake, and a pedestrian walkway has been paved. We stop at a point diagonally situated across from the Wilderness Temple to the east; we can see the lights of the Train Station nearby. We are thus about halfway between the Palace/Square Temple and the Wilderness Temple across the lake. The sky is lit by almost continuous, silent flashes of lightning, and the wind has intensified.

Slowly the procession approaches. People are strung along the road in small clusters—perhaps a hundred in all. Mala women, from the lower reaches of the social order, in particular, are conspicuous: Paidi Talli is their goddess. We recognize our friend Paidiraju's family. The drumming intensifies as the *jangiḍi* is brought down to the lake by a narrow footpath. It holds a large burning flame along with turmeric, a raw mango, twisted wicks, a puddle of oil. They place the basket on the sand and clear a small space where Satyanarayana and Bhaskara Ravu sit, smiling, at rest. Already the first young men have entered the lake. They ask me if I want to join them, but by the time I understand the offer they are already far into the water—and anyway I am not so certain that I am ready for this immersion, although Big Lake looks a little cleaner than usual, by night. A group of five or six, including Srinivasa Ravu—Bhairagi Nayudu's son-in-law, a priest in the Wilderness Temple; Venkat, Bhairagi Nayudu's son; Paidiraju; and another man we don't know, Appa Ravu—wade some 150 meters in, the water reaching up to their waists. A much larger group, mostly teenagers, stands 50 meters behind them, watching. We wait.

Here is the outer limit of language. I can report what I saw, but will even I understand these sentences? A birth. But before it, there is patience, the most remarkable ability to wait until the moment is ripe. We stand around the *jangiḍi*, studying the dark lake, the sky, the backs of the men dimly seen from afar. All is easy, relaxed, the night breathes in cool air, the hot season is forgotten, people are happy, serious, expectant. I wonder, without urgency, how long they will wait, and how they will know. Occasionally a cry breaks through the darkness. "Hey Paidimamba!" Are the men deep in the water praying to her as we were told, inviting her to approach? A ripple passes through the crowd of boys closer to the shore. Has she come? Again, silence. We wait. Ten minutes pass, fifteen, more, there is no need to hurry, you cannot rush a regal goddess, when she is ready she will come.

Sky and water merge. Where is above, where below? At the moment of birth, who can say? Somewhere within this watery darkness, they say, a spark will flash. We stand. Even *waiting* is too harsh a word for this moment, this mode of uninterrupted being or breathing, this awareness. Such gentle silence is rare in India; perhaps only in the high mountains can one hear it. We cannot see the spark amid the lightning streaks, but there is movement now in the lake, the boys standing in the rear rush forward, the smaller group of men disappears into the water, a series of soft cries pierce the darkness: "Jai Paidimamba!" Some minutes pass. There is splashing, a flurry of movement. The first to be dredged out of the water is Srinivasa Ravu; he is unconscious, his cupped hands heavy with mud. Then Venkat, Paidiraju, Appa Ravu, all of them drenched, muddy, beyond communication. They are dried off. But it is Srinivasa Ravu who has brought her and, as if delivering a child, the women, working quickly and efficiently, take the mud from his hands into the *jangiḍi*, they clean and wash and make order, they mix the goddess into the turmeric—she has arrived with turmeric and vermilion of her own—they knead and mold her, they give her food, red rice, eggs buried within the muddy mass. Close behind me, a string of colored firecrackers explode, one by one. I am startled, after so much gentleness; brought back to me, the old contingent memory-stricken me, I can't help remembering the sound of stun grenades thrown at us by soldiers at the peace demonstrations in Israel-Palestine—*peace*, that other word, that abstraction, if only there were peace. A strong scent of fresh turmeric fills the air.

I have seen many strange things, most of them in India. This is another, stranger than many, perhaps because of its still wonder. It seems to me that I have witnessed the tentative, precarious birth of something you might call time or, alternatively, world. New time is born into old time, the desiccated residue of the year; Handelman might say that the new cosmos is born into the old one, which will have to grow it, nurture it, allow it to germinate, ferment, mature. With infinite tenderness they have lifted this goddess with cupped hands out of the muddy lake, brought her to shore, cleaned her, wrapped her, fed her. Now they will carry her to her Square Temple, where she will sit for months, slowly infusing the pots with her presence in a long osmosis of self filtering into self, coalescing. Again, they will wait—for many weeks until, in the autumn, she will come, first in a dream, then as the Sirimanu tree. In any case, she is here, with us.

The first bird cries of dawn, a rush of wings, then the cocks crow. We take Bairagi Nayudu home, park as near to his house as we can, but still there is a painful walk for long minutes through the lanes; I hold him firmly by the arm, he rests on me. It is not every day that I walk a living goddess home. The effort has exhausted him; this year, like last, he could not enter the lake. It is time to resolve the issue of his succession, not an easy business. I wonder if he is wondering whether he will come to the lake or the temple next year. He has spent his whole life as a servant of Paidi Talli, who comes on him when the moment demands. Tonight Srinivasa Ravu was the one to hold her in his hands. Perhaps the presence is too much for anyone. As we drove away from the lake, I noticed a teenage boy, dressed in black, huddled, head on his knees, on the curb, sobbing.

May 16, Rajahmundry

Home—the deep sense of well-being. It is humid, of course, but no worse than Vizag. The electric current comes and goes. Patanjali Sastry and Smile come by to catch up. Nirmala resumes her magnificent dinners. I clean the house, put the new books on the shelves. A stillness descends.

On the train, I sit next to a family, and we start to speak. He asks me about agriculture in Israel; there is little I can say. My agricultural vocabulary in Telugu is limited, now, to rice cultivation. Before I get down at Rajahmundry, he produces two *cinna rasālu* mangoes: our Andhra speciality, he says, pushing them into my Madras gunnysack with the laptop and my books. They are soft, pliant, golden red, the gift of this season. Rajeswari says that although people love to complain about the heat, their feelings are actually more complex. They love the mangoes, the particular, enhanced intensity of *avakāya* pickle at this time, and the breeze. I think she is right. And since I have been staunchly maintaining that the heat is, in the end, quite bearable, Krishnayya, who suffers from it keenly, has been teasing me: there is no such word as *ĕṇḍa*, heat, in the Telugu lexicon, he says. Andhra is a cool, northerly country. Some confusion exists in our minds, that is all.

May 19, Rajahmundry

At night, strong winds appear, lightning flashes, drops of rain. Perhaps these are the "premonsoon rains" the papers like to describe—an oddly oxymoronic category. It is nothing like real rain, more an intimation that something is shifting, a dress rehearsal, slightly parodic. In Tirupati, far to the south, the goddess Gangamma has celebrated her annual festival; she comes into the city in a series of psychedelic guises, *veshālu*, in which she wanders the streets, slowly swelling into her true, undisguised self; when the guises coalesce, when one incarnation of the goddess touches another, the first rain should fall. But here in Rajahmundry people are reluctant to give up their horror of the heat still to come. They talk of *rohiṇi-kārtĕ*, the astral time span still a few days off. The proverb says: "rohiṇi-kārtelo roḷḷu baddal' avutāy" (In the Rohini days, mortar stones split into smithereens [because of the heat]).

I exploit the cool evening for solitary walks to the Kadiyam Road, stopping to chat with the pan shop lady on my way back. She is very curious about Israel. How does one get there? Could you walk or take a bus? Do I have a job there for her son? How much is the *esa*? What, I ask her, is an *esa*? She repeats it several times, trying to enlighten the dull-witted foreigner, and at last I understand: a visa. The *esa*, I say, is not the problem. She wants to know if we have castes in Israel. No, I say. This seems unlikely to her. "Here we have Kapus, Sayebulu,[4] Mangalivallu, Tailorlu, Gollalu, and others. Do you not have these different kinds of work over there?" All are there, I say, but no castes; people are basically a single mass. She ponders this strange configuration, perhaps not quite believing me. "There are definitely two castes," she concludes. "Females and males." I concur.

Venkatesvara Rao comes early in the morning for a long, rambling conversation. He, too, is interested in Israel, in academic life there, perhaps a little envious of the striking freedom I enjoy. As always, his precise, cultivated sensibility astounds me; there seems to be nothing he does not know in Telugu literature, and in classical music. He has brought a faded photocopy of his Telugu *ghazal*s. I persuade him to come back in the evening: Smile, Patanjali Sastry, and I want to hear him sing these poems. Before he goes, he picks up K. Siva Reddy's book from my table—appropriately, proleptically, it is titled *Varsham Varsham* (Rain!)—and reads:

You need nothing
to write a poem.
You need no complex confabulation
of means and ways.
One sound is enough, one look is enough,
one song, one line in a song
is enough,
one falling leaf is enough
one blade of grass in the wind is enough,
a branch that snaps on your forehead is enough,
a child holding on to your little finger is enough,
look at the child's face, look at the eyes,
 look at the uncertain steps,
you need nothing
to write a poem
you are enough
 your being alive
 is enough.[5]

I order a huge quantity of *chapatti*s and three curries for the *ghazal* party. As usual, Smile brings the beer and wine (the Pondicherry red wine that everyone insists on drinking chilled; not that it would be much better at room temperature). We have barely sat down and poured the wine before the current goes, as keeps happening throughout the day. In total darkness, to make a start, I recite two lines of Hafez:

shab-e tārīk va bīm-e moj va-girdābī chunān hā'il
kojā dānand ḥāl-e mā sabuk-bārān-e sāḥil-hā

[Black night, monstrous waves,
merciless riptides:
Can they know our terror

who stand, light-handed,
on the shore?]
Dīwān 1.5

The lights go on. Apparently, someone knows.

Venkatesvara Rao begins with Telugu *ruba'iyat* and moves on to his own crafted *ghazal*s, sung in various classical rāgas. They are limpid and heart-wrenching, the language strangely transparent. Smile and Patanjali Sastry know many of these poems by heart and sing along. Other honored names are invoked: Krishna Sastri, Sri Sri, and the great *ghazal* singers of the early twentieth century. From outside, a cool breath of evening comes to listen at the doorstep. The neighbors downstairs are also spellbound by the songs, as they tell me later when I go for my late-night walk. Ghost of Ghalib, the master of the Urdu *ghazal* in nineteenth-century Delhi, in a Telugu garb:

Near you, I forget myself. I go home.
In my distraction, I walk right past my door
when I go home.
I won't follow you, but let me know the way you go.
I'll sweep the path
and go home.

I have no work with you. My tongue wants sweetness.
Calling your name with a full throat,
I go home.

Look at these eyes: They are only clay vessels.
Seeing you, I turn them into lamps
and go home.

When I wait for you in vain,
I leave this heart as a teardrop
and go home.

For Rentala, there is no more good or bad.
Gauging everything
by how *you* see it,
I go home.

May 19

Every time I come back to Rajahmundry by train, I tell the auto rickshaw driver to take me to *Minister illu*—the Minister's house. J. Rammohan Ravu is Minister of Roads and Buildings, a Congress man, and his house is just around the corner from my street. Rajahmundry is proud of this minister—he is a well-liked and admired politician, known to be attentive and efficient—and his house is a landmark known to all. Today Tataji, in town for a wedding, calls and asks me to pay a courtesy call on the Minister, whom he knows ex officio.

Rammohan Ravu has just come back from complicated medical examinations in Boston. It seems that they have now diagnosed the problem, and it is not as serious as was feared. The house is crowded with visitors, suppliants, well-wishers. A policeman records the name and place of residence of anyone who enters. He struggles with my name, asks me where I come from; as several times before, I am proud to say: "Rajahmundry."

It is a beautiful house, spacious, with a large staircase of fine stone leading up to where the Minister sits. A life-size portrait of Shirdi Sai Baba graces the wall. I am introduced, confirm the odd fact that I speak Telugu, ask about his health. "Now I am fine," he says. He is a strong, classically built Andhra man, sturdy and almost fierce, and the room is full of such men—so very different, I think to myself, from the much milder manner and appearance of the Tamil people I know. A woman arrives, bends down to touch his feet. I sit beside him watching the constant flow of petitioners. The man is accessible and prepared to listen. They speak of their problems, produce papers for him to sign. He consults his adviser-*mantrin*s, signs with a flourish. To my eyes, the whole scene could have been transplanted here from the Nayaka courts of the seventeenth century—a *darbar* audience, the king sitting in judgment, hearing cases, making decisions, with courtiers standing respectfully at his side and armed *sipahi*s stationed at the threshold. The atmosphere is brisk, businesslike, intense. Has anything changed from the Nayaka pattern? Yes, much has changed. For example, there are, so far, no ornate Telugu poems describing in detail the daily routine of this modern king—how he gets up in the morning, studies himself in the mirror, walks through the streets while young girls and housewives grow faint with desire. Such *abhyudayamu* works, remorseless in their progression, were standard fare at the Nayaka courts. Perhaps such compositions will yet come from the pens of today's suppliants.

I would be happy to ask the Minister if he likes Telugu poetry, or classical music, but there are more important matters to be attended to. The stream of visitors swells steadily. There is no lapse in the Minister's attentiveness and patience; perhaps this *darbar* will go on for some hours. After some minutes we take our leave. It is good to meet your neighbor. A slight fragrance of royalty wafts down my street, glowing with that deep, soft luminosity of morning in the delta. Some mornings, like this one, for some reason, we also get sudden, sour whiffs from the direction of the river, the Andhra Pradesh Paper Mills upstream. It is cloudy again; the paper says there will be scattered showers. This summer, says Ramacandra Murti, Tataji's friend, is no summer at all.

May 20

Thoreau: "The greatest part of what my neighbors call good I believe in my soul to be bad, and if I repent of any thing, it is very likely to be my good behavior."

I wake late, five thirty, moments before Ratnam's soft morning mantra: *pālu*, milk.

Heavy with dreams, I drag myself out to the Nehru Road. A few drops fall. Dense clouds. To the east, over Kadiyam and NH 5, they are gray and unsteady; but behind me, over the river, they are a riveting black—not dark gray, not blue, but purple-black and stationary, as if mesmerized by the Godavari. (I can understand.) Is "summer" over? A wistful note creeps into conversations—as if people were being cheated out of some beloved, delicious torture. Against the lurid backdrop of imminent rain, I wind my way up to the highway, like a Pahari *abhisārikā*, a lover braving night and storm on the way to a rendezvous.

Near the top, I come across a man on a bicycle loaded, like a camel or a mule, with five bulging brass pots in various sizes. The pots hang from the handlebars, the seat, some hook at the back. Something is wrong with the balance. He pours milk with a blue plastic cup from one of the larger pots into the smaller ones, patiently, slowly, not wasting a drop. Perhaps he has far to go. I wonder how he fared. At the very moment I reach home, the storm lets loose. Suddenly the usual coordinates of sanity have no meaning—up, down, inside, out, left, right, before, after, all is a single wind-driven torrent. Within seconds my bedroom is flooded, though the windows are barely open. There is no way to staunch the wound in what was once a firmament: *ambaram sāgaropamaṃ sāgaraṃ câmbaropamam*, the sky is like the ocean, the ocean like the sky. (As for the battle of Rāma and Rāvaṇa—the heart of the epic tale, which the anonymous poet, completing this verse, tells us can't be compared to anything but itself—I suppose it is still unique.)

Of course, the power fails, too, and in the wild raging of the storm day has reverted to night. In the dark I struggle to mop up the flood coursing through my flat. Lightning strikes somewhere close by, and a long thunderous roll shakes the street. Are there peacocks dancing—as they are said to do during the monsoon—to the drumbeat of the thunder? Aghast, I stare at the swirling sheets of rain. I surrender. What else can one do? Absurdly, my mind dredges up images of the mandatory wet-sari scenes in Hindi films: always moments of pseudoseduction, stereotypical and a little silly. More to the point is the sudden vision of sun-parched fields drinking in this bounty. Vimala, a Telangana girl, after all, used to speak of a distinctive ecstasy, the instantaneous, defenseless opening of the arid and hard to being drenched, to feeling.

But it is more than that. Time in Andhra has a rhythm in this Uttarāyaṇa half-year, a strong syncopation that has to be lived to be known. It is something like an uneven alternation of clenching or bunching and release. Summer tightens and blocks: even the wind or the air is said to be clenched tight, *gāli bigincesindi*. Then something cracks open, and the deep waters that were mysteriously veiled until this moment flow in all directions. Time is a snail, bunching, stretching, stopping, bunching, stretching again. Perhaps this is what the philosopher-linguist Bhartṛhari meant by the two contrastive movements he defines in time—*pratibandha*, occlusion, and *abhyanujña*, release. The rhythm of temporality moves through recurring, slow blockages to temporary bursts of acceleration, a precarious letting go. And time is probably only one instance. Thought, too, may move in the same spastic beat, clutching preceding, conditioning release.

When the torrent finally abates, the air is cool; Rajahmundry feels, for the moment, like Paris or Berlin. The street has gone green-gray.

* * *

Much of yesterday went on the Tamil novella of G. Nagarajan, *Nāḷai maṟṟum ŏru nāḷe* (Tomorrow Is One More Day)—another meditation on time, as the name suggests. Or on timelessness:

> Wherever you looked, there was change. Only in his life, it seemed, was there no change at all. Everyone had left him and was going off somewhere. They all knew where they wanted to go and how they wanted to get there. He alone did not know; he and Mina. . . . All that he and she had was "today"; they couldn't even catch hold of "tomorrow."[6]

Bhartṛhari again: time, like speech, is actually undifferentiated, a oneness. For Nagarajan, sheer human misery produces this mystic state. Kandan, his (anti-)hero, lives a grimly episodic awareness, full of want. Like his inventor. Nagarajan died in 1981, at fifty-two—burned out by life. I like his Tamil: spare, despairing. Like all the rest of his generation, the blight of Marxism bit into his mind; but it was the suffering around him that drove him mad. The sensitive ones took this path, dreaming of some absent entity, the "people," the "workers," some illusory force that would bring change, would make "tomorrow" real, different from today. I can somehow imagine it, despite the immense damage they inflicted on words, on truth. Just look around. Look at the milkman on his bicycle—and he is one of the lucky, at least he has milk.

On the wall of a liquor shop, after Kandan's epiphany: "masūtiyil vīṇ aṭitta nerattaic carāyak kaṭaiyil carikkaṭṭtuvomāka" (In the arrack shop, may we make up for the time wasted in the mosque). Shades of Hafez; or, with a wicked twist, Thoreau. To apply to me, substitute *library* for *mosque*.

Abbie translated the novella, and then she, too, died, at fifty-one, magnanimous, forgiving, transcending, to the end. Ramakrishnan and I will publish the translation in her name. The time has come; we meet next week in Madras. Doubts arose as I read. Nagarajan is dead, Abbie is dead. Some other blockage, a caked and arid place in me wonders if it has meaning. Abbie wouldn't like such thoughts. When I read to the end, in the dim daylight after the rain, I knew we had to go ahead.

May 22

R. Sri Venkatesvara Ravu comes in the evening for a long talk. I read out Pĕddana's verses about Varuthini's love illness, *viraha-vedana*, which occupy me throughout my days; I try to describe what I think is so new: the intensification and three-dimensionality, and the indirect probing of

Varuthini's mind through the experience of sunset, nightfall, moonrise. He agrees: the third chapter of the *Manu-caritramu* is in an altogether different "style." I point to 3.19:

mṛganābhi-pankambu mĕyininḍan aladina māyā-kirāti maicāya dĕgaḍi
nava-pincha-maya-bhūṣal' avadharinci naṭincu pankajâkṣuni-cĕlvu
 sunkam' aḍigi
kādamba-nikurumba-kalitayai pravahincu kāḷindi-garvambu gāku sesi
tāpincha-viṭapi-kāntāra-samvṛtamainay anjanācala-rekhan avaghalinci
kavisĕ mariyunu gākola-kālakanṭha-
kanṭha-kalakanṭha-kari-ghaṭā-khanjarīṭa-
ghana-ghanâghana-sankāśa-gāḍha-kānti
gaṭika-cīkaṭi rodasī-gahvaramuna

[Blacker than the blackness
of the Tribal Huntress in disguise,
who smeared her whole body
with black musk,

accepting homage from the black beauty
of Lotus-Eyed Krishna, dancing with black
peacock feathers on his crown,

unsettling the pride of the Black River
with its flocks of black geese,

swallowing up the slopes of Black Mountain
and all the forests of Night Trees,

darkness spread the deepest
black brilliance of crows, peacock's throat
and cuckoo, elephant herds,
blackbirds, or massed monsoon clouds
through all concave space.]

Blackness nested within deeper blackness, or superimposed on other blackness: the syntax circles back upon itself, so that sound itself serves to mold or trace these pockets of intensified outer darkness. But

Varuthini's mind must feel like this—as she heats up in the torment of unappeased desire, as the burning night wears on, parts of her are lost, beyond reach, blacker than any known black, black lurking within black. And then there is the list in the end, inconceivable cumulation of superceded *upamāna*s—the old standards of comparison—emptying out into a dark infinity. A verse like this, it seems to me, is far beyond anything that could be called description.

RSVR loves Tikkana, especially the *Udyoga-parvan*; he recites Tikkana's version of the Golden Rule.

ŏrul' em' emi ŏnarcina naravaray apriyamu tana manambunak' agu dān
ŏrulakun avi seyak' uniki parāyaṇamu parama-dharma-pathamulak'
ĕllan

[What is the highest good among all the paths of goodness?
When someone does something that hurts you,
you don't hurt back.]

He recalls this verse whenever there is some uncertainty or difficulty in his life. He speaks of the distinctive characterization in speech and gesture that Tikkana perfected. RSVR has the perfect ear of the autodidact—uncorrupted by the "tradition." Also an evident courage in selection. He ranges from Tikkana to Telugu haikus, on which he has written a brilliant essay. With mild forbearance and dispassion, he speaks of the two schools today in Andhra—those who believe literature should deal, first and foremost, with social problems, and those who feel that literature is its own justification, an autonomous aesthetic domain. It is clear to which party he belongs.

He quotes a letter from Olga—erstwhile Paigambara poet of the revolutionary days in the sixties—to the haiku poet B. V. V. Prasad: "Your *Rālina pūlu* came to hand while I was in the midst of a thousand anxieties and a hundred fears. In a second, my mind was filled with such immaculate, serene sorrow." She ordered a hundred copies of the haiku volume to give to friends.

So, for at least a moment, she crossed the lines: one erstwhile revolutionary has managed it. In his essay, RSVR talks of the mental readiness, *mānasika samsiddhata*, that is the true, necessary condition for reading a haiku. Not a meter, not a form, the haiku, he says, is a genre that dispenses with explanation. The real test is with Nasara Reddi, a haiku poet from Nellore who learned Japanese in order to translate directly into Telugu. Sashi also speaks of him with reverence. I must meet this man.

RSVR asks me if I don't find nights, alone in the flat, a problem. He would be deeply unsettled, he says. No, I say, I love the silence and the freedom, though sometimes I "pine for" my wife (I have gotten into the habit of using the arcane Telugu expression, *bĕnga pĕṭṭukŏnu*, in such contexts, relishing the slight ironic touch). I know he finds all this mysterious—my coming and going, my uneven Telugu, my half-baked musical awareness, Eileen's miraculous, fleeting appearance and subsequent disappearance, my disembeddedness from a world of crisscrossing family ties and obligations, my Jewishness (whatever it is). He admires Lin Yutang and Dale Carnegie, has read them many times. Borges is an unfamiliar name—I think few in Andhra know him—but he has heard of Mandelstam. I give him some Haydn quartets, an experiment, and promise that soon we will listen to one movement together.

* * *

The last landmark before the highway is a small wooden tea stall on rusty wheels, the planks painted blue, with the glorified inscription "Hanuman Sapata Shop" (*sic*) in white, sprawling letters. It tends to huddle in the dubious shade of a large thorny bush by the roadside. Today I reach it very early, about a quarter of six—Ratnam, the buffalo girl, came at a quarter past five—but there is no chance of catching the little family still asleep. A fire is burning. The wife crouches over a boiling kettle. Three medium-size tin pans sit on the ground next to a stack of firewood. Jars with sugar, masala, and dry snacks and a stained plastic thermos line the wagon's flat surface, where the tea glasses wait to be filled. A young child, naked from the waist down, pokes at the flame with a stick. A red sun is already burning away the remnants of morning gray. The husband sits and waits, positioned next to a vast building site; trucks come and go, laden with red earth. In the distance, a radio is playing a morning prayer in Sanskrit, *suprabhātam*; a thin, melodic whine drifts through the mango grove. Perhaps someday there will be a grand "Sapata Mall" on this site, all stone and plastic. Will the wagon man have to move on? In the meantime, it is already hot, the sky has reverted to its clenched, withholding mode. I push from my mind the thought of these three standing, pouring tea, through the scorching hours of the morning and the stifling heaviness of afternoon. As always, without even a greeting, I continue past to the Kadiyam Road.

* * *

There is another Patanjali (with the initials K.N.Y.), from Vizianagaram, a good novelist, a satirist, a friend of Patanjali Sastry's, bound together by the name. An understated man. Once they asked him to write a film script, so he wrote it, and the film was produced. When it came out, they interviewed him on TV.

"So you wrote the script for this movie?"

"Yes, I wrote it. But they changed it. They left in only one of my lines."

"One line in the whole script?"

"Yes."

"Which one?"

"*Selavu*. Goodbye."

May 25

Sashi Shekhar arrives by overnight bus from Hyderabad, carrying poems: Nasara Reddi's, inscribed in a small notebook (the poet dictated them to Sashi over the phone). Just three days ago RSVR had mentioned this man as the greatest of the Telugu haiku poets. We read two verses, for a start: at once it is clear to me that this is the kind of voice I have been waiting to hear. There are hints of Mandelstam. A very complex simplicity. Some of the poems, though they are very short, were written with astonishing patience, over years. This is a pace, a rhythm, I admire.

In the afternoon we go by auto rickshaw to Korukonda and Kapavaram, some 15 kilometers from Rajahmundry. Sashi wants to show me the Buddhist sites in Andhra—he is the world's authority on this subject. We start by climbing the Kapavaram hill. Pre-Mahāyāna caves, then the red-brick remains of the *caitya* hall, *stūpa* mounds, a period of florescence in the first centuries AD. From the crest, the delta spreads out at our feet, a green-red tapestry dotted with sharp hills. The sun sets. We see that the temple to the Man-Lion, Narasimha, on the next hill has been newly painted. We imagine the life of the monks who lived here—no doubt busy with their rituals much of the day and night. But it was in places like Kapavaram that the Mahāyāna crystallized as we know it; that the great metaphysicians Dignāga and Nāgârjuna lived and thought. For the local people, Kapavaram is Pandavula Metta, the Pandavas' Hill, an echo of the epic world of the *Mahabharata*: the five Pandava brothers must have lived here during the years of exile in the wilderness.

Krishnayya waits at the bottom of the Korukonda hill, and as usual his inquiries bear fruit: there is an eighty-year-old ex-Devadasi dancing girl from this temple still somewhere in the vicinity. We will look for her. He speaks to an old man, Peddapati Krishnamacaryulu, who often saw the Devadasis dance in the Narasimha temple at the foot of the hill: *bāla-bhogam* in the morning and *pavaḷimpu-seva* in the evening. Each time ten to fifteen Devadasis performed before the god. In addition, there were special ritual events in the temple that were marked by their dance. They lived on the income from *manyam* land given to the temple by the king. After the government banned the Devadasis in 1947, under the utterly mistaken view—inculcated by the lunatic reformers—that they were prostitutes, most of them migrated from this area.

After dinner, more Nasara Reddi, until late. Is it the poetry, the heat, my incipient departure from this place for two weeks? Something has stirred me up, and for most of the night I lie awake. In the morning, clouds, raindrops, a cool breeze. Walking uphill toward the highway, I think again of Pĕddana's discovery in *Manu-caritramu* 3: with Kanakaiah, I am still stuck in the description of Varuthini's hallucinatory desire. The lover she longs for is gone; like me, she cannot sleep. The verses tremble with intensity and a sense of novelty, a newly invented expressive world drenched in moonlight and delusion.

The moon moved through a world
drenched white by its rays
as if Dark Time were a doctor
who had perfected a pill from mercury,
processed and condensed, and let it dissolve
in a cup of milk so it could easily
be swallowed—to give lovers
potency and youth unending.
(3.25)

We see directly into Varuthini's highly charged mind; we see the world through her tortured eyes. These verses are mantic, charged with effectual power. Earlier Telugu poets also acted on their world—Śrīnātha sang a whole temple into existence—but in Pĕddana the verses seem to operate quite differently, solidifying an autonomous world, real in its own terms, that is internal to the poem and to the listener's mind. Each individual verse, as in the past, is a mode of doing or using or acting; but it acts first, and perhaps only, upon itself. Perhaps it is this self-contained, self-propelling quality that identifies the *Manu-caritramu* as "fiction."

My "true" name emerges yesterday in the afternoon, when I tell Krishnayya I was born on Bhogi Day in mid-January, the day after the solar festival of Sankranti. Males born on Bhogi Day, says Krishnayya, are named, alliteratively, Bhogeśvara Ravu, lord of enjoyment. The title seems right on all levels. How long it took for me to find it!

May 29, Chennai

Ramakrishnan says that if he had to choose one, emblematic image for what has happened in his city over the last two decades, it is this: "When I visit a friend and am offered a glass of water, I have to ask if it has been boiled or purified."

Not so long ago, this wasn't the case; even in the 1980s one could drink the tap water in Madras—to say nothing of his childhood years, when on his way to school he would drink from the street taps, in any neighborhood.

On the other hand, some things don't change so much. At Kartik Fine Arts in Mylapore, a *kacceri*—sung by Bhusanakalyanarama; and the accompanying violinist, a young genius, Akkare Subbulakshmi, is a Chola bronze come to life. She smiles regularly as she plays, clearly relishing the music, the moment, her friendship with the other artists. The singing is clean and intense, too much for me; the *rāga*s they are playing, Kiravani and Hindolam, push me into the abyss. Carnatic music is structured for severe ecstasy, sheer precision enhancing emotion to an unthinkable pitch—but only when it is sung slowly enough, and with a certain lightness of touch. It is strange, but right, to think of ecstasy not as a function of breaking out (as the Greek word would suggest) but as breaking *into* bonds.

Ramakrishnan speaks of Nagarajan as we work, slowly, through the opening of the text. A tall, strong man who deteriorated through ganja, drink, nameless grief. Loved by women. Each time Ram saw him he would buy him a new dhoti; he slept in the streets, never washed or changed his clothes. "He never gave you the impression that he was unhappy."

Madras days, all the old richness. After forty-eight hours, my Tamil starts to reemerge. Until then, muteness torments me. I hear the sorcery outside me, a music like no other, liquid, cascading, the sound of truth, but my tongue is rigid, wordless. When the shift takes place, it is like drowning in memory: Mandaiveli, our first home in India. The Carnatic masterpieces Eileen used to sing with exquisite gentleness. Nothing will ever reach so deep.

With Rajamani I go to meet Vasunatan, Personal Assistant to the Minister for Endowments, to seek permission to photograph at Tiruvarur. He is kind, attentive, aware. An old Madras building, a taste of the Raj and its bureaucracy; there are the whirling ceiling fans, thousands of cardboard files—old, dog-eared papers spilling out of them—stacked in heaps on metal shelves, a small army of clerks. A sign in Tamil says that visitors are not allowed to speak to subordinates without the permission of the head clerk. Temple priests in dhotis wander the corridors. Paper cumulates, ferments like a goddess, fades, curls, is filed, dissolves. He promises a letter of permission within the week.

After two days of cloud and sultry heat, today there is sun—but summer is clearly ending. In Kerala, Hyderabad, tremendous rain. I fly out tonight, to some possible, tangential world.

June 12, Berlin

Yesterday, Claudio Lange in the atelier, a new series of paintings on frames. Each time I come to Berlin, I make a pilgrimage to this rather holy spot (Claudio would hate the adjective) where I first read, under Claudio's tutelage, the little-known poet Cernuda. What galaxy am I visiting? Rajahmundry recedes, and is anyway inexpressible, even to those who are close. For a few hours, I am carried along in the sweet clarity of northern Europe. Objects don't merge or collide. Space envelopes unobtrusively, not the sticky elastic chrono-topos of India. It is easy and strange. At six I meet Kesavan Veluthat, probably the deepest historian of medieval South India in this generation, at the Hauptbahnhof, another surreal piece of future planted in Mitte.

We walk the streets, take the boat tour on the Spree. Stop to see the South African film *Tsotsi* at Potsdamer Platz. I am the awkward guide who has not drunk deeply enough. But in the Tiergarten he tells me how when he was twelve years old he stole eight annas from his father and ran to eat beef at the Muslim shop. How did he like it? It was awful, but there was the thrill of transgression—still there today. This was after his grandmother made him bathe a second time because he was writing lessons with a fountain pen that he had taken to school—so the ink was polluted. Being a Brahmin in Kerala, he says, was stifling; he was very angry.

Berlin, as always, shows the cracks; time, the bad time, oozes readily to the surface. Nothing is innocent, everything skewed and therefore interesting. There is a subtext: the madness *then* reminds him of certain Indian voices, now. He speaks of the Emergency that Indira Gandhi proclaimed in the midseventies, when civil liberties were suspended; when he was warned by the security goons to watch his words in class. An oral *cāṭu* verse comes to mind:

> yauvanaṃ dhanasampattiḥ prabhutvam avivekitā/
> ekaikam apy anarthāya kim u yatra catuṣṭayam//

> [Rashness,
> wealth,
> power,
> foolishness:
> each one, alone, is a catastrophe,
> to say nothing of when all four combine.]

That, says Kesavan, was what happened in the Emergency, and is likely to happen again. I think the verse is a focused meditation on political power, *prabhutva*—a recipe for calamity. Foolishness—its natural companion. Impetuousness and wealth won't lag behind.

Kesavan discovered Sanskrit poetry only later in his youth, after recovering from the trauma of memorizing Veda. A learned uncle told him he could read Sanskrit books if he wanted to. How? asked Kesavan. You open the first page and read the first line first.

VARSHA, RAINS

June 13: En route to Hyderabad

Green, soaked and soft, far below, from the window of the plane. European summer. Hyderabad will be caked brown. The captain announces the route: Munich, Vienna, Bucharest, Trebizond, Kayseri, Sivas, Van, Isfahan. All the stations of my youthful restlessness, my *yauvanam*, one by one. There is snow, still, on the high peaks in Anatolia. I remember the cold, moon-soaked midnight in Sivas, in eastern Anatolia, where we slept in the bus station, my brother and I, and woke to find the whole town staring down at us in wonder.

Was India already in me then, on the overland passage from Tabriz to Erzerum, with Hafez in my head? As if India were the magnet, and I the iron filing; unconscious, unmelted. Before I had smelled India, or seen how the angular contours of Europe round off, become continuous, thicken, cumulate, fold, and swirl. I knew nothing of that rawness that Europe so easily masks or contains, the sheer physicality of intellection. But tonight I know. On the other side of the mountains, there is desert, rolling yellows and browns, white riverbeds, Armenia, Iran. If words mean anything—but why should they mean?—it is only when the underlying echo, the music that motivates all real language, fades into silence.

Oriana Fallaci: "I have always looked on disobedience toward the oppressive as the only way to use the miracle of having been born."[1] Yes. But she is now self-blinded, enraged at Islam, at the people who live in the desert below me. Humaneness stops at the borders of Tuscany. So much for romantic courage. After this week in Brussels, Paris, Berlin, speaking from my book on Ta'ayush and the Israeli peace movement, I conclude: of all our failures, one of the worst, and the hardest to correct, is the failure to convince others that you are not a hero.

June 14, Hyderabad

Arrival at midnight, my first entry via the international wing at Hyderabad. Weary, sad, I wait an hour for my bag. Jyotirmaya sweeps me up into the city.

He had at least two great teachers: Isaiah Berlin and Mallikarjuna Mansoor, perhaps the most versatile male vocalist in the Hindustani tradition in the mid-twentieth century. At his dying moment, Mallikarjuna Mansoor asked his son to play the *tampura* drone, plucking the four strings softly, over and over—pure sound.

He would teach even in the middle of a concert; there was no division among the modes. Once Jyotirmaya was singing with him onstage and made a slight mistake. Mallikarjuna Mansoor, in the middle of the performance, said: "Do it again, correctly." Jyotirmaya sang it again. His teacher insisted: "One more time." He would not go on until it was right.

Music is the staple subtext in this house. Jyotirmaya salvaged what could be saved in the archives of All India Radio, Hyderabad—after they had witlessly destroyed fourteen thousand hours of priceless old recordings.

To reenter via this level of listening.

June 15

Raghuramaraju, professor of philosophy at the University of Hyderabad, comes for dinner at Jyotirmaya's together with other friends.

Raghu, sleek and effervescent, is trained in Western philosophy and also well versed in the classical Indian schools; recently he has branched out into various Telugu literary domains. He is especially interested in the great maverick novelist Chalam, whose feminist novella, *Maidānam*, I've been reading in Rajahmundry. *Maidānam* is surely a philosopher's text, unsettling, iconoclastic, unresolved. Chalam died in 1979. Throughout his life he was a self-consciously bohemian figure, a man of many loves (and women); in Rajahmundry they still remember the hut on an island in the Godavari where he lived alone for some two years, musing and meditating. His Telugu *Musings*, an erratic, lyrical diary, saturated with monistic nature mysticism, is perhaps his best work—Patanjali Sastri urged me to read it, and I am finding it ravishing—but it is *Maidānam*, and perhaps some of his rather sentimental short stories, that people know best.

I agree with Raghu, *pace* the conventional consensus, that Chalam, the pioneering feminist-reformer and a lifelong enfant terrible, is actually highly traditional, Viswanatha Satyanarayana the one with a modern sensibility. No one comes close to the radical vision of Viswanatha; and yet today he is usually, wrongly, classed with the traditionalists against the Marxists (facile opposition). It is the strange karma of Telugu that Viswanatha, unquestionably one of the great writers of the twentieth century, of the order of Proust or Joyce, remains unknown outside Andhra.

We talk of the postmodernist vogue in Indian universities, a mystery. How to explain it? Mediocrity seeks its rationale. But other factors apart, I think perhaps it is the underlying aggression that is so attractive—the dissolution of text, author, world. Derrida himself is another matter, far from destructive. I think of the last time I heard him lecture (in Jerusalem). For over three hours he improvised, like a jazz artist, spinning a kind of musical or mathematical labyrinth out of the magic of French phonology, leaving semantics, indeed all reference, behind. The Schönberg principle, beautifully stated by Thomas Mann: "Reason and magic meet and become one in what we call wisdom or initiation, in believing in the stars, in numbers."[2] I think something like this was alive in the South Indian poetic tradition from the beginning.

Toward midnight the talk turns, inevitably, to politics. Jyotirmaya is finishing his book on M. S. Golwalkar, one of the ideologue-precursors of the modern Hindu Right. Jyotirmaya brings to the subject a volatile mixture of horror and fascination. Darkness of the soul always has a genealogy. Jyotirmaya speaks bitterly of what he calls today's "designer victimhood"—the avid invention of a narrative of victimization, with its coveted existential advantages, in the interests of a lethal political program. Now it is India's turn; I know the protocol only too well, from Israel.

June 16

Sanskrit emergency: my student Tammy is in town, hoping to read an obscure Kerala commentary, the *Vyangya-vyākhyā*, surviving only in manuscript form, with a local scholar. But one after another, the great pandits of Hyderabad turn her away. Are they unwilling to explore a totally unknown text? Are they prepared to teach only what they were themselves taught by their own teachers? Are they reluctant to teach in English? And what of the spirit of adventure, the taste of the unknown—the sine qua non of Sanskrit studies in Jerusalem? Perhaps there is no simple answer. We keep hearing excuses of one kind or another. Tammy, living at Jitendra and Jhansi's, is getting close to despair. Jyotirmaya puts me in touch with Aravinda Ravu, the city's Chief of Police, who is finishing a Ph.D. in Sanskrit in his spare time. He insists on speaking Sanskrit to me, rather than Telugu, on the phone. He may well be the first Sanskrit-speaking policeman since the days of Kālidāsa, but he is too busy to teach Tammy himself, and somewhat surprisingly, his influence with the pandits doesn't go very far. Aravinda Ravu, it turns out, has other claims to fame as well, including a Homeric ferocity in the war against the Naxalites.

Sashi takes me to the Raga Coffeeshop at the Rukmini Riviera Hotel, where we sit for some hours over beer. He needs to get away, he says, from the inbred atmosphere of Hyderabad, to see the world from another angle. I agree. In the meantime, he is immersed in all things Telugu, utterly in his element. He has been reading *The Sound of the Kiss*, our translation of Pingali Suranna, and he has rather a lot to say about it. Three mavericks, he says, came together, or rather, colluded, in this book: Pingali Suranna, Narayana Rao, and I. None of the three has disclosed anything of the personal trajectory that led him to this book; no wonder the novel is so tantalizing. Every character discovers that he or she is living inside a preexisting story, whose contours slowly become apparent—a story invented by God and first narrated to the goddess Sarasvati. Presumably, this must be true about Narayana Rao and me as well.

At the table next to us, two officers from the Department of Tribal Affairs are drinking steadily and, it soon transpires, eavesdropping on our conversation. One of them interrupts us in order to ask me point-blank: "I hear you speaking many languages, Telugu, English, Tamil, and something I can't identify. How is it possible?" Did Eileen call on my cell phone? I can't remember. I am tempted to tell him that I belong to a somewhat peculiar Lost Tribe.

June 17, Rajahmundry

Hyderabad in the early morning looks washed, clear, glistening. We reach the airport in fifteen minutes, a world record. This jumble of Iran and Palampet, of Persian, Dakhni, Telugu, Amharic, is suddenly whole and perfect—the perfect beauty of the incongruous. Nothing ever satisfies like an elegant dissonance.

At breakfast Jyotirmaya says that his happiness quotient directly reflects his proximity to good Indian food. Thinking it over, I think he is right: we taste the world each day, and we also speak it; here the tongue lingers over the playful, the subtle, the thick, the unexpected, the almost inconceivable. Since the taste—of food or language—is so full, in and of itself, and so engaging, I find that I momentarily stop wanting more, ever more, and grow gentle, almost content. Sometimes the result is a strange self-possession, as when I stood yesterday in the swirling road at Malakpet, not needing to be elsewhere, and the rickshaws and the bullock carts spun dizzily all around me, and a cacophony of Telugu and Hyderabadi Hindi flowed through my mind—but then the "self" is only another (irrelevant) theory.

Horizontal light, I learn from a magazine on the plane, is bad for us. Vertical light gives depth and resolution. From above, I watch the dry upland slope downhill into green paddy fields. The Eastern Ghats are covered with trees, large clumps of forest. The Godavari, from a distance, could be the sea.

Landing in Rajahmundry is uncannily like it was in Iowa long ago. I suppose only I can see the resemblance, or would think of it, but it is the same—a small flat space amid other flat spaces, green, soaked in horizontal light; also intimate, so much so that anyone can walk out onto the tarmac, inspect the big plane that has swept down from the outside for a moment's rest. The bags are handed over by hand, a family matter. Panchayat elections are about to take place, one of the Election Inspectors has arrived; they are waiting to receive him with white garlands, already rather wilted in the heat. No sign of rain. Satyanarayana, who has come to collect me, complains that the summer—Rohiṇi-karte, when rocks shatter in the heat—has gone on for double its usual length. Yesterday toward evening there were dark clouds and a big wind, but nothing came of it, and today is again sun-drenched, humid to the point of choking.

A sweltering noon hour, high noon; we drive, giddy from the sun, through the parched fields.

Look:

> Because she fears the noonday heat,
> even Shadow cowers under our bodies
> and won't come out, not even a little.
> Traveller, why not rest for a while?[3]

Homecoming, already perhaps my fifth or sixth; each time a wave of contentment crests in me, I am back where I belong. Two weeks away—the house is covered in a thick layer of dust; dead cockroaches lie, feet up, where they came to the end of their karma. The bookshelves and the kitchen sink are shaded by thick cobwebs. Someone has turned off the refrigerator, no doubt to save the electricity, so there is not even a bottle of cold water. But the electricity is working, and Godavari flows out of the taps. I rush to wash the floors, rinse the dishes and cutlery, put away the flotsam-jetsam of Europe. Kanakaiah says he will come this evening to read.

Sastry asks me about the weather in Hyderabad: it is, I say, about 35 in the day, and dry. "That's nothing!" he exclaims in envy. So it seems I have arrived, after all, in time to taste the last days of strained anticipation. I have read of them. I will wait.

* * *

The chief priest at Tirupati, at the apex of a vast army of priests and other functionaries, was once a highly regarded doctor in London—so Jyotirmaya reports. The god came to him in his dream and called him home, and he went happily. And what would I do if Venkaṭeśvara came to me in a dream?

If millions of Spaniards can misread the *Quixote*—and they do—and Germans get lost in *Faust*, caught between Mephistopheles and his other self, why should Andhras not think that Pĕddana sides with Pravara against Varuthini (Kanakaiah's view), or that Rajesvari in the *Maidanam* is Tara reborn (this is Raghuramaraja's thesis)? And yet the original, as Borges says, is unfaithful to its translation. The culture makes its choices. Do I, the heartsick philologist, have the right to reconstruct?

* * *

Night.

The stars are clear, at first innocuous. Then I remember: this means no clouds. It is sticky, the air heavy. She stands, crisp gray hair, in the orange light of a bulb outside, with enormous dignity, very slowly straightening out the sari drying on a line.

I stop to buy boxed mango juice at the stall near the Minister's House. Priyanka, a young student, her hair in pigtails, hands me the juice and says softly, a melodious blessing: "maḷḷi raṇḍi" (Please come again). The same gracefulness and self-possession, but fifty years younger. A little drunk on all this splendor, bathed in the humid night air, I stagger homeward. The buffaloes are lying, monolithic, as if deliberately settled by Henry Moore in the chaotic courtyard surrounding Ratnam's thatched hut.

OK, OK, so you're happy. So what. And then?

No then.

June 18

It was too hot to sleep. At five thirty I hear Ratnam clanging the outside gate, afraid to come in and climb the steps because Raja's dog is barking. Maybe the dog, too, is hot, its nerves taut; in the past, she was mostly soporific. I go down in my *lungi*, vessel in hand, to get my morning milk.

Smile comes to talk of politics and the old days in Eluru: who is left to be admired? "People liked JFK, but—leaving aside the many he killed for nothing in Vietnam—look how he slaughtered the blond actress I loved."

Sastry is in a new campaign against the industrial expansion at Tuni, which will ruin the coast. He wants them to dump their wastes not deep in the sea, as they are planning to do, but somewhere where the farmers can recycle them. Whose responsibility is it? I ask. There is a government committee on the environment; but they have no power. Only the private activists stand a chance of stopping the damage. Shades of Israel. If it's something worth doing, like making peace or protecting innocent civilians from the settlers or saving the environment, you always have to do it yourself.

* * *

Forty-four degrees Celsius yesterday, 45 today, and tomorrow? At night, the paper says, it goes down to the mid-20s. A bizarre physical well-being, a certain joy, seems to come from giving in to the heat, not fighting back. I float through the morning. Kanakaiah is elusive. I read and reread the Pĕddana verses for today. A short stroll in the sun shakes up the anodyne. It is like summers of childhood, before there was AC in the world. Will our children believe us when we speak of this? They will never know the blessing of such surrender.

Bioy Casares: "I believe we lose immortality because we have not conquered our opposition to death."

* * *

The paper adds a wrinkle to a story of some weeks ago; a Hyderabadi engineer working for the Americans in Afghanistan was kidnapped and killed by the Taliban. When we first heard the news, everyone felt for the young, shocked widow. Nothing had prepared her for this calamity. What has Hyderabad to do with the Taliban? An utterly external, senseless reality had intruded into *our* world. But another shock was in store. It now transpires that the man had a second wife, one Svapna Reddi, with whom he had a baby daughter, Nitisha; Svapna is claiming five lakhs in compensation from the state. Bigamy, says the *Deccan Chronicle*, is widespread, and most of the men, at least, claim that it's no business of anybody's except the two (parallel, conjoined, perhaps conflicted) families. The Telugu term has a soft ring to it: *chinna illu*, the little home. Andhra and Tamil politicians, as in other matters, are apparently exempt, de facto, from this law (1955). *Plus ça change*: "Individuals with one wife are considered eunuchs, not men" (Vireesalingam, 1875).[4]

* * *

The suddenness of the change seems unlikely. At midday, the heat is unmitigated, the streets silent, empty, brilliantly alight, as if frozen into a kind of golden, fiery dry ice. Almost nothing moves. One hardly breathes. The leaves of the palm tree across the street are still. The paper has forecast another sunny day, without relief. I doze in and out of the *Naishadhiya*.

Then, first, a shadow falls. I look outside. Dark clouds frame the flame of the forest. A trace of wind. The electric current fails at once, as usual. The gold disappears. Thunder sounds, far away.

I go outside to the Kadiyam Road. The streets are alive again, people staring at the sky. Some smile, tiny lightning streaks of white against dark. I see a long flash of lightning above the trees.

The animals seem to feel it. Two dogs scurry across the road. Several white cows wander into the street, heads down, mooing. Birds flutter on the branches.

A crystal expectancy. We have been waiting for many weeks for this first sign of a crack in the molten gold. We have breathed in this liquid fire, and it has come out through all our pores. We are exhausted, and we are ready, fully ready.

But nothing. As if the waters had not yet broken, and the world was, again, resisting. Locked. I say to the sky, "You can do better than that."

Within the stillness, with the first drops, a certain dusty fragrance rises and falls. Pungent, like sweat. Substantial. Elusive. I want more. I think of Kālidāsa, the moment when summer ends, *śuci-vyapāya*:

tad-ānanaṃ mrit-surabhi kshitīśvaro rahasy upâghrāya na triptim
 āyayau/
karīva siktaṃ prishataiḥ payo-mucāṃ śuci-vyapāye vana-rāji-
 palvalam//
 (*Raghuvaṃśa* 3.3)

[No matter how many times
the king of the earth
sniffed at her mouth,
fragrant with earth,
he wanted more

like an elephant sniffing a forest pond
when the first drops fall from the sky
at summer's end.]

Dilipa's queen is pregnant and thus has a longing to eat earth, which (this being India) leaves behind a fragrance in her mouth. Dilipa simply can't get enough of it. I know now how he felt—also how the elephant must feel. These few drops, *pṛṣataḥ*, are not enough, though soon I can taste them, too—musty, full-bodied—and then I hear them, a patter, hardly more than an urgent whisper, as they strike the ground.

And then it stops. False alarm. In the battle to hold back or give birth, the resistance has won. I ache with disappointment. In the mauve sunset, I go out to buy a pen at the paper store. I ask the boy behind the counter, "Will it rain?" He assures me, "paḍutundi" (It will fall).

So perhaps the *Naisadhiya* divination worked after all. I just didn't take it seriously. Here is where I broke off reading to rush outside. Nala stands before Damayanti for the first time after entering her palace. He has his mission to perform, but he is almost dying with desire. Which force will win out?

ayodhi tad-dhairya-manobhavābhyāṃ tām eva bhaimīm avalambya
bhūmīm/
āha sma yatra smara-cāpam antaś-chinnaṃ bhruvau taj-jaya-bhanga-
vārtām//
8.53

[A battle was taking place
between Control and Passion,
with Damayanti as the stake.
Her eyebrows showed who won.
Love's bow was snapped
in the middle.[5]]

Control, holding back—*dhairya*—admirably captions this afternoon. Still, I say to myself, as with Nala, the mad moment will finally break through.

June 19

Can the sky cry wolf?

At nine o'clock this morning the current goes. I am lethargic, my intestines hurt, and I am, above all, hot. Not even a fan to alleviate the heat, which is pitched somewhere in the mid-40s, no doubt, and rising. By noon I am completely prostrate and even beginning to consider modifying, in extremis, the Shulman principle: that it is not enough to read the *Symposium* in Greek, one has to read it in Greek *in Greece*. Similarly, mutatis mutandis, with Pĕddana and Śrīharsha.

At 2:30, again, gusts of wind, gray clouds, the colors change. The power comes back, goes, comes, goes. At 2:51—monsoon.

Today the smell is more intense. Sweetness of dust, decomposing animal matter, rain. There is much banging of shutters and doors. It grows dark. Light has left the world. A tremendous wind wracks the palm trees across the street; the fronds twist, bewitched, around the trembling axis of the tapered trunk, a green-gray *tāṇḍava*, Śiva's End-of-the-World Dance. Incredibly, the men on the building site opposite my house go on working, soaked to the skin, through the deluge. They are nailing down planks. I have an impulse to rush outside into the flow, to bend and swirl like the palms.

When the first shock wave passes, you hear the staccato of the drops smashing into stone and wood and the hushed swish of wind and branches and the growl of thunder, a deep birth cry. Birds spiral down into the trees. Lightning shivers against black sky. Two monkeys peer out from high on the palm branches across the street, immobile, like in Kampan's famous simile:

> The she-monkey sleeps through the rain
> in her cavern, while the male sits, still
> as the Yogi who has stubbed out
> all feeling.
> (4.10.76)

The temperature falls some 10 to 15 degrees Celsius within seconds. A sweet, slightly scary coolness settles into the skin. You can breathe again, you can think; unlike the frozen monkey, you can even feel.

There are the aftershocks: gentler drops splattering on the red earth, a caressing breeze; bodily blockage drains away, the anxious wait is over; in the heart, a letting go.

June 21

I wake to low thunder and dark sky. Up to the Kadiyam Road; strong breezes, the air cool at last. It will rain. At the Hanuman Sapata Shop, a fire is, as always, burning, but today it looks thin and unusually brilliant against the gray-green horizon. All the endless pots and pans and jars and bottles and cutlery and rags and plates and baskets have been miraculously stacked on the wagon's tiny shelf, to protect them from what will come. It is like a demonstration that space is expandable, that you can squeeze anything into any small piece of it. It works for people, too.

Past the mango groves, workers, mostly women in bright saris, are working the fields, taking advantage of the imminent rain. Long rows of green pulses and vegetables are being carefully nurtured, weeded, hoed. Someone has erected a tall silvery scarecrow, actually one of two—one humanoid figure covered in something like tinfoil, the second a brown, nondescript companion. Don Quixote and Sancho Panza, incongruously transplanted to the Andhra Delta. Probably in the villages the rice seedbeds are ready by now. And Paiḍi Talli? She is germinating, too.

When the rain comes, this time it is gentle, gracious, and continuous, a generous bounty. Lakshmi, on the phone, thanks me: "With your coming, the rains came, too." It is god's grace, I say, and she readily agrees. The paper, with its usual prescience, promised clear skies.

On the other hand, the *Deccan Chronicle* supplies daily nuggets of wisdom. Jean Genet: "Crimes of which people are ashamed constitute their true history. The same is true of man." (Not, perhaps, of woman.)

June 22

Krishnayya arrives, loaded with Perantallu. They seem to be as abundant as trees in northern coastal Andhra. Better still, he has found an eloquent informant, a semiliterate woman from Vijinigiri who speaks a rustic Telugu, mostly incomprehensible even to Krishnayya, but who is a mine of story. We will seek her out and listen.

Rain remains a weighty theological issue. One Raghava Reddy writes to the *Deccan Chronicle*: "Sir, after *varuna japam*s [hymns to the rain god] were conducted in various parts of the State by the Hindus, God offered his blessings in the form of rains ('Priests Seek Divine Help for Rains,' June 20). This is a reminder to all those who claim to be atheists and for those who do not believe in God [apparently, two separate categories—DS]. Last year, when the Muslims organized mass prayers on the lakebed of Himayatsagar for rains, their prayers were answered. This clearly points out that God does not distinguish between religions."

Good to know. On the same page, Tom Friedman writes that "philosophers are important, but not in bulk."

Thus primed for the day's work, we are about to open the computer when the electric current fails. Load shedding again? It may be hours before it returns. Krishnayya, as often, tells me he is not surprised. He had never heard of load shedding before he went to Calcutta in the mid-seventies. "This never happens in Andhra," he told his friends, who wisely said, "Just wait."

I tell him he is a little jaded. (He has been explaining to me, convincingly, why my teacher Kanakaiah has disappeared; this, too, did not surprise him. There always comes a moment, he says, when the mere existence of a set task weighs too heavily.) He is all too aware of my Pollyannaish tendencies, particularly pronounced when I am in Andhra, so he says: "Right, actually everything is splendid. It is not that the current has gone, we simply can't quite see it. If we meditate long enough, it will become apparent even to our eyes, though they are veiled in *māyā*, the distorting delusion that is ours from birth. Besides, it's very cool in South India, we're comfortable, and at any moment God himself will knock at the door."

"And if we open the door, what will he say to us? That the current will soon be restored?"

"No, he lives in a Hindu heaven. He'll say: 'ikkaḍa kūḍa karent ledā' (So there's no current here either?)."

* * *

Word arrives from Jerusalem that Henry, a dear friend, is starting chemotherapy. Since the news of his lymphoma, "reality" seems to me paper-thin; far more so than usual. I am with him, or he with me, every hour now, but I cannot save him from the everyday agony, the terror.

Israelis would normally say something fatuous like "Be strong." I write to him: melt and flow. "Strength" is part of the problem. The South Indian recommendation is to soften. But does it help?

He is staring at death, unable to avert his gaze. He is younger than I. The veil has been torn away. I think again about the Advaitic temptation—the wish to believe that there is some singular, godly aliveness hidden within us, a level of being, nonpersonal, that cannot be injured or destroyed. Such "nondualism," experienced in Rajahmundry, is somehow intuitively persuasive, and almost comforting, at times intoxicating; one melts effortlessly into the organic, decaying whole. The other compelling choice is the hardheaded, remorseless Nāgârjunian attack on the mind: what passes for reality is no more than our crystallized projections, in which we invest futile energy and thus fall into suffering; what is "true" is only the empty space we can perceive if we clear away all habitual intellection. Nāgârjuna, too, belonged to Andhra. It's not so easy to decide between this lyrical, romantic Advaita that lulls you into a liquid self-congruity and the cool clarity of the Mahāyāna in which "self" itself is part of the delusion: *mundu goyyi venaka nuyyi*, a pit before you, a deep well behind you, as the Telugu proverb says. One should perhaps want to be free. But I think of death as a violent interruption, awkward, noisy, and always too soon. It will not let me finish the thought or the dream. I want to resist. Like my father, I will resist. Until I find the means—whatever broken syllables happen to turn up, however dissonant the music—to complete the poem.

But perhaps freedom is like the monsoon; unlocking, unblocking, unclutching? I can feel, without analyzing, the Mahāyāna therapeutic, utterly seductive. It may even be true, unlike reality. I am certain to resist.

June 23

To the small town of Dhavalesvaram, downriver, for dinner at Janardana Ravu's; Kamesvari's exquisite touch. On the way, traffic locks into stasis; many buses, packed with passengers, stand helpless on the road. They say this is now the pattern every evening on the road from Rajahmundry to Dhavalesvaram. Krishnayya recalls the days he used to walk from his house in Dhavalesvaram, by the river, to the Arts College in Rajahmundry; there was pitch blackness, forest, empty space between the two towns. Hungry demons roamed here undisturbed, a serious threat to lonely passersby like Krishnayya. Now it is an uninterrupted urban stretch. After some time we abandon the auto rickshaw and wend our way by foot along the drainage canals and over the mud and sand by the roadside; even this passageway is nearly impassable in the crush of frustrated pedestrians. Dhavalesvaram itself looks a little dreary, a warren of dust, pigs, alleys; and some elegant old houses. The River is even closer than in Rajahmundry, the real heart. What was it like to grow up beside the Godavari, to share your thoughts with her each day, as if with a slightly capricious aunt next door? I think Godavari still speaks directly to Krishnayya, still runs through his dreams.

I wake at four thirty, head buzzing with Telugu. No room there for more sleep. So when the light turns gray, and you still can't tell a blue thread from a white one,[6] I am standing on the balcony watching the line of white (or blue?) cows staggering slowly along the street on their way to work.

R. Sri Venkatesvara Rao and Kanakaiah appear almost simultaneously in the late afternoon. Venkatesvara Rao has read the *Prabhavati* afterword[7] and is full of interesting responses. He is intrigued by the notion of *pratyekī-karaṇa*, individualization, which we suggested as an innovation of the sixteenth century. We speak of *rasa*, the liquid "essence" of aesthetic experience, and of *sādhāraṇī-karaṇa*, the depersonalized universalization that, according to the great Abhinavagupta, is what releases the *rasa* (that exists inside each of us) when we hear a poem or see a play performed. Kanakaiah, perhaps sensing my hostility to the notion, says that every spectator at the drama has his own karmic memories, *vāsanā*s, so the experience can never be truly depersonalized; even Abhinavagupta recognizes this. RSVR says that he always identifies with the main hero, the *nāyaka*—in a play or a film or a story—and assimilates the *nāyaka*'s likes and dislikes; within that process, there are moments of true generalized awareness, a kind of contrapuntal rhythm, or ebb and flow, as his own idiosyncratic consciousness recedes before that of the imagined hero. The idea interests me. Eventually I express my skepticism and say that there is no such thing as *rasa*; Abhinavagupta was a Tantric metaphysician, his poetics derived from his praxis. No, says Kandaiah, fully at home in his world, the Telugu *kāvya*s like *Prabhāvatī-pradyumnamu* and *Manu-caritramu* come from somewhere else, another stream; they are close to the maverick poetician Kuntaka and the theory of *vakrokti*, crooked speech—that creative distortion in language that is the hallmark of real poetry. Śrīnātha, he says, is the first to apply this principle in Telugu.

We all have the same, immediate association; we pause for a moment to recite together Śrīnātha's *Bhīma-khaṇḍamu* verse, *hara-cūḍā-hariṇânka-vakratayu . . .*

A little crooked
like the crescent moon on Śiva's head,

sharp as the contours
of the firm, quickened breasts of the goddess
roused to fury at the end of time,

yet soft and delicious:

good poetry is all of this together,
dancing
wherever poets live.[8]

Kuntaka and Śrīnātha lead, says Kandaiah, directly to the medieval Andhra school of poetics, to Viśveśvara and the *Camatkāra-candrikā* (Moonlight of Amazement)—also to the great Telugu *prabandham*s of the sixteenth century. I agree: Viśveśvara lived at the Reddi court in Racakonda, in Telangana, toward the end of the fourteenth century, a contemporary of Śrīnātha's. I think Kandaiah has intuitively reconstructed the basis of the Andhra school, and he proceeds correctly to its most distinctive feature, the concern with *śābdika*—phonic-musical-magical—effects. Syllables combined scientifically have immediate results in the world. A poet who knows the magic of the combinations can bless or curse, kill his enemies, revive the dead, make the barren fertile. Kanakaiah has some direct access to this linguistic metaphysics. Perhaps the school is still alive, here in Rajahmundry.

* * *

Local Panchayat elections will begin on June 28; the courts have removed the last impediment. Auto rickshaws draped in banners, with blaring megaphones, roam the streets. These elections are generating some passion, yet the system as a whole is somewhat opaque. Where does power reside? You can see the checks and balances, the active role of press and judiciary, the voter's decisive moment. A real center, strong in certain ways, exists in Hyderabad—yet how much control does it really exercise, or seek to exercise? The Andhra "state" is certainly not dependent on a Weberian-style Brahminic legitimation; historically, all Andhra polities drew their authority from other sources, including, before all else, the pervasive presence of the wilderness with its charismatic and often outlandish virtuosos, still very much at work today. The wilderness, and its tribes and outlaws, are never outside the system but rather integral to its functioning, on all levels, sometimes in very violent modes. A vast intelligence network, manned by spies of various kinds, appears to function more or less effectively, perpetuating one of the main colonial mechanisms of rule; together with a stolid bureaucracy, this ramified network provides a modicum of structural continuity to today's Andhra. Still, not much of this picture relates well to a notion of the modern democratic national state with its flag and postage stamps. I think the state as we know it is an artificial superstructure; the reality down below is one of ad hoc accommodation between warring systems—especially the bandits in the forest and the caste politics of the towns. And yet these two systems are really one.

* * *

Telugu seems more and more like Greek: a diffuse spectrum of local dialects, highly diglossic, even more so than Tamil (contrary to conventional wisdom); yet mostly mutually intelligible. The so-called *grānthika-bhāsha*, an artificial prose concocted by the pandits, never stood a chance; but this does not mean that what is today thought of as standard (*vyavahārika*), the official language of the media, has a much better chance. It, too, is likely to crack open and allow for some new linguistic coagulation (and with it, the birth of new creative literary forms). All the literary styles are relatively restricted crystallizations out of the nonstandardized oral continuum, which has its own integrity, based on a norm of radical variation. In short: a forest language, or rather the language of many islands in a sea of wilderness, as in Greece and the Aegean; but the Andhra ocean is composed of rocks and trees. Tamil was always, as the Tamils have claimed, more stable, the diglossia more obvious on the surface but actually far less extreme. One might meditate on diffusion as the cultural substratum in a wilderness-based political-linguistic economy.

June 25

Kanakaiah's visits are by now totally unpredictable. He darts in for half an hour, recites three or four verses, and rushes off. I roll the verses on my tongue, hoping they have come to stay.

Sashi earnestly asks, as we walk up and down the street in the dark: OK, so there are a thousand years of *kāvya* production, it is weighty, it is important, but why should I think of it as poetry? Why stretch out what is so much better compressed? A. K. Ramanujan mesmerizes him, the short Cankam poems and the Kannada *vacana*s. Why did Raman not read (or translate) *kāvya*?

I read Sridhar's *Purāgānam* (Ancient Voice) with him (Sridhar was once his close friend):

ninnaṭi nirāsaktata minhā
mar'em ledu

nannu nen'ayinā
palakarinca ledu

nālona
purāgānam edo
kŏnasāgutundi

kŏmpadīsi
mīk' ĕvarikainā
vinipistund'emon ani
tappincuko tirugutānu

ayinā
ĕkkaḍik'akkaḍa
ĕppaṭik'appuḍu
paṭṭubaḍipotū. . . .

[But for yesterday's languor,
nothing

Not even I could make
myself speak

In me
some ancient voice
goes on

I wander
lest someone
hear it

yet
ensnared
everywhere
everywhen. . . .]

One has to put aside all his early revolutionary poems with their *tupāki* rifles in hand in order to read this one in its clarity.

Probably much of the so-called poetic production of the second half of the century falls under this rule.

But Sashi's problem is unconvincing, and it is not a matter of definition, either. I admit to him that I'm unlikely ever to spend a month reading *The Fairy Queene*. Pĕddana, however, is as close as the buffalo girl next door.

* * *

The Jalari fishermen have a myth about the male deity Potaraju; Krishnayya tells the story as we have tea in the late afternoon. He heard it directly from the lips of the Jalaris in Vizag, on the beach near his home. Gods and demons were fighting; the demons had swallowed the ancient Vedic texts. The gods wiped out the demons except for one, Kŏmma Rākshasaḍu (Horn Demon), who was missing. They searched for him everywhere, finally found him, and made him cough up the Vedas. *Okaksharam angiṭlo arigi poyindi*: Alas, one phoneme was worn away on his palate.

This comes straight out of my dreams: always there is the one letter of the inscription that I can't read, the one critical word that is missing from the dictionary, the one volume that has been lost, the only one that really matters. For these fishermen, however, it happens twice: first the voracious Rakshasa himself goes missing, then the crucial phoneme that he once "knew" is also gone. It seems to have been inscribed on his palate—orally? Both spoken and inscribed? The Vedas have this incompleteness as a matter of principle. Which phoneme was it? The Jalaris say you would have to ask some Jalari pandit. In fact, the question is probably redundant.

* * *

Krishnayya leaves in a flurry for Madras, for his visa appointment. A sudden stillness. I think I will ride Smile's bicycle up the Nehru Road. The colors have changed again: green and dark blue (clouds), dark-red waterlogged earth, soaked brown thatch, pastel facades, red rooster feathers, mud-black buffaloes, white afternoon sun—no more gold. Relief. When I told Smile I have been enjoying his cycle, he quoted Ismayil's poem:[9]

dīn' nenu tīsuk'ĕḍutunnāno
nann' idi tīsuk'eḍutundo
nāku telīdu.
nā kavitvam lāge.

ākāsānikī roḍḍukī madhya
cakrālu tirugutāyi.
adhika bhāgam ākāsamlone.
angulam mera mātram
anṭipĕṭṭukunṭundi nelani.
nā kavitam lāge.

vidhullo tele sāyantrapu mohāla
rangula gālipaḍagalu digipoyi
mem gūḍu cerukunnāka
oka cakram bhūmmīda ānci
oka cakram kalalloki telci
niddarotundi.
nā kavitam lāge.

[Am I taking it
or is it taking me?
Don't know.
Like my poetry.

Between sky and road
wheels revolve.
Mostly in the sky.
Only a finger's breadth
touches the earth.
Like my poetry.

Kites soaked
in evening tones
float down to rest.
After we reach our nest,
a wheel on the ground,
another floating into dreams,
it sleeps.
Like my poetry.]

June 26, Guntupalle, Buddhist Caves

Lakku, most amiable and erudite of drivers, wiry and voluble, picks me up with Sashi before seven for the day's trip to Guntupalle in West Godavari. The sun is back, the river alight as we cross it westward. Sashi is a bit disappointed at the weather; he thinks Guntupalle is best seen under thick cloud.

Seacoast, delta, mixed zone, dry land, wilderness: the road traverses all of these in turn. Guntupalle is poised on the cusp of wilderness, thick forest leading north and west into Telangana. The Andhra Buddhists seem to have had a preference for such sites, the hilltops that are wilderness thresholds, with a commanding view of the green plains below. By ten o'clock we are there. From below, the caves look like black gaps in the dense foliage. The sun is burning, the sky a profound, clean blue.

Guntupalle is the largest of all Andhra Buddhist sites, and one of the longest to be continuously inhabited: from the second century BC until the eleventh (Nannayya's time). Moreover, in all likelihood the great logician Dignāga lived and was buried here; his own works describe him as living on "the great Nāga mountain," *mahā-nāga-parvata-nivāsi*—the Nāga in question being perhaps the elephant's back that seems to have congealed as this mountain, with its horseshoe loop, precisely reminiscent of Ajanta. There are some sixty caves carved into the hills, some for solitary virtuoso meditators, others for more sociable types; at the top of the hill, a large *stūpa* burial mound, the remains of an assembly hall, and other red-brick monastic structures. The rock face itself sweeps sinuously through the hollowed-out chambers, almost liquid in its soft swirls. One particularly attractive cave-"villa" set apart from the others must, Sashi says, have been Dignāga's home. It is more than likely that Nāgârjuna, the most penetrating of the early Mahāyāna philosophers, visited here on one of his official tours. Nāgârjuna—who saw the world as a lattice of interwoven projections emerging from our minds.

It looks like they had a good life, serene and serious, with this heart-rending view of unending green below, dotted with ravishing flashes of *Turai*, Flame of the Forest—far too beautiful, one might have thought, for a monk bent on release. But I find it hard to imagine Dignāga sitting in his cave, mapping out an abstruse, metaphysical logic. Logic appears so utterly impoverished and insubstantial—truly empty—against this shimmering setting of rock, tree, field, and sky. Maybe that is what *emptiness* means, the cultivation of a contrast stark enough to undermine thought. Forest may be empty by definition, resistant to conceptual forms. But this wilderness is, they tell me, full of bears, who sometimes come down from the top of the mountain toward sunset. They are dangerous. How did the monks face them? A small poisonous viper coils itself through two stone recesses on one of the ancient *caitya* buildings—Dignāga reborn (my suggestion)? Sashi says maybe the snake has finally found some peace. Murali, the main caretaker-guide, says young couples from the village often sneak up here to make love amid the ruins (and the bears, snakes, frogs, and lizards); he says he has had the good fortune to come across them many times: the final, Tantric stage of Māhayāna Buddhism in practice, another happy mode of emptying the mind.

In the early afternoon we stop for a courtesy call in the village. Rajput warriors from Chhattisgarh in middle India migrated to Guntupalle some centuries back; they, in fact, were the original owners of the land the antiquities sit on. Murali is descended from these kings. He takes us to visit their vast, cool house, built in 1920, decorated with finely carved teak lintel and pillars. We are offered water and sweets in dignified, almost silent gestures of hospitality. We see only the men: tall, manly, even fierce, just like the paintings of their ancestors, with their enormous drooping mustaches, hanging on the walls inside.

Here, in the flatland of the paddy fields, another Buddhist community once lived—perhaps the laity that supported the monks uphill. We walk through the fields in search of antiquities. A modern goddess, "Tara," sits in a shrine painted yellow and daubed with red dots, surrounded by fields. Once they took this image up to the caves, so we are told by an old farmer; then for three years, crops failed, until they brought her back. He is proud of his goddess and of his goddess-nurtured home. A little further along the footpath we see long white Palnadu slabs, carved and, in one case, inscribed in Ikshvaku-period letters. A thrilling moment: the stones speak from out of the distant centuries. They have been lying here for nearly two millennia, waiting for us to happen by. A few other peasants join us; they bring a bucket of water with which to clean the inscription (so I can photograph it and Jitendra decipher it). Nearby, scattered amid the grass and shrubs, half buried, are a very old red-stone Tara, most elegant of the Buddhist goddesses, and a standing Buddha, largely worn away by time, rain, sun. It is like an empirical, routine demonstration of nonpermanence, this stone emptying itself out, giving up its carved image. A few more minutes and we reach a prone stone column. "Strange what enlightenment a discovery brings, this sudden ray of light."[10]

We are walking on top of a buried Buddhist city, with its shrines and shops and streets and homes. They break through the surface, demanding attention, calling up memory, like long-forgotten friends. A slightly lugubrious romanticism surges through us. The ghosts are waiting, eager to tell their tale. Sashi tells me I must quickly send an archaeologist from Israel.

At Pedda Vegi, the old Chalukya capital [formerly Vengi], there are the red remains of a stūpa burial mound and a temple, literally side by side; also a very old *linga* shrine and a compact, well-preserved sun temple. They are among the earliest surviving temples in Andhra. More red sandstone, much eroded, more insistent voices. Fragments of statuary, bits and pieces of divinity in seemingly random poses, line the temple's outer wall. Along with all the living gods and goddesses of Andhra, we have these once-upon-a-time deities, flotsam and jetsam that have washed up here close to their buried homes.

By now it is late afternoon, we are exhausted from the roads and the climb. At Jangareddigundem, Sashi introduces me to a village bar. We file through a dark restaurant into an even darker room at the back. The familiar gray-streaked pseudomarble tabletops, grimy and sticky; red-glass ceiling lamps, most of them burned out; in the far corner, on the wall, a small square box with framed pictures of indeterminable gods, a red lamp burning beneath them; a few whirling fans and a dysfunctional AC unit, covered with dust; dark green curtains blocking the windows, though through a door to the courtyard the granular, gray late-afternoon light filters in. Men sit, drinking, smoking, eating, chatting (no women come to such places in coastal Andhra, in marked contrast with Telangana). We order beer and finger chips; a waiter in white brings us four glasses. Sashi asks if they are clean; the waiter peers into one, trying to see in the gloom, fails, swipes his finger inside and pronounces them to be fine. Why is it that this somehow captivating space feels so continuous with Dignāga and the meditation cells above us on the hill? "Form is emptiness, Sariputra, and emptiness, form." Thus spoke the Buddha. A small TV perched close to the ceiling is showing dance clips from Telugu films in lurid color. I stare at them, entranced, as I sip my beer. Lakku recognizes a song-and-dance sequence from *Keśava Reḍḍi*. "Do you know the name of that actor?" Sashi asks me, and of course I do not, so he tells me, with a smile: "Nāgârjuna."

June 27, Rajahmundry

Sleep-starved. The morning passes in a daze. Two hours at Reliance-Webworld, reading the e-mail; if I let it go a day, it turns into the sorcerer's apprentice. Reliance-Webworld is air-conditioned to the point of freezing; one sits huddled over the computer, trying to stay warm, while outside the world languishes in a humid, simmering heaviness.

My business relations with Ramakrishna, the washerman down the street, seem paradigmatic. The day before yesterday I told him clearly I was leaving for two weeks and needed my clothes back before that. In the classic *dhobi* mode, he pointed to the sky: what if it rains? Noncommittal. But this morning as I approach, he smiles. It is ready. Or rather, it will be ready. Good, I say, I'll come back within an hour. OK? OK. I head for the e-mail. Rush back to catch him before he disappears for lunch. He sees me coming and strikes his head with the palm of his hand. What happened? I completely forgot. But you told me so confidently last week that you never forget anything, you remember even which plastic bag each person uses to bring his clothes. Did I say that? It's true. But I forgot. So when should I come? Anytime. Evening, *sāyantaram*? Yes, I'm here till eight o'clock. Will it be ready? Yes, surely. I come back at four thirty. He sees me and darts into the house, a dark shack covered with thatch, returning with my still unironed clothes. Putting aside whatever else he was doing, he lifts the hot, heavy, ancient iron and attacks Shirt Number One. I stand beside him in the sun; it is hot, and this will take some time. I say: You know what, I have to buy something across the street, I'll be back in five minutes. Please finish them now. Yes, yes, he says. Six minutes later I return. He has put aside the shirts, including Number One (one sleeve completed) and is poking around doing this and that. Belatedly I realize that unless I stand beside him as he works, inflicting on him the burden, or possibly the neediness, of my presence, he will never iron my clothes. So I stand and chat. How much does it cost to go to Israel? Twenty thousand rupees, more or less. In that case it must be quite close to Dubai. Yes, I say, it is indeed quite close. Meanwhile, his little boy, naked from the waist down, comes running to him, crying for peanuts; the nut vendor, on a beat-up bicycle, has just arrived; he measures out unshelled peanuts and *marmarālu* seeds in the iron cones of an earlier time. The child's eyes deepen and expand in joyful anticipation, despite his mother's grumblings at the wasted money. The nut man goes his way, I look back at Ramakrishna's wooden stall. The shirts, believe it or not, are ready, beautifully folded and reinserted into the plastic bag in which I brought them a week ago. He never forgets. I pay him (a little more than he asked) and take my leave.

It is like all the rest of human relations in India—de-objectified, personalized, almost intimate. The task does not exist in its own right, or as part of a formalized program. It exists only in the personal space between him and me. When I step out of that space, the task slips out of his awareness. This ironing business is not some Weberian routine, though Ramakrishna is at it all day long, every day. It is something between him and me, utterly dependent on my presence beside him. I think this is how the government works. Sashi says there are three daily trains in the evening from Rajahmundry to Hyderabad, to accommodate the endless stream of people who go to petition the Secretariat. They keep at it for years, though nothing happens. Their physical presence is a necessary, recurring condition. If something *were* to happen, it would be like Ramakrishna's awakening into action when I stand beside him. From bottom to top of the system, objects (rules) are highly dubious entities, utterly dependent on something else; and the currency of direct bodily and emotional contact is the only effective tender.

June 28

With the rains we have an influx of crickets, cockroaches, and crows. The latter circle in raucous black parties of ten to fifteen, then swoop down near the yellow divider along the Kadiyam Road. The cockroaches are enormous, like small rodents and, with their long fluttering antennae, particularly repellent. Many mornings begin with a cockroach hunt in the kitchen, my substitute for the old colonial tiger *shikar*. (The cockroaches are of course particularly fond of the kitchen.) But the black crickets are the most impressive. In searching discussions with my neighbors, we have failed to resolve the entomological puzzle of classification: are these *cimmeṭlu*, as the more scientific and pedantic claim, or *miḍatalu*, grasshoppers, the majority view? In any case, they are aggressive, tenacious, and immune to most countermeasures. They congregate at sunset, or a little earlier, at the base of the steps leading up to my flat. At first they have the aimless look of reserve soldiers reporting for duty—I remember the feeling all too well—but soon, donning combat gear, they begin to move in formation, wave after wave, up the stairs. Like trained commandos they pass through the iron grate and attack the wooden door and windows. No matter how tightly I have sealed the house, some miraculously find their way in. Once inside, they have an unnerving love for bedsheets, towels, and shirts; and they can jump or fly to quite astonishing heights. When one gets into your shirt, you frantically shake yourself out—not an uncommon sight at social gatherings—but the horrible sensation lingers on; your skin prickles with the fatal combination of memory, imagination, and everyday sweat, and sometimes with the actual continuing presence of some die-hard, resourceful cricket lodged in back or neck. By morning they are gone, the steps clean except for a few cricket corpses left behind on the battlefield.

* * *

At seven thirty, as I am boiling water, the power goes. This is so common an occurrence that it doesn't even occur to me that the circuit has shorted out. But the neighbors have current, so I soon realize that the problem is in my flat alone. Raju goes in search of an electrician, who finally appears at four and changes the fuse, in the old mode I remember from Jerusalem of thirty years ago—the same white, rectangular fuses with their slender copper wires. But the day drained and dribbled by in waiting, mostly fruitlessly. I call Kanakaiah to tell him I'll be away; he recites a litany of problems and disasters that have kept him from coming to teach. They are always there, and always true, though not always equally salient. Meanwhile, I have been thinking about Varuthini's continued suffering; she has survived the dark night of longing, and now her girlfriends, still trying to comfort her, announce the onset of dawn:

Look at this row of lamps:

Yesterday, at sunset,
    they stole the sun's red glow.
Now he's coming back
    to claim it.
So they've hidden it in the corners
    of the eyes of women
    worn out by a night of love
    (who after all owe them something
    for the daily gift of soot)
and in exchange have taken on
their paleness
as a mask.
    (3.56)

Sun, lamps, women: the last two bound up in reciprocal obligations and exchanges. Another threesome. The lamps stole the sun's red glow in the evening but are reluctant to return it, so they hide it in the corners of women's eyes. Now we know why women who stay up all night making love have red eyes. These women have to perform this service for the lamps, since they use black lamp soot each day to make up their eyes. Light comes from or through another, never from oneself. Pallor, like color, is a movable substance, to be bartered or offered in payment for services. Yet pallor is also a mask, hiding the intensity of a dying flame. Perhaps it is this oddly tactile texture of fancy that is so captivating in Pĕddana.

Late evening, Sashi arrives, a little lugubrious (my departure). We try our hand at a Nasara Reddi poem, from the other quotidian moment of transition:

DINÂNTAM

jīvitam mīda āsa kaligince
driśyal' appuḍ'appuḍu leka poledu.
kāni ave
na maraṇāniki dohadam cestunna
vishayam maravalenu.

anāsaktamgāne talupulu tĕrici
gadiloki praveśistānu.
gadi ninḍā dummu.
kāsta dulupukuni
paḍukunṭānu
ĕgire minugurulni cūstū.

[DAY'S END

It's not that there are no
occasional scenes
that raise hope
for life.
But neither can I forget
that these
crave my death.

Listlessly
I open the doors
and enter the room.
Full of dust.
Shaking some off,
I lie down
watching the fireflies.]

Much harder to translate than Pĕddana; there are precise silences at every point. In each such silence, a weight of utterly unbearable sensation.

An "I" speaks, or intimates speech, too sad or empty for words; it is truly an end (of a day, of time itself). And there is even a rationalized reason for the emptiness: the opening double negative ties the occasional, sporadic experience of hope to certain death in the gnomic manner of the Sanskrit figure of universalized projection (*arthântara-nyāsa*, literally "shifting to another matter"—which always, however, comes *after* its concrete instantiation in a Sanskrit poem). But the real contrast, an intimate echo, is with Kalidasa's end-of-day verse from the prologue to the *Śākuntala*:

subhaga-salilâvagāhāḥ pāṭala-saṃsarga-surabhi-vana-vātāḥ/
pracchāya-sulabha-nidrā divasāḥ pariṇāma-ramaṇīyāḥ//

[These summer days—
when diving into water is so delicious,
when the wind from the wilderness
bears the scent of trumpet flowers,
when you can doze happily in the shade—
are best
as they draw to a close.]

That unexpected, residual love for the hot season that I have now discovered in myself comes through at the pregnant moment when the day ends: here a moment of celebration. Nasara Reddi has taken up and reframed a motif that runs through the classical texts—thus we have Piṅgaḷi Sūranna, *Prabhāvati-pradyumnamu* 4.116:

ambudhilonik' antaṭanu hamsuḍu ḍiggĕ dinânta-majjanâ-
rthambunu bolĕn aṭṭiyĕḍa dat-taṭin āraga gaṭṭinaṭṭi ra-
ktâmbaramoy ananga tanarārĕ kaḍun kaḍasanjaṭhīviy an-
tam boḍa sūpĕ tārakalu tat-patanodgata-binduloy anan//

[The sun jumped into the ocean
like a Yogi taking his ritual bath
at day's end, and the sky was
the ochre robe he hung up to dry
and the stars, the drops of water
that splashed as he dove.[11]]

Sūranna's stars have become Nasara Reddi's fireflies; and the sweet shadow of the trees, which Kālidāsa prescribes for late-afternoon naps, is replaced by a lonely bed or cot in some modern, dusty room. Why is it so dusty? Has he been away for a long time? For that matter, Nasara Reddi's speaker can't seem to fall asleep.

June 30, Hyderabad

From Rama Brahmam, scholar and poet in the Telugu Department at the University of Hyderabad, I learn that the color of gold in heaven is dark green, like the leaves of the Jambu tree (hence one of the Sanskrit names for gold: *jāmbunada*). My student Tammy has been reading her Sanskrit commentary with this gentle, curious, incisive man, but today she has the afternoon off—*śishṭânadhyāyana*, Rama Brahmam jokingly calls it, the vacation one gets when august personages come to visit. So I take her and Maya to Khairatabad to see the mosque, the loveliest building in this city of superb, gritty monuments, some now crumbling under the brunt of traffic and pollution. The minarets, happily asymmetrical, sway slightly in the evening air. Hundreds of pigeons are at home in the latticed windows in the upper stories. The mosque was built by a woman—Khairattunnisa Begum, the daughter of the great Sultan Muhammad Quli Qutub Shah—in honor of her teacher, Akhud Mulla Abu 'l-Malik. The tomb prepared for him nearby is, however, empty, since this beloved tutor died while on pilgrimage to Mecca. Perhaps the empty tomb adds to the mysterious spaciousness of the mosque, a mirage of light and upward movement in the heart of the crowded neighborhood of Lakri-ka-pul.

Dinner at Jitendra and Jhansi's. Jitendra has many adventures to report; he has walked the wilderness alone, traveled on the trespassing fishing boats to Pakistan. "This thing they call fear," he says, "I'd like to experience it sometime."

On the way back from Dilsukhnagar, late at night, to my hotel in Secundarabad, Paradise Corner, the auto driver gets lost. He stops every few minutes to ask people on the road: "Paradise kahān hai?" (Where is Paradise?) Mostly they say, "sīdha sīdha" (Go straight). One person suggests: "Go straight and turn left." I am glad someone knows the answer to the question.

July 1, Hyderabad, Bangalore

An open letter to the public from the Chief Minister, Y. S. Rajasekhara Reddy, to crown the Congress campaign in the Panchayat elections: "Congress believes in talking less and doing less work." After twenty-four hours, they issue a correction; but the true intention comes through all the same.

* * *

The young scientist Milinda welcomes me to the Indian Institute of Science in Bangalore. It is cool, quiet, green, serene, a thick forest in which scientists have planted their labs; another paradise. Furry creatures scurry across the paths, and at night the snakes come out. Milinda gives me the Indian theory on this matter: if you tread firmly on the path, the snake will recognize that you are a superior being in the hierarchy of creatures and will humbly yield.

By evening, a deep silence takes hold, so rare in India; only the occasional exotic birdcall rings through it. Raghavendra, my life-scientist friend from Berlin, has provided me with this hiatus from the wet furnace of Rajahmundry, and I remember: it is even possible, at times, to think.

Raghavendra, a quiet visionary, amazingly effective and humane, works on wasps; he arranges a tour of his lab. His doctoral students know all the wasps by name or number; they spend days—happy days—gazing into their nests. The day is divided into a long series of five-minute observation "bytes" followed by one minute off. It is a classical Indian temporal rhythm, straight linear sequence dissolving regularly into unstructured time-space—like the ten-month year, *samvatsara*, of the classical calendar, always followed by two months of monsoon. Great dramas transpire in the nest: Potential queens, call them Varuthinis, manifest aggression; the males, like Maya-Pravara, mostly rest, mate, and fly away. A mild functionalism responds to changing contexts. Raghavendra tells me he speaks Kannada with his mother when he agrees with her, English when he disagrees.

Jim Ponet arrives from New Haven after midnight—his first entry into India. For many years, since we met and a unique friendship was forged in the Israeli army, I have been telling him he must come here; now it has happened, and I am in the unfamiliar role of guide, wanting to introduce him to my gods, one by one. We will retrace a pilgrimage route through the Kaveri Delta. Of how many human beings could one say, as one does about Jim: he knows about god, or God?

July 6, Lepakshi

Sharp rain greets us as we reach the great gentle Nandin, a stone bull sitting patiently at the entrance to the village (just inside the Andhra border). An immense boulder is still poised precariously over these houses—Lepakshi's prime wonder. What is it to live in the shadow of this remarkable rock? Raghavendra says the earth is 4.6 billion years old, and life appeared 3.6 billion years ago. It took a billion years to cool down. How long, then, has this rock been solid?

In the temple, late afternoon, golden light trickling softly in, I recognize Srinivas, one of the priests, from my first visit years ago. He is standing in front of the masked Durga, finishing a *pūjā* for three visitors who then depart. We are alone with him and the goddess, who inhabits a pillar close to a mirror that stretches the length of the wall. The old silver mask I saw on earlier visits has been exchanged for a newer, golden one; and this one, like its predecessor, is coquettish, cheerful, light. I ask him if he could remove it for a second, as he did for me once before. Perhaps it is the silent ambience, the empty ease of this space, the Telugu, perhaps it is the dim memory I have called up, but he immediately agrees—and again I find myself standing before the black-stone goddess of infinite sorrow at the moment she is spearing her would-be-lover, the buffalo-demon Mahishâsura. The contrast between face and mask is astonishing; even more so the deep reflection of both face and mask in the mirror. She lives there, inside the mirror. Pilgrims who come from far away to visit this goddess make their offerings to her reflection.

Lepakshi, built in its present form in the decade of the 1540s, has the perfection of the incomplete and the intense vision of the blind. Virupanna, the builder, tore out his eyes—so they say here—because when Aliya Rama Raju became king of Vijayanagara, knowing nothing of his predecessor Acyuta Raya's order to build the shrine, he was enraged at the expense; he sent soldiers to blind Virupanna. When the latter heard of the king's command, he said, "If my master wants my eyes, I will offer them to him myself"—and proceeded to gouge them out and dash them on the wall of the unfinished Kalyana Mandapa, where Śiva and Parvati were to be married. The stains (*lepâkshi*, "smeared eyes") are still visible, and as for the wedding, it has been postponed: the creator god Brahmā, the officiating priest, still stands at the entrance of the *maṇḍapa*, ready to greet his guests. For all the glory of the Natya Mandapa on the way in to the shrine, it is this stunted, stymied space outside that moves me most. This, and the monolith shading the huge *linga* behind the main sanctum. The cook, they say, was late with lunch, and the stonemasons used the extra hour to carve the *linga*, its many-headed cobra parasol, the coiled pedestal, and the delicate reliefs on the rock face. When the cook emerged from the kitchen, she stared in disbelief at this superhuman achievement, and the force of her gaze, *drishṭi*, cracked the great rock in three places. You can still see the cracks.

It takes boldness to leave a masterwork unachieved; to make its incompletion the key to its wholeness. The temple straddles, somewhat uneasily, inelegantly, the cusp of the hill, which tradition claims is the carapace of a tortoise. The pillars of the Natya Mandapa reveal the uneven stress of the stones. One pillar, they say, was cut away from its pedestal by the British, who wanted to understand how this temple managed to keep itself standing; you can see the column resting uneasily, directly, on the pavement. The entire edifice is like that boulder—perched on the edge of space, refusing to fall, willing its beauty. A blind person could see it. It is good to be back, for these few hours, in Andhra.

July 9, Tirukkataiyur, Konerirajapuram

For many years I have been meaning to see Teraluntur, where my favored poet, Kampan, is said to have lived and sung the ten thousand verses of his Tamil *Rāmāyaṇa*. In the end, the village, simmering under a relentless sun, is very different from what I had pictured in my mind—plainer, more disordered, the traces of the poet somehow tacky and pale. At the entrance to the Āmaruviyappar temple, just inside the *gopuram*, stand two black icons said to be Kampan himself. He is bearded, with fresh vermilion on his forehead; his hands are folded in blessing or entreaty; he wears an incongruous pink sari, plaited with blue and gold. So that is what he looked like. An old Śrīvaishṇava Brahmin in the temple sings a few verses, including the famous *taniyan* to Lord Rāma:

naṉmaiyun cĕlvamum nāḷum nalkume
tīnmaiyum pāvamun citaintu teyume
cĕnmamu' maraṇam iṉṟit tīrume
immaiye rāmav ĕṉṟ' iraṇṭ ĕḻuttiṉāl

[Goodness and fullness are given day by day.
Badness wears away.
Rebirth and dying will end
here and now—if you speak these two syllables,
Rā + *ma*.]

By midmorning we are in Tirukkataiyur, near the coast, where Śiva killed Death. Couples come here to perform a second wedding when the husband reaches the age of sixty. In every corner of the temple we find bare-chested older bridegrooms and their garlanded wives—and, of course, the *purohita* who performs the swift ceremony. Facing Kāla-samhāra-mūrtti (Śiva as the Death of Death) in the circumambulatory pathway outside is a shrine to the victim, Yama Dharmarāja. When Yama—that is, Death—died, the burden of population on the Earth became unbearable, so for her sake Śiva revived Yama—but assured him that he would kick him to death once again if he, Yama, caused any further disturbance to Śiva's devotees.

Hoping this is true in some more or less literal mode, I lie on the ground, hands cupped before me, and ask that He pay a little attention to our friend Henry. The paving stones, worn away by centuries of pilgrims' feet, are burning with black sunlight. Death of Death, a massive, elegant, dark carving, strangely intimate warrior, a god one might trust, seems ready to burst from the rock and descend into the dense crowd standing before him—as once, long ago, he emerged out of the black *linga* to do away with Yama.

Here, too, there was a poet, Abhirāmi Bhaṭṭar, the author of the *Apirāmiyantāti*. They say that one *amāvāsya* night, before the new moon, when Sarafoji, king of Tanjavur, asked this goddess-struck singer to tell him what day it was in the lunar month, the poet became confused and said it was *pūrṇima*, full moon. He then started to sing his poem while suspended by an iron chain over a blazing fire pit; after every verse, he broke off one more link in the chain—an attempt to force the goddess to rescue him before he plunged into the flames. When he reached verse 79, the goddess Abhirāmi, listening with avid interest, took off her round silver earring and flung it into the sky—a full moon apparent to all, even the skeptical king.

> viḻikke aruḷ uṇṭu apirāma-vallikku vetan cŏnna
> vaḻikke vaḻipaṭa nenc'uṇṭu ĕmakku
>
> [Abhirāmi has compassion for us
> in her eye,
> and we have the heart you need
> to worship in the Vedic way.]

That Death could, indeed *must*, die is as bold a statement as any Tamil shrine could make; but even bolder, deeper, is the recognition that Death must be revived.

* * *

After lunch I indulge in an Ayurvedic massage, my first. A solemn, muscular masseur from Kerala pays obeisance to a lithograph of Vishṇu on the wall before spreading me out on a long wooden plank, slippery with oil. Much more oil, hot and pungent, bottle after bottle, is kneaded into my skin, pore by pore. I emerge after an hour, reborn. How was it? Jim asks me.

"I'm out of adjectives," I say, "but I killed him."

"Who?"

"Death."

* * *

At Balu's insistence, we drive to Konerirajapuram, the old Tirunallam of the *Tevāram*. Here King Purūravas, lover of the divine Urvaśī, came to be healed of leprosy. If sheer beauty can heal, this site rising out of the paddy fields can certainly cure most earthly ills. An immense bronze Chola Naṭarāja stands to the left of the main shrine. The metalworkers were bravely trying to complete the image before the deadline set by yet another obtuse king, but they were still weeks away from this goal. On the last day an old man appeared, very thirsty. They had nothing to offer him. "Never mind," he said, "I will drink this molten copper." He did so and at once turned into the life-size dancing god. But the king was angry when he heard this story, so he struck the image with his sword—hence the mole (*maccam*) and scars one sees on the god's body today.

Temples piled on temples, gods on gods, who could contain them all? It is dark when we reach Tiruvilimilalai, famous as the place where Vishṇu tore out his lotus-shaped eye to complete the full set of a thousand lotuses offered to Śiva each day. Inside the shrine, pilgrims speak in whispers, as if overcome by wistful memories; the night is fragrant and quiet, the village huddles inside the ancient homes in the Brahmin *agrahāram*, but in the sky over the *gopuram* there is a brilliant, white full moon, no doubt set in place for our sake by a thoughtful goddess.

July 10, Tiruvarur

We begin the day with Lord Murugan as Guruguha, the son as teacher, in his temple at Swamimalai; echoes of Muttusvāmi Dīkhsitar, the great composer who uses "Guruguha" as his signature in each of his compositions. *Suprabhātam*—Sanskrit chants of waking—echo from the radio as we walk through the village after dawn. Women are drawing *kolam* designs at the threshold. Geese cackle, buffaloes lumber along the street, cyclists swerve to avoid them. Some stare at the two strangers walking quickly toward the temple. Strangers: yet the residues of many years, the subtle memories and fragrances of light and breath, are with me at every step.

By ten we have reached Tiruvarur. We pick up Venkateshan, who will do the photography this time, at the Selvi Hotel. The town looks almost scrubbed, far tidier than in March, and the temple, too, has put on a new face. The sun is pale and hot. We wait for the Executive Officer, who has to confirm our permission to photograph the paintings. I am alone with Venkateshan; Gurumurtti, Maya, Debbie, Rajamani, all my friends and companions have fallen away, each for a different reason. But I have the letter of permission from the Commissioner in my hand.

At least the EO is here, in his office; I was worried that he might be away. I have sent a letter announcing my arrival, and I know from telephone conversations that he received his own copy of the Commissioner's explicit, no-nonsense letter. It should be a simple matter, now; but as the minutes drag on, I become tense, imagining all that could go wrong. We don't have much time, only today and, if necessary, tomorrow. This is probably our last chance. And there are the traumatic memories from March.

The clerks and peons shuffle papers, answer the cell phone. It is "tenders" morning, one explains; the EO is very busy. I say we have sent all the documents, we need only five minutes to pay our respects. Ancient, long wooden tables, some piled high with bound brown ledgers, inhabit the dark, dusty room outside the office. Two girls flit in and out, past a computer screen. An ageless clerk, spectacled, in white dhoti, pores over a vast bound volume of accounts.

After less than an hour—an achievement?—we are summoned. A friend of the EO's beats us to the door and slips in to take a seat. Venkateshan and I march in, smiling. Another nameless friend sits to my left. The EO greets us summarily, I hand over the letter. He has read it before, we are certain of that, but he now reads it again slowly, as if looking for something. Minutes pass.

"You have to pay twenty thousand rupees," he says at last.

I try to assimilate the shock. This is the first we have heard of any fee, let alone so large a payment. We have been over this issue many times, in Tiruvarur and Madras, with him, with the Commissioner and the secretaries and assistants. Why did he not mention a fee before?

I say to him, "That is a huge sum. You did not mention it in March. The Commissioner said nothing about it. When we discussed these matters, you told us that only the Commissioner's consent was lacking."

"But *she*"—a mysterious Englishwoman whose name he cannot recall—"paid up." And he puts aside the letter, signs a form or two, plunges into jocular conversation with his two friends, pointedly ignoring Venkateshan and me. He laughs. The conversation bubbles back and forth. We sit and wait.

It is, of course, deeply insulting, and I am angry, also wondering if this will go on now for more hours, days, weeks, months. And were I to pay, would permission at last be granted? I contemplate making a scene, giving free vent to my mounting rage. He laughs loudly, spinning words, with his friends. I see, however, that he is very well aware of our presence.

I interrupt him. "Sir, let us finish this matter. You know I have come twice to Tiruvarur for this purpose. You know the Commissioner has granted his permission. You have named an exorbitant sum. Let us find a way to settle this."

He ignores me. No hint of a reply, of having heard. Cascades of Tamil. More private jokes. Venkateshan signals to me to be calm, to wait.

Ten minutes pass. Mental calculations. Twenty thousand rupees is nearly five hundred dollars. But this, I am quite sure, is only his opening bid. I could use some advice, but there is no one to give it. I know I have to act, it is up to me. On his desk, among stacks of papers, a plaque in Tamil praises godliness and patriotism, *tevīkamum tecamum*.

Again I break into his chitchat. "Sir, this will not look good outside Tiruvarur. Surely you know. Let us settle the matter now. We have only a few pictures to take and we will go. Twenty thousand rupees is too much for five or ten photos."

He turns to Venkateshan. "Who are you?" "The photographer, I came with 'Sar.'" "Where do you live?" "In Chennai." "On what street?" And so on, a useless, rough, meandering barrage of questions. Venkateshan answers calmly. Finally the EO turns to me.

"How much can you give?"

I calculate, exaggerate—10 percent of his price? It is too much, but I say, "Perhaps two thousand, perhaps three."

Readily he agrees. "Make it two thousand. You notice I am only asking for two." I put two thousand-rupee notes on his desk. He wants to know the exact spelling of my name so a receipt can be written out. It is not the money that I mind.

In two hours the work is complete. I comb the Tevâcirayan *mandapam*, looking for more pictures, sketches, inscriptions. There are none, only faint traces of paint that have been plastered over. Decades of unconscionable neglect have nearly destroyed the Mucukunda series, but a record will now remain.

July 11, Tanjavur

Two Chola masterpieces, the Kilaiyur image of my beloved poet-model, Cuntaramūrtti, and the Velvikkuti Pārvatī, grace the gallery of bronzes in the Sarasvati Mahal—almost a pair, perfect alone, perfect together. A living, rather stormy poet stands, self-confident, across from a lithe, living goddess. Each time I reach Tanjavur I come to see them as a pilgrim, overcome with marvel. I could stare at them for many hours.

All day long a strong wind swirls the dust, the streets stretch and crack in the heat. The Tamil saying goes, "āṇi mācattilum āṭi mācattilum aṭṭikkiṟa kāṟṟile ammikkallum nakarum" (In the months of Ani and Ati, the grinding stone moves in the wind). No rain. *Āṇi* fatigue? Earache, neck ache, eager for home.

July 12, Mylapore

Sunrise on the marina, after the Tanjavur train deposited us in the big city at 5:00 AM. The morning joggers are out en masse. A small party of policemen on horseback rides in grand style over the white sand. Kaṇṇaki, the violent heroine of the ancient *Poem of the Anklet*, the *Cilappatikāram*, is back. In the story, she tears off her left breast and hurls it at the city of Madurai, burning it down, after the Pāṇḍya king has her innocent husband executed for theft. Embodying Tamil womanhood, Kaṇṇaki's stone image (actually a rather tacky modern version) stood for years on the beach. At the advice of her astrologer, Chief Minister Jayalalita had the statue removed so that rains would come. Her violent, burning gaze, *drishṭi*, was the problem—thus the astrologer. Indeed, no sooner was Kaṇṇaki taken away than the rains began in earnest. The newly elected CM, Karunanidhi, has ordered the statue reinstated. As a result: this year, no rain.

Horror in Bombay: over 150 killed in terrorist bombs on the commuter trains.

July 13

Ramakrishnan reminds me that A. K. Ramanujan died thirteen years ago today.

There is always a gap, Ramakrishnan says, between language and experience. Great writers elevate experience to great language. In modern Tamil, they usually bring language *down*. It seems to me that the very idea of intensifying through linguistic precision is mostly lost—to say nothing of polishing, chiseling, discipline, *ullekhana*, the ninth-century poetician Rājaśekhara's ideal of professionalism. We work through the morning on Nagarajan; with each reading, I admire the man more.

At midnight, rain, lightning, relief; but the days are very hot. At C. P. Ramaswamy Shastri Institute, I speak of Ta'ayush, with little resonance.

Israel, as usual, is remote; there are far more pressing problems here, or in Bombay.

July 14, Kalahasti, Tirupati

Inside the Kalahasti temple, wandering, in the afternoon. People are welcoming, curious. This experience recurs each time I come here; some magic inheres in this place, an ease, as perhaps befits the home of a goddess whose hair is "fragrant with wisdom," as her name tells us (Jñāna-prasūnâmbika in Sanskrit and Telugu). A woman says to Elana: "Are you happy after seeing the god? When you see the god on the hill, you'll be still more happy." Another woman insists on offering Elana her *naivedya* of bananas and cooked rice. Is it because of Elana's brilliant blue eyes, or a sensed affinity? A few raindrops greet our arrival, not enough to cool.

In Tirupati town, we visit Govindarāja, brother to the great god Venkaṭeśvara uphill, together with Chenna Reddi; it is midday, and hot; we sit quietly with the god after *darshan*. Chenna Reddi says, "He is tired, he needs to rest." I feel the same. But it is good to be back in Tirupati, connected again. On the train, we read Annamayya's first poem:

You can't embrace it, you can't reject it.
You'll never escape Love's command.

Women's faces are lamps held up in the market.
Their breasts are golden pots on the front porch.
Luscious mouths, shared honey.
We make love to bodies. Make no mark.

Warm curries on the plate, lovers' quarrels, displays of pride,
spots of shade in the hot sun, occasional hours of love,

strings you can't break, mysterious smiles,
pain in the midst of goodness, words within words,

oil poured on fire, hopes that never end,
the space inside desire, like drinking butter
when you're thirsty:

finding the god on the hill
is the one good thing that is real.[12]

It is perhaps the most lyrical list I have ever seen; the copperplates class this *padam* as a love poem. So one comes to Tirupati to find what is real. *Darśanam*, seeing: in Telugu it is an active mode, *darśanam cesu kŏnu*—something one does. Seeing and being seen—this intertwining of selves.

July 15, Tirupati

This time, it seems, He didn't want us to go away.

Tickets for Suprabhatam, the predawn service, are almost impossible to come by; but by late afternoon Seshagiri Ravu and Chenna Reddi have miraculously managed to inscribe our names. Without such special tickets, it is now a ninety-hour wait in line for *darshan*; and there is a terrific rush up on the hill, the city packed with pilgrims. At 9:00 PM we ascend the mountain. Security is fairly strict, though not up to Israeli standards. We pass the spot where the former Chief Minister, Candrababu Naidu, survived an assassination attempt.

It is another choppy Tirupati night, like the first time I came here, with Narayana Rao, in 1985. It was nearly midnight when we arrived, the queue almost empty, and we sailed easily past the entrance, straight into the sanctum. Such things don't happen any more. Why the crush in mid-July? I ask Chenna Reddi. He says that previously there was always an ebb and flow, periods of slack, periods of great pressure. Now there is only steady, and steadily increasing, flow.

We try to sleep for an hour or two in one of the bungalows earmarked for privileged pilgrims, but I can't let go of my wakefulness. Is it the proximity to the god? I remember well this tautness of anticipation in body and mind. Eventually I renounce sleep for tonight. At one thirty we move toward the gate. The dark is cool, caressing, a profound change from the sticky immersion down below in the town.

Clutching computerized tickets, people are streaming toward the entrance. They seem groggy, like me, but one also senses a gentle solemnity—not a common Hindu mood. There is a certain orderliness about this moment, no pushing or bodily haste, little noise. We go through the first gate at two o'clock and begin the long walk from enclosure to enclosure, along fenced-in aisles, through airportlike security (they send me back outside to hand over my cell phone charger to the locker attendant; and they scrutinize with interest my USB device). Behind us is a young intern from Bangalore. Many seem intrigued by the presence of three obvious foreigners. We are asked to sign a form saying that we are devotees of Lord Venkaṭeśvara; but suddenly there are no more empty pages in the vast register, so they wave us through.

Finally we emerge into the antechamber, through the golden doors. It is 3:00 AM: time to wake him up. "Uttishṭha nara-śārdūla!" (Arise, O tiger among men) The chanting from inside the sanctum, behind a simple curtain, has the freshness of chamber music, of a living prayer, utterly unlike the mechanical perfection of the cassettes. Many among us chant along with the priests. First his dark green mattress is taken out, then the cot that supports it; Lord Venkaṭeśvara has had his daily allotment of a half-hour's sleep. Priests enter from the door on the left carrying brass pots of water for the *abhishekam* anointing.

Wake up, come back to us, stay with us.

I hate crowds, and standing hemmed in by the throng in the tiny antechamber, I let my thoughts wander, impatient. I note an uncharacteristic monotheistic note of doubt. Why should god *not* have an evenly textured, continuous presence? Why should we have to wake him? This will be my fourth *darshan* at Tirupati. The remembered strain of waiting, the fear of being crushed, the sleeplessness, and a strange inner isolation, a brittleness of surface—all these slowly come back with full force as the drone of text swells and peaks. "Govinda!"—again and again the pilgrims cry the name of god, each time the curtain is briefly drawn. The priests are playing with him, with us, veiling, disclosing, veiling again, as if his opening to us had to be gradual, a little coquettish, not a single splendid, stable revelation. The crowd's gentleness in demeanor, a truly remarkable forbearance, is punctuated by ever more intense cries of "Govinda," rolling like a new kind of thunder, human, rising in pitch. Children sleep in the arms of their fathers. Patience is wrapped in urgency; I feel the restlessness around me, in me. Then the curtain is drawn open to stay.

On the right, the women begin to enter one by one. Then it is our turn. It happens quickly. We stream through the dark passage that connects antechamber with sanctum, the guards molding the flow with their hands, literally lifting us from behind, a little roughly, across the threshold, to the constant chorus of "jaragaṇḍi, jaragaṇḍi" (Move on). . . .

This roughness, Ponet says later, is helpful, a way to ensure that we will not be overcome by god.

He is different this time. Fully encased in gold, with the exception of his black face. I remember—wrongly?—seeing him as mostly black rock, fully alive. But there is no time or space to study him. My body turns with the arc, already departing, pushed from behind by the constant, urgent flow of human beings toward god. Ahead of me, men are twisting backward, striving for another second of vision, and another, as the current carries them out and away.

I find myself outside in the cool night. Kamesvari, very quiet, as if containing intense feeling, points to the *śikhara* capital towering over the sanctum, brilliant gold against the black sky. Like him. Like the Andhra *mangal-sūtra* that wives wear around their neck: black and gold. The deepest colors, perhaps, of Andhra herself, the colors underlying the red soil and the green paddy fields and the gray-brown rivers and green-blue sea. A steady flash of golden light against, within, the dark. Suddenly I cannot speak, cannot find words anywhere in the seeming silence of the mind. A wave of joyfulness crests and breaks, my eyes tear. It is, I think to myself, at last, though "thinking" does not describe it, as if—but it is not "as if"—I have a found a friend.

Slowly, relishing the enchantment, we visit Yoga Narasimha, the Man-Lion; the Annamayya storeroom where the copperplates inscribed with poems used to be kept; the Ayina Mahal, or Chamber of Mirrors. We sit for a while with the god; we collect our round, heavy *laḍḍu* sweets. Kamesvari, in particular, seems loath to leave the enclosure. As we emerge, we see hundreds sleeping in front of the temple, most covered head to toe in blankets. For what seems like a long time, we wander over the mountain, barefoot, looking for Chenna Reddi and the lodge. More and more sleepers, on the roadside, on the ground beside the bus stand: thousands have spent the night in the open near the temple. There are confusing directions to the Seshadri Nagar Complex, our bungalow, and we get lost. Elana says, "Finding God was quite easy, *much* easier than finding our way home."

It is turning light as we get into the car to head back toward town, and now the first sign is given. The engine won't ignite. The driver tries every means, cleans the contact points, reconnects the wires, washes away the accumulation of dust and grease from the battery; nothing helps. "He" doesn't want us to go. After an hour, we find a share taxi heading downhill. It spins with the mountain curves, a dizzy descent, and when it reaches the bottom, the engine fails. The vehicle won't budge. The driver is unable to restart it. A second sign. The town spreads at our feet, white in the early morning; the breeze off the mountain has died down.

July 17, Rajahmundry

Home by six thirty on the Tirumala Express. The house is dusty, forlorn; and there is no electric current. I check the neighbors' situation; they have power. So something has shorted out again in my flat. It is Sunday, it will not be easy to find an electrician. Already the day is hot; luckily, a good breeze is blowing, as I confirm by watching the higher branches of the trees, slowly dancing. (During the hot season, studying the branches for movement became a reflex.) By nine o'clock the whole building is without power. So it goes throughout the day. I conclude: I will *never* be *not hot*. I come back at six thirty after an evening walk around Kambala Cheruvu, and miraculously the current has returned, without human intervention. Perhaps the Tirupati *pūjā*s are having some (slightly delayed) effect. Raju arrives, at last, with an electrician, who is hard pressed to explain the mystery; he will change the whole fuse box tomorrow, as a precaution. I attempt to activate the domestic system: Ratnam will bring milk at dawn, but the washerman is sick, or on leave, or both; he finds it hard to convey to me his reasons for refusing to work. I stop for tea at Nirmala's; she is completely unimpressed by my report of the ninety-hour wait for *darshan* at Tirupati. Some matters are not amenable to calculation. Satyanarayana says, "We must go again, next year, to see the god."

July 18, Podalada, Antarvedi, Palakollu

Smilegaru's Poetry Tours of South India, Continued: On our way to the ocean, we have midmorning tea in the village of Podalada with M. S. Suryanarayana. He has composed a long poem on Dokka Sitamma, a Brahmin woman of the old time who cheerfully fed everyone, high or low—a local heroine. Suryanarayana is thrilled with our visit; a short, wiry man, he literally jumps for joy when he sees Smile, who released his book in Rajahmundry. He knows Narayana Rao and has heard of me. Literature and philosophy, he says, are dead in Andhra, in all of India—dried up, a wasteland, there is no one left who can feel. I tell him that one good reader is enough; this hardly consoles him. He shows us his large library of modern Telugu works, some now quite rare, stacked in piles in an upstairs room overlooking the coconut and mango groves. He lives the literary life with great passion and in profound isolation. Podalada itself is splendid, perfect, shimmering with green. Ravulapalem, Palivela, Ganti, Udimudi, Gannavaram—the route itself is a poem, charged with mantic names. Paddy fields, ripe for transplanting, soak under the sun.

At Antarvedi we pay our respects to Lakshmi Narasimha, another embodiment of the Man-Lion Vishṇu; we buy his *yantra*, a geometric field of auspicious vectors, for Henry, for healing. We climb to the top of the lighthouse to see the Godavari meet the sea. Elana asks the right question: at what moment does it cease to be river and become ocean? Hot noon colors: a thousand straitlaced palm trees, the broad, muddy sweep of the Godavari, her surrender. I wonder how long it takes a drop of water to travel here from, say, Nasik (where Misha and I paid our homage to the river, years ago). But does the drop of water exist?

At Palakollu the ancient *ārāma*-temple is closed, but eventually they allow us in. An older man in a red dhoti expounds the local *purāṇa* narratives with great fervor. He has been twice to Amarnath in Kashmir. Palakollu, with its crystal *linga*, is Kshīrârāma, the Milk Shrine, with its own fragment of the great *ātma-linga* of the demon Tāraka, splintered into five by Śiva's arrow. The temple has been renovated recently, a towering new *gopuram* put in place; inside, another set of scattered *objets trouvés*, random pieces of god. Near here, at Gunapudi/Somârāma, the black *linga* turns white on new-moon nights. The stories of the five *ārāma* shrines mix in his narration with the secrets the snakes learned from Śiva and Parvati at Amarnath. In the West, there are people who give courses at universities on "myth," whatever it is. They should come to Palakollu.

So now I've seen three out of five *ārāma*s, these ancient Buddhist sanctuaries turned into homes for a Telugu-speaking Śiva. Like Daksharama and Samarlakota, Palakollu is a little eerie, unbalanced, the old Buddhist substratum barely hidden under the haphazard surface. The city itself has the sense of long-term, organic growth, the steady cumulation of centuries, like Rajahmundry; a few tall nineteenth-century buildings, still delightful, black with mold and decay, survive on the main street with its shops and horse-drawn carriages. Palakollu is where Smile, as a young cadet, became engaged to Yasmin.

* * *

Late evening, the current fails—why do the citizens of Rajahmundry put up with this so passively?—so we sit, sweating, in the dark. Elana has noticed the inscription on one of Paluri Venkata Gopalakrishna Visvanatha's posters in my flat: "You have to have a dream so you can get up in the morning." Last night I dreamt of Nasara Reddi's poem:

> tonight
> alone
> heaping up stars
> swished by
> fishtail.

In the dream it was as if this were the missing Tamil piece I've been seeking, the one that made sense of all the rest, binding the stars to their orbits.

July 19, Papikondalu

Second ride up the Godavari from Pattisima into Khamam district—what is known in Rajahmundry as Boat Shikar. The APTC "launch" was fully booked for today, but Elana, with dependable serendipity, happened into Mayor Chakravarti's office while looking for the Rajahmundry Museum—and he at once graciously intervened and secured three seats. Channel 9 News then interviewed the rare tourists to this town. We are greeted with great solicitude when we climb onto the boat at Pattisima. There is a first stop at the Virabhadra-Bhavapurusottama temple, fresh in my mind from the April visit. I study the colors of morning: mud-brown-red of the river, sand-colored sand, black crows, black-green shadow of the clouds on blue-mauve hills, a whole palette of greens, reddish soil, gray cloud. Suffusing it all there is that faint tinge, almost invisible but always palpable, of infrared-almost-gold.

I had forgotten. No sooner are we afloat than the floor show begins—exhibitionistic disco dancing to the sound of Telugu cinema music, carried at deafening volume over the announcement system. The discord with the silent landscape of river and hills slowly becomes unbearable, a sacrilege. Narayana Rao's rage at the new middle-class philistines of Andhra seems, for a moment, almost credible. The moment passes. It transpires that the entire boatload is a single, cohesive group of jewelers, gold merchants, from Narasaraopetta, with extended families. We have unwittingly infiltrated a tribe. Soon the boundaries give way, Elana and Jim are enticed into dancing, and I am adopted by Manikandhara, a young enthusiast. He wants me to know that the Char Minar in Hyderabad is number 54 among the Wonders of the World. He knows the whole list. The Eiffel Tower, he says, is number 8. Have I been to Paris? I have. Is the Eiffel Tower truly a wonder? Well . . . I ask him to tell me instead about Narasaraopetta, he says it is a very lovely place. I believe him. I'd like to get to know it.

We stop to pay our respects to the river goddess, Gandi Pocalamma, then to take on food at Devipatnam. Traces of Sitaramaraju, the early rebel against British authority: then, as now, to go up the river from Rajahmundry was to enter deep wilderness, with its violent rebels. Upstream the going is slow, the sun hot, the screeching of the cassettes wearing and wearying. After lunch a young astrologer gives a "spiritual" (*adhyātmika*) discourse, rambling on for over an hour. "I will give you my cell phone number, I will give you my card. You can call me with any problem. I have 95-percent success rate. Problems with health, with business, with examinations, with marriage, I can manage them all, do not fear. I need to know only your name and your horoscope. Just a minute on the phone will do. There is a mantra for everything. If you worship the Sun God at dawn for thirty days, all trouble will disappear. If you have some deficiency in your horoscope, I will know the remedy. Gifts of gold from merchants are always an excellent thing. Tomorrow is the beginning of Sravana month, a good time to give to Goddess Laksmi. The goddess is close to us during the first two weeks of Sravana. The *jīvâtma* is one with the *paramâtma*. Every *dāna* donation has its goal. Even a small gift brings results." Every time I think he is ending, another stray association, another confident boast, takes hold of his mind. He has been doing this since he was a child. He passes through the boat, and many reach for his card.

The Settis are on their way to Bhadracalam, Annavaram, Simhacalam. Each year they come on some such trip. The women are decked in heavy gold, saris aflame. With the exception of one skinny dancer, they look very well fed. They are eager to see us eat as well. When we say goodbye after dark on the Pattisima landing, they embrace us, tears in their eyes, before disappearing into the night.

Smile arrives within minutes, Godavari prawns for us in his bag. We have stared all day at the river, following her delicate shifts of feeling; we have seen her emerge out of muddy brown into a near-transparent evening sheen. But this is not enough—Smile wants to ensure that Godavari is inside us, and not in some ethereal mode like memory or, let us say, a diary note.

July 20, Rajahmundry

Another good dream two nights ago, after the late-night curries and Bacardi. Smile drives me home on his scooter. A cool night. Suddenly I know the answer to Shlomit's question in March, when I was home in Jerusalem: "gilita mashehu?" (Have you discovered something new?) It is not, I realize, a matter of some sharp moment, some special insight. This broadening, this going deep, the spectrum that has opened up, friends, poets, critics, Andhra—perhaps never have I known a time so thoroughly bound together into my own singular, dissonant harmony. I dream that I have been allowed to select whatever part of myself, in all its wholeness, that I want to be buried—not in a negative way, but as if being put, at last, into its right place. Very moved, I choose the Ashkenazi Jewish part, which goes into a silver box, contents wrapped in green banana leaves.

There is an afternoon excursion to Daksharama (again) and then along the river to Kotipali, where the Moon set up a small *linga* to atone for sleeping with Tārā, his teacher Brihaspati's wife. His prayers bore fruit: Śiva gave him the particular luminosity they call *chāyā* (reflection; shadow), best seen, they say, in the waxing moon. Shadow is thus a kind of light, first radiating outward from the god's black stone. One needs, perhaps, a certain penetrating vision to see it properly—or, even better, a precise, transparent memory where the story of origins can be filed for ready reference. Perhaps seeing the light is also a function of telling the story.

Tonight is like old times in Rajahmundry: Endluri has published his third volume of poems, this one about his trip to America, *Aṭa jani kānce* (quoting Pĕddana); and since the book was already "released" there, overseas, what remains is to mark the event here with his friends. Smile and Patanjali Sastri are happy to celebrate with a bottle of rum and fried chicken; Kanakaiah arrives a little later, untempted by these delicacies but glad, I think, for the party. My flat is somehow extraterritorial, hence well suited for such pleasures. After some hours I am exhausted, again, by the sheer weight of my ignorance, but also intoxicated by the poems that are flying around the table—a few lines by Tilak and many whole poems of Ismayil, who is lovingly remembered tonight. Some of Smile's delight clearly derives from a risqué boldness, no doubt refreshing when it first found its voice:

TEA CUP

Under the welcoming banners of her eyes,
she stands with a cup of tea
for me.
In that teacup, truly,
waving hands of steam:
my life.

A bit bitter,
a bit sweet,
a bit alive,
very very hot.
I can't take in such heat.
If it cools off,
it's no use.

Now, like an eyelid,
a thin membrane hides
the surface:
like eyes dreaming a dream,
like my lover's pussy,
like a dove held in one's hands,
tremulous.

This is the right moment
to drink tea.[13]

Eventually Smile can't resist reciting some of his own poems, very good ones; and we again urge him to go back to writing. Yesterday he promised me that he was about to embark on a novel. Patanjali Sastry has mapped out a play, which came to him in a flash a few days back. He knows he is a very good short-story writer and playwright; his collected stories should be out within a week or two. The richness that washed over me at our first sitting, in February, has, if anything, grown still more rich. A circle is closing. Malamoud writes that he will be back to visit next week. But listening to the poems, I am thrown back to my early years in Jerusalem, in the late sixties when, for me and for my impassioned friends, Hebrew words (read aloud at night) had this high voltage.

The rum is finished and my guests depart; Kanakaiah stays on to read a few verses of *Manu-caritramu*. I can't help it: their precision, their complexity, their discipline, their lucidity—all bring relief, the old music welling up and overpowering even the sadness of not knowing. The contrast is pointed and severe, even if little by little I am beginning to feel my way into the twentieth century. Gratefully, I see Kanakaiah off into the night, happily holding the *laḍḍu* sweet I brought him from Tirupati.

July 21

Morning walks resume. At six o'clock, nine white cows lie, crumpled, soporific, near the divider on Nehru Road.

Last week, Chhattisgarhi Naxalites murdered thirty-three tribals at Errabore. Why, I ask again, has the Andhra government given them so much slack? Why let them act at will? The government could easily end this stalemate. Patanjali Sastri says that when the peace talks with the Maoists failed, two years ago, government troops cornered the entire Maoist leadership in the Nallamala Forest. They could have finished them off, but a delegation of poets intervened to save them. Note the pragmatics of writing poetry in South India.

* * *

Before J. and E. leave for Madras, Yasmin takes them shopping for Andhra earrings at Tanishq, across from the Pushkara Revu. (In the old days, this building was inevitably submerged when the river flooded.)

Smile and I wait outside, at first patiently, then . . . He tells me how Lord Krishna wanted to take his wife Satyabhama out for an evening spin in his chariot. "Aidu nimishāllo voccestānu" (I'll be down in five minutes), she says, putting on her earrings. When she finally appears, a certain Krishna Rao, in pants and shirt, is waiting for her, and the chariot has become an Ambassador car. How many cosmic aeons have passed? "Don't worry, my dear," he says, "I may not look quite the same, but I'm still Krishna."

July 22

After midnight, at last, a soaking rain, lightning, monsoon storm. The exploding raindrops wake me, I throw open the door, drink in the benefice, the fragrant street, joyfully sink back to sleep.

Āndhra Padya Kavitā Sadassu, East Godavari Branch, along with the Cultural and Development Association, is holding a series of ten lectures on Telugu classics in the Community Hall, Round Park, Prakashnagar. Lecturers come from all over the delta. Last night one Pingali Venkatakrishna Ravu, from Vijayavada, speaks on *Manu-caritramu*. The hall is packed; well over a hundred Rajamundrians (many pensioners) have come to hear this first discourse. Could one hope for such a turnout for a lecture on *Naitatam* in Madras? Here the canon is alive and well; many in the audience (even I) whisper along as the lecturer sings the verses (elegantly, in something akin to Hindolam *rāga*). He is far from original, but originality is not the point. The exercise is quite different from Hari-kathā or *purāṇic* narration; this lecture genre is primarily lyrical and responsive, and rather personal, though I am always struck by the severely normative tones regularly attributed to these ultimately radical, unsettling poets and their works. Perhaps the veil of the normative—a fantasy of dharmic orthodoxy—is what allows for the strong cultural continuity, even if the sensibility has changed. Listening intently, I remember how different Telugu poetry is from Sanskrit or Tamil; how strangely enhanced, gently hypnotic, and profoundly musical it inevitably is. Perhaps it is the consistent syntactical dissonance in relation to the meter that provides this intoxication, an exotic adumbration of the complex counterpoint one hears in Haydn and Mozart. One's mind follows the recalcitrant, discursive syntax even as the ear, and perhaps the rest of the body, attunes itself to pure music, the latent rhythmic drone. Telugu verse is, no doubt, the most effective of incantations. I wish I could recite like Venkatakrishna Ravu.

July 24

So now it is the turn of the cockroaches. Some secret attaches to these seasonal cycles. It rained a little more this week, although in general Andhra is on the verge of drought; the monsoon has largely failed. Something, in any case, has sped the breeding and maturing of these hideous creatures with the beautiful Telugu name, *boddinka*; for a while there were none, but now, each day, I hunt them down. This morning I was startled by a cockroach so big I was sure he was a frog, hopping toward the bathroom. In addition, the white ants are definitely making progress in the kitchen, leaving a wide swathe of chewed-up wood, plaster, and tile behind them. Fuzzy centipedes, *jĕrrulu*, are suddenly plentiful, inside and outside the flat.

I have been writing—first time in weeks—and suddenly the *Naiṭatam* moment makes sense to me. Nala wanders, invisible, in Damayanti's palace until he sees her; but he is sure he is only seeing the hallucination that has haunted him for weeks. She, for her part, cannot detect his presence; and yet the garland she throws in the air, aiming at the neck and shoulders of *her* hallucination of *him*, naturally falls around his (real) neck. Why should it? But then, how could it miss? The Pahari painter shows this moment lucidly—the flurry among Damayanti's attendants, the clear reflection of his unseen face on the walls and the shiny floor; her hopeful, unerring tossing of the flowers. Now both of them are nonplussed. He can't understand how a garland cast in the air by a delusion could come to rest on his body, and she sees the garland disappear as it touches his body, which no one can see. This intrusion by something akin to reality causes the two levels, mental fantasy and physical enactment, to bifurcate and replicate:

anyonyam anyatravad īkṣamāṇau parasparenādhyuṣite 'pi deśe/
ālingitālīka-parasparāntas tathyaṃ mithas tau pariṣasvajāte//

[They kept seeing one another
as if they were somewhere else,

though together they occupied one
shared space.
And while their two fantasies,
false, mutual, and internal,
gripped one another,
these two people
truly embraced.]
(6.51)

Two interlocking fantasies embrace one another as the necessary condition, it would appear, for the imminent meeting, face to face, of two real lovers.

But in the Tamil text, despite the exact repetition of Śrīharsha's given context and its structure, the point is rather different.

He happily embraced her—the all-too-familiar
delusion. She clung to his chest, thinking
that was as it was.

Indescribable ecstasy welled up.
He let go of her, staring
at the brilliant vision.
She, grieved that she could see
no form, gently withdrew
her bangled arms.

Suddenly we are watching two distinct individuals, each driven by cognitive error, but each also intact and aware that part of his or her mind is aflame. Damayanti receives the clinching phrase: she is thinking about what is "as it was"—probably thinking that the apparition she holds in her mind is or should be real as well as true, though she sees no trace of Nala with her eyes. In sixteenth-century Tenkasi, this distinction becomes entirely relevant, and not in some merely theoretical sense. Still, what she cannot see may be in doubt; what he sees is real but classed as delusion. The mind, by now a distinct, entirely subjective entity, relatively autonomous, knows that such mistakes happen to it or in it quite routinely. More important, it is capable of linking such errors to the active, personal imagination.

Time is getting short, less than six weeks to go, and everything is unfinished—*Manu-caritramu* unfinished, Telugu unfinished, I have read only the first hundred pages of *Veyi paḍagalu*, memorized only a handful of verses, Paiḍi Talli remains unwritten, only a few notes on *Naiṭatam*. . . . How can I leave? Andhra and me, two illusions embracing?

July 25

Wasted hours, too many hours, reading Graham Greene, *End of the Affair*. I took the book off Patanjali Sastry's shelf upstairs; an old paperback, stained inside with big blots of mold, the usual condition, admirably suited to the profound corruption of the writing. Perhaps it is the corruption that is so compelling; I couldn't give it up. Apart from the cruelty, there is the primitivism of his obsession with what he calls God. What religion would predicate everything, or for that matter anything, on belief? Ponet taught me years ago that if you have to believe, you don't think it's true. India is good therapy for the Western faithful. Sometimes I think the whole problem in the Mediterranean religions comes from insisting on using the capital letter.

* * *

The Andhra Police managed to kill Madhav, the top Naxalite, in an encounter in the Nallamala Forest—a major victory. Perhaps the terms of symbiosis are being revised. Some say the police have, at last, poked a significant hole in the "Maoist corridor" stretching from Andhra up to Nepal (does this corridor exist?). But today's paper promises free education, courtesy of the government, to Madhav's son Kartik (who never knew his father). This, too, is interesting. K. G. Satyamurthy, who founded the whole pestilence years ago, says Madhav, normally surrounded by fierce bodyguards, was not protected by his comrades because of caste politics. Upper-caste Naxalites, that is, were quite ready to allow him, a low-caste man, to die. For an egalitarian bunch of terrorists, the accusation is bitterly ironic; and rings true, another element in the continuing mystery of irresolution.

The mystery has other layers, however. On one side there is the fanatical fury of the Naxal hunters in the police: one hears of police stations that keep labeled bottles containing the pickled genitals of dead guerillas. Apparently Madhav's body also suffered this treatment; and by the time it was handed over to the family, it was so decomposed as to be unrecognizable. Fierce hatred shapes the ongoing battles in the forest. On the other hand, there is the inextricable interweaving of these two systems, which, some say, goes right up to the top. No party can win an election or set up a government without the Maoists' support. What, then, do we make of the considerable violence on all levels? You need them, people will say, and you need to show them their limit. It is really a matter of symbiotic self-calibration. To my eyes, it looks like a precise reproduction of earlier periods in Andhra, say, the time of the Reddi and Velama kingdoms (fourteenth–fifteenth centuries), which showed the same interdependence of savagely conflicting forces, the same primacy of the wilderness do-or-die mode. Like then, the modern replay includes an aspect of struggle between coastal Andhra and inland Telangana, the latter supplying most (not all) of the pickled genitals.

* * *

Light rain at dawn on the Kadiyam Road; the colors have changed again. Now, regularly, I see the blue-black skies that Sanskrit calls *nīla*; and a luminescent green as the crop ripens around the quixotic scarecrow. A new black butterfly has come out of the forest, by the hundreds. The *moduga* tree is shedding its flowers, the ground glowing with small red flames.

July 26, Annavaram

Charles and Annie arrive by the night train from Chennai. After lunch Krishnayya takes us to Annavaram to meet Kapilavayi Ramasastri, a learned *śrotriya* Brahmin with unparalleled experience of Vedic rites. Krishnayya's great-grandfather was a stonemason here at Annavaram. I didn't think we would make this trip: On Sunday, Krishnayya came to take leave of me, then went off to Dhavalesvaram to see his mother. He told her he was leaving for America for a year. She said: "Don't go. You don't need to go. You don't even need the money." The next morning she died.

Ramasastri lives downhill in an orderly, spacious house. He sits, legs folded, on the swing as Charles asks him about the *ab-ishṭaka-yajña*, a rite structured around bricks made of water. Perhaps nowhere else in India is the rite still performed, but Sastri has himself witnessed it (some thirty years ago). He knows by heart the Vedic passages that lay down the rules. There are six different kinds of water to be made into "bricks" (actually held in Nagavalli clay pots), including the first, special category of rainwater that falls while the sun is shining. Together, they make up a kind of altar, water poured over water.

As he speaks, his wife, son, daughters, and sons-in-law hover behind him, and possibly for the first time I see what is meant by *brahma-varcas*, the bodily radiance of the Brahmin. These people literally glow with a delicate, inner luminosity. Their features are clear, their eyes alive, their demeanor dignified, aristocratic; they know they are the bearers of an ancient vehicle of truth. Gentle confidence, an assurance born of centuries of study and practice, radiates from the way they stand, walk, sit. With his son, Ramasastri sings for us from the Sama Veda, a haunting, winding verse from some moment long before *our* world was created. An extraordinary, energetic peacefulness permeates the home, their words, their gifts to us, like water poured into water.

I ask him about Vedic education: do they teach the Vedic accents by three separate head movements, as in Kerala? No. One should recite in perfect stillness. They pour lime juice on the boy's head as he recites; he is to hold himself motionless so that not a drop is spilled down face or neck. What about Paninian grammar—do they learn this along with the Vedic text? Not much. It takes a long time to master it, and they don't have time. But they insist that the student recite only what he has understood.

In the old days, I say, there were kings who used to support such rituals, give money, initiate them. What about today? Even now it is true, says Ramasastri. Zamindars still give to the Vedic Brahmins, and modern politicians sometimes patronize the sacrifices, to their advantage. I ask about various specific rites—the large-scale Vajapeya and the Asvamedha, the ancient horse sacrifice, with its obscene moments; all these, he says, are forbidden in our time, the corrupt Kali Age.

At five o'clock we go up the hill, where Sastri is to participate in a *homa* offering celebrating the god's three-day-long birthday. It is very good, Charles says, to celebrate a birthday for someone who is never born. A party of priests is reciting mantras at the top of its lungs (why, always, so loud?). There are cameras, bright lights, a certain extraneous fuss: someone has come from Hyderabad to make a CD recording such rituals at this temple. We sit for half an hour, then climb up into the temple for *darshan*. Another two-tier shrine, very modern; you can see the feet of Brahmā, the root, down below, standing on the Vaikuṇṭha-Nārāyaṇīya *yantra*; then the middle part, a Śiva-linga; and above them stand Śiva himself, a fiercely mustachioed Vishṇu, and Śrī. There is a story to be told here, but it is hidden, for now, under the hypermodern, middle-class veneer. Still, the original, engaging awkwardness or asymmetry shines through, as in so many Andhra shrines. Vanadurga, the Wilderness Goddess, perhaps the original presence, presides over this mountain from outside the temple enclosure.

When we come back to the priests in the *mandapam*, they are starting the *manthana*, the rubbing of fire sticks to produce fire for *homa*. I have never seen this before—the hard *uḍumbara*-wood pole placed into the *aśvattha* base, with two bare-chested Brahmins sitting on either side, pulling the pole with green ropes, back and forth, *pravritti* and *nivritti*, to generate flame. After a few moments, smoke comes out. Ramasastri is one of the main "churners," and across from him sit several young, muscular, handsome Brahmins; they take evident joy in this physical activity, attacking the ropes with gusto. The male pole drills and swivels inside the female base, thick white smoke is born, but for some reason—is it the presence of these foreign witnesses?—this evening fire does not appear. There is no sign of the spark that must be latent in the wood:

> vahner yathā yoni-gatasya mūrtiḥ na driśyate naiva ca linga-nāśaḥ/
> sa bhūya evendhana-yoni-grihyaḥ tad vobhayaṃ vai praṇavena
> dehe//

> [Just as the tangible form of fire, latent in the wood, cannot be seen but its potential existence is never lost and can be grasped over and over by means of the fire stick, so both [levels of reality] can be grasped in the body by means of the syllable OM.] (*Śvetâśvatara Upanishad* 1.13)

They try again and again, they pare and hone the tip of the pole, they check the fire-black receptacle where the tip is placed, they recite the mantras, the Nagasvaram horns and the drums reach toward a climax—and still no flame. They break a coconut to deal with *drishṭi*, one more try, but it doesn't work. Just in case it really *is* our fault, we thank Ramasastri and take our leave.

Pururavas, ancient king and lover, first learned the art of churning fire, a rather ineffective consolation offered by the gods for the loss of his beloved Urvaśi, a nymph from heaven who came down to earth for his sake but was taken back by the gods. Fire connects this world to the gods' world, but I am sure Pururavas, like any man, would have much preferred the girl. Sometimes even a fiery connection is all too tenuous. Sometimes the spark stays locked inside. We come down the hill in the dark, turn right onto the National Highway, toward Rajahmundry; within moments we pass a melodramatic blaze just off the road. Perhaps the mantras worked after all, though like all other forms of language, they have a tendency to be displaced.

July 27, Rajahmundry

Kanakaiah lectures in the Round Park on Madaya Mallana's *Rājaśekhara-caritramu*, "the most neglected of all Telugu *prabandha*s." I have never even seen the book; from his description, clearly a *kathā* work, in the *Kādambarī-Vikramârka* line. He thinks Mallana preceded Pĕddana and the rest of the sixteenth-century poets. He has a lot to say, the lecture is over two hours long, and the audience slowly begins to drift away. The usual honoring, garlands and bananas, rolls on for another half an hour after the end. But unlike the earlier lecturers, Kanakaiah is focused and full of substance. He clearly sees the novelty in the great Telugu *prabandha*s, their distinctiveness when compared to Sanskrit and Tamil; early sixteenth-century Andhra-Karnataka (the terms didn't apply) saw a radical departure from all earlier precedents and norms.

He comes by early in the morning to ask how I felt about the lecture, to pursue its theme a little. I tell him that listening to him, I wanted to read the text; he is happy at this response and says, "That is enough for me, I am satisfied." We speak of newness, of the discursive turn in *kāvya*, the "birth of literary fiction"—Margalit Finkelberg's term for fifth-century Greece. Some of the change, he says, comes from Kannada of this period. He thinks the poets have turned dramatists, and the *prabandha*s are very close to plays—dramatic, rich in dialogue, interested in character; and he sees they are deeply intertextual, citing, conversing with one another. Like the Russian novels of the nineteenth century, I suggest, and he nods; this classically oriented Telugu scholar, so much at home in the self-contained world of the Andhra Delta, knows his Dostoyevsky and Tolstoy.

July 28

Patanjali Sastry takes us to Sitanagaram to the ashram of Cittibabaji. Tomorrow they will lay the foundations for a Panduranga temple; 108 stūpas, they tell us, are already in place. They will also soon have 108 cows. It is gray and cool today, the ashram soaked in peacefulness. Baba's bed and wooden sandals are kept in a separate room; but a wealthy businessman from Vizag donated a large sum for building the vast sanctuary, with bearded stone image of the Baba, pink flowers scattered at his feet. Baba was an Avadhūt renouncer, thus belonged to no established *darshana* or school; and he was not given to teaching. The presence is what mattered. I ask if there was no *sampradāya*, no line of teachers, and at once the answer comes: yes, a Sufi *sampradāya*, he was in the line of Tājuddīn. Eclectic, unpredictable, profoundly original, esoteric: the Andhra hallmarks.

On a terrible road along the river we drive, from pothole to pothole, to Polavaram, where work on the dam is under way. It will be the largest man-made water reservoir in Asia when it is finished, and huge tracts of territory will be submerged, large tribal populations displaced. Great round segments of pipe rest, a little menacingly, in the brown mud, as if deposited by a race of giants. From here the Godavari reveals all her sweep and majesty—Pattisima to the south, Papi Kondalu to the north and west, row upon row of intersecting purple mountains. Soon much of this open-hearted landscape will disappear under water. The sheer scale of the project attests to a boldness of vision; and, as so often, I wonder: if they can change the face of the earth at Polavaram, if the planners and engineers of Andhra have the expertise and the resources and the managerial skills to do this, why can't they supply electric power in a steady way to the little town of Rajahmundry? Why can't they clean up the drinking water so that people would stop getting sick with typhus and the endless other waterborne diseases? It is a cultural choice like any other, and the collective will seems paralyzed.

Just before nightfall we see the deltaic vista from another angle, on top of Korukonda Hill. It is a steep climb to the summit, and the famous Narasimha (Man-Lion) temple is closed; but its outer walls are exuberant with carvings that seem not to care about the classical canons—they are whimsical, unfettered. The monkey-king Vālin staggers, almost happily, to his death. Rāvaṇa, nonchalant, carries off an unflappable Sītā in his chariot. Today is the first day of the month of Śravana, the heart of the monsoon, and we can see dark rain slanting down into the fields. Black buffaloes wallow in the shallow ponds, hardly more than dots in the rust-colored water. Again, the mesh of hills receding north and west. Red-tiled roofs of the village, and just beyond—torrents of green. We look down at the hilltop of Kapavaram, which I visited with Sashi; you can clearly see the red bricks of the stūpa base and other buildings. The two mountains seem to be conversing, perhaps debating, with each other; Narasimha growls at the Dhyāna Buddha, sitting in meditation—who, one supposes, transmutes fierceness into forbearance. But many of the meditating sculptures, most of them beheaded, on top of Korukonda also have a Buddhist look, as if the early Mahāyāna were the substratum here, as if emptiness preceded the Yogic Lion. Who can say? And what would it mean to be here first? To empty out a lion? In the wind that waves us down the mountain, I hear, without quite noticing, the faint roar of the Bodhisattva.

July 31, Hyderabad

Morning lecture at the History Seminar in Central University: Ramulu, Aloka, Murali, Jyotirmaya, Rakesh, Ramaraju, Rajagopal, Vasanti, and a crowd of students. There is an energy, a scintillation, on campus, far more than what I remember from an earlier lecture, some years ago; still, it moves.

I take myself into town, to Abids, the Visalandhra Book House: but most of what I am looking for is long out of print. Great Telugu books are rare—more rare than manuscripts, as Narayana Rao likes to say; and this is true no less of the modern classics (with notable exceptions) than of old *prabandha*s. Fortunately, Murali is digitalizing the Sundarāya collection, possibly the best in Andhra; soon the whole of nineteenth- and early twentieth-century Telugu printing will be online.

Jitendra takes me before dinner to his office, where we rummage through his books, piled in delicious disorder on, under, and around his shelves. He gives me a priceless copy of Tam. Tevapperumallayya's great commentary on *Manu-caritramu*—a taste of old Telugu Madras, from nearly a century ago. The cover has crumbled, the ants have eaten their way through many pages, but the beauty of the old Madras printing shines through—to say nothing of the singular clarity and insight of the words. I am carried back in time: some forty-five years ago I was the boy who rummaged sadly through the remnants of my grandfather's collection of Yiddish and Hebrew books. Most had been given away to a seminary in Chicago when he died, but there were a few survivors, often a single volume unaccountably left behind out of a precious set. In my adolescent dreams, mostly rife with unreachable girls, I would sometimes find one of the missing volumes, or a lost page from one of his Yiddish poems.

All India Radio in Vijayavada apparently has tens of thousands of hours of recordings from the 1940s, '50s, '60s. One can only hope they are preserved in minimally adequate conditions. Sashi's great-grandfather, Sivasankara Sastry, gave a series of radio lectures on the *Yoga-vāsishṭha*, the great Kashmiri meditation on illusion: if only we could find them. And there are archives in the stations at Tirupati, Kadapa, and elsewhere. They should be sorted, selected, transferred to CDs. Jitendra has a friend who, in a single year, collected seventy thousand old gramophone recordings from all over South India; and let us not forget the thousands of unread, unpublished manuscripts in Tanjavur, Vetapalem, in private collections . . . As we walk the streets of Dilsukhnagar, as the lights come on in the houses, I have a vision of catastrophe: time, a tidal wave, is washing away these books, poems, concerts, lectures, interviews, recitations, incantations, all of them unique and irreplaceable. As the wave crests, Jitendra, Murali, and one or two other driven souls, with me lagging far behind, frantically grasp at a few fragments that might still be salvaged. And if some are, indeed, rescued, perhaps someone might also try to understand them.

The magnitude of the task, my inadequacy, my greed, wanting to take it all in, wanting to know: these the heavy rocks to be rolled uphill.

August 1

Eileen arrives at twelve thirty, we disappear happily into Hyderabad—*ajñāta-vāsam*, the unknown mode of dwelling, hidden from the eyes of all my friends—and the city, a gracious Iranian princess in translucent veil, happily takes us in.

As night falls, we wander into Khairatabad; the mosque is even lovelier than last time (and so it is each time: the definition of a masterpiece?). The cupolas, just slightly out of line, are a gentle beige-brown against the gray-black monsoon sky. Pigeons perch, as always, on the stone latticework ascending the minarets. Eileen says: Like a person, it needs its trees, its birds, its sky. Men are scrubbing their hands and legs in a kind of fury before the evening prayer. For a moment I am overcome with nostalgia for Isfahan, Tabriz, the wanderings of my youth. A young boy says to me in mixed Urdu-Telugu: "It is very beautiful. For four hundred years it has been very beautiful."

August 2, Rajahmundry

We land in a soft, steady drizzle which intensifies toward noon. At last, this is real rain; the city drinks it in eagerly; everyone we meet seems refreshed, happy at this much-delayed bounty. They compliment Eileen for having brought it with her. Patanjali Sastry greets her with a firm "Welcome home."

Smile comes toward sunset with a bunch of small *cakkara-keli* bananas, exploding with their distinctive, granular sweetness. Talk turns to N. Jayaprakash, the former IAS officer, District Collector, who did what no one else would do: he resigned his high post in order to found a serious reformist movement, Loksatta, first an NGO and now an incipient political party. Sastry says he is banking on people's disgust with the inept, mostly corrupt system that has been in place for many years. He is a man of transparent integrity with an agenda of grassroots change, a focus on health care in the villages. Nobody can predict what will happen, but I notice today, as in other conversations in Hyderabad and elsewhere, the tentative tingling of hope.

* * *

Late at night, in the mustard glow of the lamp beside the door, under Damerla Rama Rao's sketch of an Andhra girl and the chubby goddess Nirmala Devi, we listen to the Muttusvami Dikshitar *kriti*, *Ehi Annapūrṇe*: the gentle percussion of the rain outside mingles with Bombay Jayashri's unerring microtones. They say this was Dikshitar's final, or perhaps penultimate, composition, sung on the day of his death in Ettayapuram.

> ehi annapūrṇe sannidhehi sadāpūrṇe . . .
> viśveśa-manollāsini cid-ānanda-vilāsini . . .

[Come, Annapurna, ever full,
goddess who lavishes food,
become present to me
through your game in God's mind,
the happy play of awareness.]

Full, fuller, fullest. What was it like to sing this utterly trusting song, to make the goddess come alive, in the hour of one's death? The story has it that on that same morning the Maharaja of Ettayapuram, where Dikshitar was living, came to see the composer; the king was agitated and distressed because the royal elephant had broken out of its chains, escaped from the elephant stable, and was now trumpeting wildly in the cremation ground outside the town. "Don't be afraid," said the composer; "no harm will come to your family." He sent the king away and began to sing the haunting song, tears in his eyes, his students accompanying him; and the goddess appeared in his room as a blaze of white light.

I guess the wild elephant inside him was about to break loose, and Dikshitar knew it. The musicologists like to say that the trumpeting of the elephant is fixed on the note *ni* (*nishāda*), the highest in the *rāga* scale—the pitch situated on the verge of infinity. The bewitching *rāga* Punnāgavarāḷi, in which this song is set, begins and ends its scale on *ni*; and Jayashri's voice lingers on this same *ni* when she reaches the word *sanniDHEhi*, "Become present." It is true: one can die of the sheer, overdetermined intricacy, or the lucid intensity, or the humane magic, of Carnatic music.

August 3, Tisha Be'Av, Rajahmundry

All night, even in my sleep, I hear the soothing drum-drone of rain.

Before dawn a squirrel, or maybe a large lizard, somehow finds its way inside; its scurrying and swishing through the bedroom push me over the brink of waking, out of dream. At six, after the milk arrives, I check out the Kadiyam Road. For a few minutes the rain has stopped, but I am nearly alone on the long slope uphill—except for silver Quixote and Sancho Panza, standing unperturbed in a sea of green. The thatched huts of the watchmen are soggy through and through (I hope they are dry inside). Rich coffee-and-cream rivulets stream downhill. A strong gray wind sweeps through the cashew trees. Dogs circle erratically, restless, up and down the empty road. Wet and empty, full of rain. It is the season for lovers; Rajahmundry is mostly still in bed. At the odds-and-ends shop there are no morning papers, and the shopkeeper, my friend, apologizes: "Cyclone, Sar."

August 5, Rajahmundry

Two days of continuous rain, lashing winds, belated monsoon. Timing is all: for the newly transplanted rice seedlings, this deluge is a disaster; we needed the rain a month ago. But in Telangana, the drought is now over, the *kharif* crop back on schedule.

Electric current comes and goes. The train lines to Vizag and to Hyderabad are cut, the tracks flooded. It is cold; I find it hard even to remember the intense heat of May and June. Whenever you go out, your feet are immediately drenched, the streets swirling with rain. Yasmin says to me that, having tasted the full blast of summer in Rajahmundry, I should stay on to feel the cold season. If only I could. Now each day has the shadow, the raw bittersweetness of incipient leavetaking.

In one stormy moment a cyclist, blinded by rain and wind, loses control and crashes into me from behind, opening a wide gash in my right leg. He apologizes, chagrined, but I can see it was not his fault. And what was I doing walking down the road in the middle of all this?

Ophira arrives from Kerala just before the trains shut down. I take her to say hello to Patanjali Sastry. Impishly he says to her: "First Eileen came, two days ago, and brought rain. Now you have come with the cyclone. Will you please tell me who else is expected from Jerusalem?"

Three times to the river to see her in spate—with Ophira, with Harshita, then later with Eileen, Smile, Yasmin, and Sastrygaru, a little ways downstream. At Pushkara Revu, she, Godavari, has climbed the steps and flooded the paving at street level; the gates are locked, no one is allowed in, though peering through the holes you can see occasional, hardy swimmers, black stick figures in a sea of brown; one or two brave souls have made rough wooden canoes out of black branches and are riding them eastward and southward in the swift current. All the way upstream, as far as the eye can see, brown torrents churn and whirl. People cluster in large groups at every point along the embankment, marveling at the dramatic swelling and acceleration of their goddess, this "necklace hanging over the breasts of the Andhra Earth-goddess" (*āndhra-vasudhā-vakshoja-hārâvaḷi*: Śrīnātha, *Bhīmeśvarapurāṇamu* 4.178). She is unquestionably a person, a woman, overflowing from time to time with passionate excitement, at other times serene, immersed in the depths of self. In the cold rain, the distance between river and sky has diminished; they are now part of a single, uninterrupted liquid force.

Sastry recalls the 1986 floods, when animals, people, sometimes whole huts were carried away by the stream. "It was *terribly* beautiful." The beauty is intrinsic, as are her shifting moods. "Each day you go there, each day of the year, she will be somewhat changed." Rajahmundry nestles, continually astonished, at her side, waiting for her to rise up, swell into her richer, fully manifest self, reach out to touch.

Is she a river or an ocean? Elana's question from two weeks ago, at Antarvedi: what is the moment of transition? Today, with swift water drowning the horizon, it is even harder to say. Water poured into water, an endless, frothy brown rush: fullness always spills over. This is, in my view, the most fundamental, the most consequential, of all Hindu metaphysical insights. The origin of life itself, of inhabitable worlds, of all our longing and restlessness—what are they but this overspill?

ramyāṇi vīkshya madhurāṃś ca niśamya śabdān
paryutsukī-bhavati yat sukhito 'pi jantuḥ . . .

[When we see something amazing,
when we hear sweet sounds,
even if we happen to be happy we are filled
with homesickness.[14]]

Yet Smile says last night at dinner that the Andhras are the least restless of all Indians (in marked contrast with the Malayalis and the Gujaratis, for example). The Andhras love their place so much, they find it so sweet, that they are reluctant ever to leave it.

* * *

Somalamma, now Śyamalamba, the first goddess of Rajahmundry, turns up outside Smile's house, behind the RTC Complex. On our way home we see women lighting small *diya* lamps—hundreds of them ablaze against the darkness in the outer *mandapam*. Yesterday was Varalakshmi *pūjā*, a day for worshiping the great Goddess of Wealth; women were busy all day inviting her into the home, *being* the goddess at home. Somalamma's shrine was once set in solitary self-sufficiency here, in the midst of the cashew groves and fields, long before Rajahmundry spread eastward toward Vadrevunagar (the Vadrevu *zamindari*), where I live. It turns out that this early temple is actually classed, today, as her in-laws' house, *attavār' illu*; her natal home is the (somewhat newer) shrine in town. In effect, the town has engulfed her, taming this piece of wilderness, leaving the once-wild goddess behind as witness.

Somalamma is Krishnayya's goddess; he grew up close to her shrine in the old town, and he knows her intimately, has often followed her annual festival that takes her from her in-laws' home back to her natal house and then, a month later, sends her back to her husband amid scenes of profound sadness and mourning. Her worshipers dance before her, jumping and crying out (*keka veyaḍam*) so as to catch her attention. This isn't as easy as one might think. Somalamma's normal state, says Krishnayya, is what is known as *magata*—a kind of spaciness and sleepiness, a mode of dreamy self-absorption and unfocused attention. It feels familiar enough to me. But in the case of a goddess, such a soporific mode may well be close to what the Sanskrit texts mean when they talk about pure, whole "consciousness," the defining feature of being fully alive.

* * *

Oleti Bangaresvara Sarma, an MA student in Telugu at the Arts College, comes to give me a daily hour of Telugu practice, with a focus on particular idioms and syntagmas that I prepare in advance. He quickly grasps what it is I need and is very happy to help me produce somewhat more complex sentences like "Even though others say he's a scoundrel, as far as I can see he's actually a rather nice person," or "Just because you have lots of money, you shouldn't look down on others." He has a flair for the idiomatic, a great gift in a language instructor, and knows how to ground my often high-flown locutions in clear everyday speech, that clarity of language that I regard as life's single greatest good. His *muttātagāru*—grandfather's younger uncle—was Cellapilla Venkata Sastri, of the Tirupati Venkata Kavulu, one of the most creative figures in modern Telugu literature. Bangaresvara Sarma knows Cellapilla's works: he has read the whole Tirupati-Venkata corpus, and he is intent on mastering all of classical Telugu. He seems to me to speak, think, and feel from some space deep inside this Telugu delta, where poetry ripens with the rice. I ask him what Telugu books he likes most, and he thinks for a moment before answering: Tikkana, Nannayya, and *Kaḷāpūrṇodayamu*. He comes from a family of teachers, grammarians, scholars, and he, too, will become a teacher, a very good one, one day.

August 6

Ophira, drawing on her own recent experience in Kalady, notices that ants have invaded my laptop. An emergency: they lay their eggs deep inside, under the keyboard, in the CD drive and other convenient parts of the labyrinth, and soon the whole computer is converted to an anthill, one lacking memory or future. Where did they come from, how did they find their way in? Who knows? We clean the machine as best we can, we lightly spray it with the anticockroach spray; dozens of blasted ants stagger unsteadily out from its depths and die on the white plastic table where this surgery has taken place. At first we think that this intervention will be enough, but within a few hours more ants are happily plying back and forth over the keyboard. Does the law of probability obtain with ants? Give them enough time and they will, I suppose, produce *Hamlet* on my laptop. Or perhaps write their own version of this diary. I wonder if they, too, would complain about the heat in May. Anyway, was not each of them an Indra—king of the gods—in some former birth, as a classical myth tells us? Now the Wittgensteinian question: if ants could speak, would we be capable of understanding them? But I am unwilling to give them a chance, I have to draw the line here. Another round of spraying, dusting, blowing, another mass exodus of dying ants—this time it seems we got them. What is left of my diary will be in some variant of human language.

August 7: Circar Express

After a two-hour delay at Rajahmundry station, the train sets off across the river in a hushed, awestruck, tentative tiptoe. I have never traveled so slowly in any form of conveyance. The water reaches up to the tracks, washes the underbelly of the great girders. After twenty minutes on the bridge, with no end in sight, Eileen asks, "*Is* there another side?" The sun is setting, the world a brown-mauve whirl of water and sky.

Eileen again: this crossing is like a hesitant, sustained, self-conscious dance. Nothing is taken for granted in the forward movement—as if the train were holding its breath, trying not to drown. It takes another twenty minutes to reach West Godavari district, and dry land, beyond the flood.

In Konasima, Razole and dozens of other villages are underwater. Upstream, the great Rāma temple at Bhadrachalam is entirely submerged.

* * *

Ophira, house-sitting as we head south to Madras, calls to report on her further zoological investigations. A continuous, high-pitched screeching in the bedroom prompted her to explore the darker reaches of the floor and cupboards; she found a thriving family of mice. She managed to extract two of the babies and bring them to safety outside in the street, but a third, left for a few moments on the porch, seems to have been spirited away by a bird of prey. She tells us she is spraying and cleaning vigorously, and perhaps for the moment the rapid, continuous devolution of the flat into forest or field has been delayed—long enough, I hope, for me to pack up and depart at the end of the month without having to do battle with snakes, frogs, or even larger creatures. (Last week in Hyderabad, I asked Ramulu if the wild forest within which Central University is situated has interesting wildlife, say, tigers. Yes, he said: there are plenty of human tigers, like at any university.)

* * *

The morning was devoted to a "class" for Jaya and Aparna on *advaita*, nondualism—specifically, Sureśvara's *Naishkarmya-siddhi* (On Achieving Nonaction), a text I love enough to be willing to expound. Ophira, very much the skeptic when it comes to *advaita*, or possibly anything metaphysical, joined us, so I mostly stuck to English—arguably the world's least *advaitic* language, recalcitrant with irreducible objects and a flat, entirely moderate and empiricist sort of common sense. Sureśvara's common sense is Indian, possibly even South Indian, though he of course finds it necessary to undermine our habitual, superficial perceptions. He begins with pain and the natural, *svarasataḥ*, wish of every living creature not to feel pain. He knows where the pain comes from—the splitting that takes place in the mind, the projection of pleasure or displeasure (never intrinsic to either subject or object) that inevitably ensues. "If you want to stop the pain"—he is confident—"read my book."

Even if the conclusion is not quite necessary, the fact of division, our mental chopping and cutting at the world, the violence we do to it, feels true. And perhaps a gentle, understated *advaita* can truly salve these wounds. Sastrygaru thinks it can—on another level, he says, than the level of god or gods, of "religion." He says this to Eileen while sitting last night at the Priyanka restaurant, outdoors in the cool dark—as if acknowledging something known to be true in a personal way not susceptible to proof, and understood from some place at once intimate and detached. As if peace were available not through some steady certainty, and of course not by striking an attitude, but in unsteady, unpredictable moments that are beyond expectation or resignation, that allow one briefly to see through the veil.

How strange, then, that the river, swelling, self-transcending, has *two* banks.

But could there be an Andhra kind of *advaita* that would explain why the intuition of oneness is the natural default, the point of departure for those who live here? The train picks up speed, I feel myself pulled through the soft, enfolding, yielding space of the delta, just beyond the river, under the rain. Add to these the constant flow of wilderness or forest, so close to any formed or structured place. And yet the strongest voices in the tradition—Nannayya, Annamayya, Śrīnātha, Tyāgarāja—maintain the dissonance and personal disembeddedness that cut through any simple sense of unity. Always there is the recalcitrant individual, never entirely one with himself or herself or the world.

Won't you remove the screen?
The one that hangs inside me.
The one called greed.

The hungry fish swallowed the hook.
The lamp is masked by a shade.
The dinner was perfect, until the fly fell in.
The mind in contemplation shifted to the slums.
Deer run straight into the trap.
Tyāgarāja remembers you.

Won't you remove the screen?[15]

Perhaps such dissonant tones are the deeper gift of the wilderness, after all, or of its translation into lucid experience; the poet emerges from the wild and maintains his or her ties to it, so long as he speaks poems, but he is no longer fully of it or even, for that matter, at home in it. Classically, the Telugu poet is a scientist: combining syllables and sounds so as to change the world, make a new world.

August 10, Tirupperur

After a few sultry days in Madras, the city groaning under an invasion of mosquitoes (bringing a pandemic of Chikungunya fever and malaria), dawn in Coimbatore is dry, humane, cool. Gurumurtti meets us at the station, takes us home for breakfast. To my joy—I had forgotten that he told me this when we met in Tiruvarur—he and Prasanna speak Telugu at home; their families, settled for generations in western Tamilnadu, come from the Andhra Delta, and they take pride in their mother language, pass it on to their children.

Eileen and I passed through Coimbatore once before, in 1972, on our way from Cochin to Ooty; I still remember, with a shudder, the two-rupee-a-night hotel room near the grimy train station. Today's visit redeems that memory; the city is easy, friendly, clean, and full of interest. For decades I have wanted to see the Perur temple, and Gurumurtti turns the dream into dreamy concreteness. The purple Nilgiri hills, sudden and jagged in their ascent from the flatland, travel with us from the big city to the temple outside it. We are in Konku land, far from the settled world of the Kaveri Delta. A splendid Naṭarāja dancer has his own, high shrine, with two sages, Gomuni and Paṭṭimuni, at his feet; his hair is not splayed out, as in so many of the bronzes, but sedately combed back, thus intimating serenity even in the course of his fierce *tāṇḍava* dance. A beautiful Jñāna-Bhairava, black with wisdom, stands close to a fine stone Cuntaramūrtti—my poet—who looks rougher, far more individualized, than in the Tanjavur bronze from Kilaiyur that I love. He, Cuntaramūrtti, passed not far from here:

ĕnkeṉum pokiṉum ĕmpĕrumāṉai niṉaintakkāl
kŏnke pukiṉun kūṟai kŏṇṭ' āṟalaippār ilai

[Wherever I may go—
even if I reach the Konku region!—
if I think of our great lord,
no bandits will strip me
or prey upon me.]
(92.3)

Then, in the eighth century, as perhaps even now, this was an unruly, somehow peripheral place, full of brigands, the roads unsafe, a spillover from the stony Deccan uplands. It is usually in the periphery that human beings invent something new. At Perur Śiva became a Pallan peasant, working hard in the paddy fields, in order to hide from his poet-lover, Cuntarar; and Nandi, the stone bull at the entrance to the temple, though sworn to silence by the god, was the one who hinted to Cuntarar, with a silent movement of his eyes, to look for Śiva outside, in the fields.

This story, an old one at Perur, is told by the lyrical and complex eighteenth-century poet, Kacciyappar, in his book on the temple, *Perūrppurāṇam*, which I read years ago in London. Kacciyappar, they say, composed the book as a last resort, when there was a severe drought in the Perur region; hearing this flood of Tamil poetry, Śiva released the Ganges from his hair, where the river can always be found, and soaked the fields here with rain. As usual, the South Indian poet's first concern is a practical one; as usual, poetry is effective, consequential, revitalizing, especially when the listeners or readers find themselves on the boundary between life and death.

We have dinner, after my talk at the Rotary Club, at the home of the genial Satish, a wildlife adventurer, back from Africa and New Zealand. On his computer we see a long, downloaded video clip of the snow leopard—the most elusive of cats, the one Peter Matthiesson walked for weeks through the Himalayas to see (and failed). I have Matthiesson's marvelous book with me for our days in Coonoor. Today anyone can see the snow leopard hunting deer on a computer screen, after dinner; there are no words to describe the wonder, or the sacrilege of instant accessibility. But Satish would still, I am sure, be ready to walk the mountains in the hope of seeing the living beast.

We ride the bus through Mettuppalaiyam, higher and higher, cool, cooler, cold. Eileen likes the white mist hanging on these mountains. The Chinese landscape painters are supposed to have lived long lives—thanks to the mists they put into their paintings.

Am I in India? There is the brown-red earth on the hilltop across from me. Cypress, cedars, pine, eucalyptus recede in a warm blue-green mélange across the slopes, close to the sky. Much of the original *sola* forest has been replaced by tea plantations: the hills are divided into neat, wedgelike segments, dark green tea bushes punctuated by erect, vertical silver oaks standing guard. Tea is ripening madly everywhere around us, perched as we are in this sloping maze of greens. Low clouds sit, phlegmatic, on the higher peaks in the distance. It is still the month of Śravana, sometimes there are short bursts of rain. We sit and stare, we breathe the mountain in, we whisper blessings for Mr. Mahi, who has given us his house and this soothing vision of trees, clouds, sky.

At Wellington, we stop for groceries at the Staff College, down from the black war memorial that proclaims how "glorious" it is to die fulfilling one's duty. I guess some people still believe this (how can they? By not thinking). Soldiers in khaki sweaters come and go beside the army canteen, which could so easily be an Israeli one, entirely familiar. Suddenly the Lebanon war comes back to me, probably because there is space here for the memories to surface in the wide open, cool, protected quiet, and because another miserable Lebanese war is unfolding day by day. Young soldiers are repeating the horrible progression that we followed then, twenty-four years ago: the knock at the door in the middle of the night, the bus ride through the dark to the emergency storerooms, the long hours spent sitting on the cement floor, loading bullets into the clips; and then the hot drive north, stomach churning with anger, with fear, the crossing of the border. . . . Suddenly the images cascade, macabre in the silence of these hills and the gray slate of rain: I can see my moronic officer stamping his feet in fury because our entry into battle had been delayed by a few hours; the Lubavitch lunatics meandering among the half-tracks on the road to Hatzbayah, trying to persuade us to pray; the grim tank driver with his pornographic reports of the first days of killing; but I also remember the strange tenderness of men jumbled together in war, and then the ones who died beside us, the wasted, useless deaths, and the useless question that cries out in the stillness—"Why?"

Why why why do we waste the gift?

Later, bumping over the mountain trail in a rickshaw, E. asks, "What are they calling this war?" It is always useful to have a name for the black rip inside reality where someone—a father, a brother, a child—has died (to what end?), for the sake of order and lucid definition, for labeling and cataloguing and filing away.

Toward evening we read the Israeli papers on the Web in an Internet café in Bedford. It seems the cease-fire is close. I dread reentering that world. Here all is peace, and the pointless question has metamorphosed, turned ironic, achieved a point: after dark I listen to an old recording of Mysore T. Chowdiah playing Tyāgarāja's "ĕnduku daya rādu ra" (*Why have you no compassion?*) in Todi *rāga* on his seven-stringed violin.

August 12

In the Lepakshi mode, I dream all night of the unfinished. Fred Hardy has slept in my flat: he died last year, in his prime, his life's work scattered in files on the computer. G. M. returns from sabbatical with his great book incomplete, only a fragment ready. He asks me if he is a poet. I say, "You write with a lyrical analytic."

> "Unfinished houses
> hold all the finished loves of this world,
> as I hold you, now, undone . . ."

I wake to the green hills, white mist on distant blue mountains: Nilagiris. We walk through Forest Dale, bus into Bedford; the names suggest we are in England, some dead fantasy of England, but this Bedford has the stained pastel facades, the dusty signboards, black auto exhaust, jumbled shops, of an Indian village. It is slightly jarring to hear Tamil spoken in this cool mountain setting; to me, Tamil naturally rolls and gurgles against a backdrop of thick, humid heat, incandescent sunlight, or suffocating, sweaty night. I always thought this overheated context helped explain the rapid-fire mode of speech, but here Tamil is no slower, no less urgent than in Madras.

Eileen said to me when we were planning the trip: "Find a place in India where no one knows you." I didn't quite succeed; tomorrow we will lunch with Ram Guha. Still, time and space have cracked open, decelerating and extending, respectively. Since this is perhaps as close as I will ever get to the fantasy of pure, peaceful isolation—days free from other tasks and other people, with only the mountains for company, and a hint of restfulness—I stop in a small stationery store and buy a long, white, empty notebook.

* * *

I am reading Patanjali Sastry's fine play, *Mādhavi*; contemplating working on a translation. But the day begins with an hour of Pĕddana *pārāyaṇa* recitation. There is time to read the verses over and over, slowly probing them with my tongue as if they were some exotic dish. Appropriately, in this spacious interval, there is new hope for Varuthini: the false Pravara, a *gandharva* disguised, is waiting to enter into *her* fantasy.

> She saw him.
> Golden as *ketaki* flowers,
> she moved toward him
> at that very moment, her belt
> gently jingling. She left her girlfriends
> behind her, slipped into the grove
> like lightning quivering in cloud,
> staring avidly as when you see
> something in a dream and then find it
> on waking.
> (3.89)

Does she know, does she sense on some half-conscious level that this man is not the lover she wants, that she, like the poet who tells the story, is playing at a fiction? There are, I think, three interlocking levels of awareness: Varuthini, caught up in a fantasy of astonishing concreteness, a madness inflicted upon the world, has the least of all; the poet knows what is fictive but forgets this in the delirium of his art; and then there is the reader or listener, who is perfectly aware of the distinction, who knows and remembers who is sane and who is mad. Literary fiction is born.

* * *

Narayana Rao has published another, deliberately provocative essay in the weekly *Vārta*—on what it takes to become a Telugu poet. People, even poets, like to say that poetry just "comes" to them without training or special effort. *Idi kevalam abaddham*: It's simply untrue. Like a modern-day Rājaśekhara, Narayana Rao speaks of the craft, of practice, of literacy. Poets are made, perhaps self-made, at any rate never born fully fashioned and mature. It is worth considering, he says, what it would take to educate a real poet. And if one could, theoretically, at least conceive of an illiterate poet (as the oral *cāṭu* tradition likes to do), an illiterate scholar or critic is a contradiction in terms.

His implication, sadly on the mark, is that this contradictory conflation is the modern norm.

After so many years of hearing and reading Narayana Rao in English, I find his Telugu voice utterly compelling. His prose is creamy and precise; he teases, chastises, whispers, debunks, then deftly strikes home. A lyrical analytic. I want him to write another book, in Telugu, on Viswanatha, Gurajada, and the failed/false revolution.

Smile reminded me last week that the people who call themselves revolutionaries ("Naxalites") today—who live in the forest, kill, play at politics—have nothing whatsoever in common with the movement of intellectuals and artists of the fifties and sixties. That march of empathic idealists has died, leaving behind only this violent debris.

* * *

Verissimo: "Excessive symmetry is either unnatural and conceals some human thought behind it, or else supernatural and conceals some mystery."[16] But there is a third possibility, the most common one in India: that a supernatural symmetry is inherently unnatural.

August 16, Mylapore

Because of the long Independence Day weekend, the early morning buses downhill are completely packed, so we end up hiring a taxi to drive us to Mettuppalaiyam. A soft drizzle sees us off. The Mettuppalaiyam-Coimbatore bus offers the usual torment of deafening, mind-deadening cinema music. It is, of course, still hot in the plains, and the light is so stark that I can hardly bear to look out the window. I miss the tea bushes, the silver oaks, the gray wind. At the airport, security is upgraded, everyone a little nervous; Prasanna's sambar powder had to be checked in a separate box and shipped in the cargo hold.

It is Krishna's birthday, *janmâshṭami*; yellow cows, painted with turmeric, wander the streets of Mylapore and Mantaiveli, led by gypsy Kuravar dressed in seedy red and a hundred tiny mirrors. Thick afternoon light seeps into all the pores of my skin. At every doorstep, a child's white footprints invite the baby Krishna to enter or record his visit. I have a habit of turning up in Madras on this blessed day. What is left of the hills, the expansive scent of memory, has condensed into a true proverb recited by Charu and Rajamani: "kaṟṟatu kaiy aḷavu, kallātatu malaiyaḷavu" (What one has learned is no more than a handful, what one hasn't learned is as big as a mountain). Instead of the mountain, some say *ulak'aḷavu*—one's ignorance is as big as the whole world.

August 19

Morning in Gandhinagar with A. R. Venkatachalapathy, certainly the liveliest historian in Madras, with delightfully unconventional interests. I have read his essays on the introduction of coffee and of tobacco into nineteenth-century Madras, but today he gives me the Tamil version of these works; and his Tamil voice, not surprisingly, is strong, resonant, rich, like good coffee. He is deeply engaged in the contemporary literary scene in Tamil; was very close to Sundara Ramaswamy (known as Suraa) and translated Suraa's fiercely controversial novel, *JJ: Cila kuṟippukaḷ* (well!). People remember, he tells me, the shock of first reading it—where they were standing or sitting at such and such a point in the novel, much as some (like me) remember where they were at the moment of Kennedy's assassination. I think *JJ* is, indeed, a shocking work, meant to unsettle the reader; when I first read it in Jerusalem, I found it remote, tantalizing, strange.

True to my one guiding principle—Never Resist Temptation—I find myself drawn deeper and deeper, on every trip to Madras, into the quicksand of modern Tamil. I cannot explain its hold over me. There is something compelling, melodic, even bewitching in good modern Tamil prose, like Curaa's (yet how rare this is). There is the truly amazing intertextuality of the modern works, almost as intense as in the sixteenth-century Telugu *prabandha*s or the nineteenth-century Russian novel. So rich a conversation *must* be overheard. And yet I am always mildly disappointed after reading in these novels for a few hours. Perhaps this sense of repeated deflation is the secret of their fascination? And why should I feel so let down?

Of course, in a way the novel lives on in South India far more than in the West, where I think it has run its course. This, too, is interesting, a tribute to the lively "coolness of the imagination" (*kaṟpanaiyin cītaḷam*; *JJ*, 214) in this part of the world. As they say, nothing is ever truly lost in India—not even the novel.

A shared, mute axiom embodies itself in nearly all these recent writers—most clearly seen in the irony implicit in the frame, the modernist reframing that dependably highlights the incongruent or the disingenuous. Alienation is the barren, predictable modern convention. It is as if the impulse to capture the widening gap between old and new experience, which drove so many of the later premodern poets, in the eighteenth and nineteenth centuries—say, Tiricirapuram Minatcicuntaram Pillai, whom we tend either not to read at all or to misread—were still driving the contemporary Tamil prose writers, old and young. Yet they seem unaware of their connectedness to their predecessors of a mere century and a half ago. And because this connection cannot be acknowledged, and because the pose of ironic alienation is itself so impoverished, the reader is regularly let down in the end. Winnicott knew so well this agony of being dropped by the artist, even a great artist, just at the point of penetrating the intimate secret of self. One could also speak of a failure of complexity, a sin unheard of in the medieval texts. In any case, *JJ* is, to me, a kind of prose *kalampakam*, ostensibly the most heterogeneous of the *ciṟṟ'ilakkiyam* or "minor" literary categories: a mixed bag, jumbling genres and tones, that on closer inspection turns out to be utterly unmixed, integral, consistent, yet also self-ironic.

We speak of Sanskrit and its links to pretension, authority, hierarchy, repression. . . . It is sometimes true, I say, I understand; but if you see only that, what you miss is the actual poetic praxis of the last thousand years—also the unique expressivity that underlies the choice of Sanskrit for writing a major poem. If one thinks of Sanskrit as a particular mode of using language, of intensifying, enhancing, clarifying, and working upon reality through linguistic means, then even Imayam's Dalit Tamil, barely susceptible to graphic recording, is a sort of Sanskrit. I think, though, that Chalapathy would not accept this.

In the afternoon, all fluid gold, Eileen and I visit the god in the Kāpālīśvara temple in Mylapore, just down the road from our old home in Mandaiveli. She offers a coconut and burning camphor to the "Lord of the Punnai Forest," one of the smaller *linga* shrines in the temple compound. On its wall, in black letters, the first verses of Kāraikkālammaiyar's great poem to Śiva, perhaps the earliest example of the Tamil devotional style (seventh century?):

> Barely born, just learning to speak,
> stunned by yearning, I reached
> your feet, Black-Throated
> god of all gods, my Lord—
> what day will sorrow
> cease?

A woman's poem, a woman poet: I translate for Eileen, and she, happy, serious, circumambulates the shrine several times. She leaves tonight for home, while I briefly revert to my eremitic, vagabond mode.

August 20, Rajahmundry, Maredumilli

Another night on the Circar Express, this time heading north, surrounded, to my delight, by Telugu speakers. The auto rickshaw driver chooses to take me to Chennai Central via Triplicane, shimmering and vibrating in the afternoon sun. It is too much for me: from how many beloved places can I be exiled at a time? Wounded by leaving, I find it hard even to read. Toward dawn the train unaccountably slows, turning into something more like a local bus; I wake up in Bhimavaram, but try as I might, I cannot see the *ārāma* Śiva shrine through the window.

For another few days, I will keep up this illusion of being settled here, where I seem to belong—no, let us leave out the "seeming." The imminent separation hangs, ghostlike, over every meeting. It is Amalu's birthday, I am called to celebrate; Amalu herself, radiantly dressed, the main celebrant, serves all the guests before sitting down to eat her birthday lunch (which she has also cooked). For dessert we have white waferlike *pūtarekulu* from Atreyapuram, one of the great miracles of the Andhra kitchen. I first tasted them while traveling around Andhra with Narayana Rao, in 1986, as if in the entourage of a beloved medieval poet; people vied with one another to host us, plying us with delicacies like this intricate, ingenious masterpiece.

Late afternoon, to Maredumilli with Sashi and Sumalini, through thick, virgin forest. Past Korukonda, we rapidly climb out of the humid plains into a fresh, almost silent world of green. Rare tribal villages are hidden by the trees. A sudden rain clears the dust: we could be driving through northern Italy, alone with the forest. As always, I am amazed at the proximity of open wilderness, almost untouched by human beings. The law prohibits cutting down trees in the forest, and it seems to be strictly enforced. So Rajahmundry sits, on one side, at the cusp of the great river; on the other side on the bank of an immense, dense forest. Were we to continue another few miles north, we would enter Chhattisgarh in the heart of middle India, another wild, Naxalite-infested world.

There must once have been something quite wonderful at Maredumilli; an endearing seventeenth-century stone Bhadrakāli, fiercest of goddesses, from here now stands in the Rallabandi Subba Rao Museum in Rajahmundry. Nothing much left of this today. A little before the village there is a metal bridge over the Pamuleru River, which is born somewhere high in the Eastern Ghats and eventually pours into the Godavari. Like all the other rivers around here, the Pamuleru is in spate, gushing and swirling in fast, brown currents. At last light, in a soothing drizzle, we climb down the muddy slopes through the forest to stand on its sandy shore. Sumalini contemplates swimming out to the jagged black rocks in midstream.

I recognize in Sumalini the adventurous, unencumbered, even daredevil strand that I know in myself; I don't know where it comes from (in her case, probably from much suffering), but it is just what I need to feel today, staving off the sorrow of departing. With Sashi and Jitendra, Sumalini has roamed the remote reaches of Telangana, living off the land, sleeping outdoors under the stars; and since the country is so wild, she carries a sharp-toothed, long machete in the back of the car. I hold it in my hands, admire the workmanship—it is an old, silvery specimen from Hyderabad of the Nizams—and hope she will never have to use it, to defend herself from sundry wilderness terrors. She escaped an unhappy marriage and brought up her son alone; she is a lawyer in the Andhra High Court, fearless and wild.

At Rampacodavaram, caught in the headlights: a gaunt old man, all in white, clutching a white-red rooster to his chest, his eyes aflame, slowly crossing the dark, wet village street.

August 21, Rajahmundry

Time, whatever it is, haunts my dreams. Aleida has remembered or reconstructed Yigal's essay on time, so we can discuss it in the seminar. I am happy for this opportunity to ask him: "Just what do you mean when you say that time has whirlpools, eddies, forgotten pockets locked within it?"

The green field halfway up Nehru Road has been harvested and thus reverts to reddish brown. When I went walking there two weeks ago with Ophira, we chatted with the watchmen, who proudly informed us that they themselves had made the silver scarecrow I have been calling Quixote and his companion, Sancho Panza. On closer inspection we saw that Quixote was boldly ithyphallic, imperiously surveying his green domain. Today he lies face-down, dormant, in the mud, and Sancho—me, that is—is nowhere to be seen.

It doesn't much help to tell myself that any closure is false, artificial.

For some reason, *aletheia* is in my mind as I walk—the nonforgetting, removing the veil, a non not-noticing, the Greek ideal. At first it seems close to the Indian notion of seeing through surface (*māyā*). Yet when you pierce the veil in Naxos or, say, Rajahmundry, what you see is utterly distinct. Naxos belongs to Diotima and her sensual intellection, the idea at play in sunlight and seashore, or in love. In Rajahmundry: the oddly asymmetrical oneness, stretched, elongated, turned back upon itself, like the Rāmappa bracket figures, like the ripening goddess drawn from the lake, like Quixote staring deep into the mud.

* * *

Smile comes, beginning the goodbyes. When you go, he says, *rajahmundry bosi potundi*: a gap will emerge in Rajahmundry.

I feel the gap in me, growing larger by the minute.

We do a first draft of his magnificent "Dragonfly":

> Fingers turn into chameleons until they find a dragonfly.
> In the green water of the lake where clouds study their faces,
> like the wind sitting for fun on the horns of buffaloes chewing their cud
> along with the evening sun:
> swarms of dragonflies.
> My fingers, looking at them greedily, turn into chameleons.
> A rainbow shimmers at my fingertips
> when I catch hold of a dragonfly's tail.

In its eyes, soft as mirrors,
the sheen of brightly colored worlds.
It thinks I'm looking into its worlds, so it bites my palm
with gentle, angry jaws.
Still, I won't let it go. If I let it go,
like a winged fish it will swim back in the wind
to the height I can't reach except in my mind.
I'd tie a thread to its tail and let it fly
but like our puppy tugging at its leash
it would fly a little and then, weighed down by the thread,
fall without a sound—
like a golden flower falling from my sister's braid.
I'm wild with happiness—
like flying from second grade to third grade,
like finding someone's rusty old coin in the dust,
like when my brother's ball, the one he wouldn't give me,
burst and wouldn't bounce.
That thin thread is the shape of my happiness.
It's getting dark, I have to go home.
If I let go, the dragonfly will fly away.
All my happiness will fly away.
I badly want my happiness to stay with me.
I crucify the dragonfly on a sharp thorn, so it can't move.
Pain has no voice, only the flutter of wings.
The dragonfly is dead.
Only the thorn remains—with my heart impaled on its point,
with my heart with my heart
with my heart.

August 23

Rajamani calls from Hyderabad; speaking about his *darshan* at Yadagirigutta yesterday; in a crush of twenty thousand people, he says casually, "Miracles usually happen."

Nasara Reddi was supposed to come up from Nellore today but cancels. I will have to leave India without meeting him, a real loss. He has sent me a packet with carefully handwritten copies of his poems, to take with me to Jerusalem.

The midday Sureśvara lesson, on the word *aham*, "I": if you could only weed out the implicit *yuṣmad*, "you"—that is, any object, any otherness—from the domain of *aham*, perhaps the word might then ring true. (Is it possible to say "I" without "you?") Or, still more suggestively: *aham* "means" only in its *vilaya*, only while disappearing, much like present time? The word destroys itself, and its meaning, even as it is being uttered. Here is a linguistics full of promise.

* * *

Another afternoon deluge washes away the gray sultriness of morning. The continuing monsoon gives us these moments of relief. The river has receded to normal levels, but still the flow is very strong, the water dyed a rich brown from the huge quantities of soil it is bearing. Strangely, every time I see it—often, in these last days—I feel it flowing more deeply inside me, nothing like a memory, more like an intimate and living presence; and what I see looks deeper too, other, utterly unlike any river I have known. Like the word *I*? As with any true perception, what is at stake is singularity. One pares away likeness and is, with a little luck, left with the unique.

At three thirty Kanakaiah comes to read Pĕddana. The false Pravara finishes his hypocritical speech to Varuthini, who accepts his conditions. These two people want each other. So at last Varuthini's desire is on the point of being fulfilled:

> In a rush of passion, she held him
> with her burning breasts,
> and they kissed, searching
> for the very roots of their lips.

I had thought Kanakaiah might be a little shy about explaining this verse, but I was wrong. He has just finished cataloguing the three places for energetic kissing—*guhye netre lalāṭe ca paricumbanam*, private parts, eyes, forehead—when Sastrygaru comes in to present me with the first copy of his new book, the collection of his stories, literally hot off the press. It is an auspicious moment: I tell him that now, after waiting for the book for all these months, following the travails of finalizing the text and the cover and the preface, proofreading, struggling to keep the piles of expensive paper stored in his office dry from the rain, printing, binding—after all this, I can now safely (but sadly) leave Rajahmundry.

Poor Varuthini, however, at the very threshold of satisfaction, is once again left dangling and forlorn. It seems to be her nature, perhaps her fate. *Viraha*, lovesick longing, brings out the best in her, and in her poet. Perhaps for this reason, the interruption feels wholly natural, even inevitable. Still, when Sastrygaru heads upstairs to his office, we try once more to release her:

Flooded by desire, she bit him,
fell, exhausted, to the bed,
and now she was begging him
as gently he slapped her cheeks
to draw out her moans,
and there was anguish, still, and absence,
given voice in words
though her whole body thrilled to his touch
and her mouth was crying out in joy
until slowly, little by little,
the sounds of praise grew softer
and she lay quiet, eyes closed, cheeks glistening,
her movements now controlled,
while her jewels and bangles also
ceased their wild ringing.

That was the first time: and he
flowed like water in her loving.
(3.116)

I have rather a lot of feeling for Varuthini; she has had to wait a long time, long enough for Pĕddana to invent the concept of literary fiction in Telugu, and even at this moment of culmination she remains stuck with an ersatz lover. Again I ask myself, at this moment of release, if Varuthini intuits more than she says, more than the poet tells us explicitly. I've discussed the problem with Venkatesvara Rao, who is sure she doesn't know. She has the image of the real Pravara fixed in her mind (*bhāvambuna nilpi*, 3.3)—a physical imprint, not (says Venkatesvara Rao) an act of the imagination. That image is certainly the key to the pregnancy that will follow—but I am not so sure that Varuthini is as innocent as the text implies on the surface. What is knowledge, anyway? Is there not always a displacement? Again, *aham*, *tat*, *tvam*, I, it, you, the self-consuming pronouns, in place only when they are out of place, never meaning what they seem. "I" wants to be "me," even I want to be me; whatever it means, this is as close as I have ever come to it, so let me rejoice with Varuthini for now, for today, while I am still here on the banks of the Godavari and the rain continues to soak and cool.

August 25, Ryali

In a heavy downpour, Maayan and I go with Satyanarayana to Ryali, over the great bridge at Ravulapalem—my last real outing in the Godavari Delta before I leave. Rice shoots are already growing high in the fields, the black buffaloes glisten like soft obsidian slabs in the rain; everywhere there is depth of green, a vast palette of shades and textures, lush, soothing, caressing the eye.

We stand before the god, close enough to touch him. He is Jaganmohinīkeśava Svāmi, Vishṇu Ravishing the World, a black-green stone carved to perfection to reveal the blending of male and female. As with the Michelangelo *Pietà* in Florence—the one the sculptor discarded because he found some minor flaw in the stone—no space on that surface is left untouched, unseen. The ten avatars frame the image on its upper curve. Dancing girls, sages, the eagle Garuda stare, unblinking, from the edges. The god's hands end in tapering, delicate fingers; similarly, his feet, which are always wet: a spontaneous birth of the Ganges, another one of those by-now expected miracles. Basil leaves mask this gentle flow. The priest sprinkles some drops on our heads. He leads us behind the image, where we see the wholly feminine bun, *kŏppu*, with a *cāmanti* flower carved in the middle. The blend is radical and complete. It is an old image, perhaps thirteenth century, a masterpiece by any standard; the temple itself is new and gaily painted in pastels, with a row of plump green plaster parrots lining the length of the roof.

At the other end of the street, exactly opposite the Keśava temple, is Umākamaṇḍaleśvara, a *linga* shrine. Śiva, fascinated and aroused, followed Mohini—the seductive feminine form of Vishṇu—here, "forgetting for a while the presence of his consort, Parvathi Devi."[17] Drops of his seed fell all over the Godavari region, and everywhere the seed touched ground it turned to silver or gold. As if in a Telugu film, Mohini kept hiding from Śiva, appearing only for a flitting second in a flower garden, in the street, in the shade of a tree. A flower fell, *rālindi*, from Mohini's hair, and smelling it, Śiva looked up and saw the god as Mahāvishṇu—hence, says the priest, this place is named Ryali, as if from *rālu*, to fall. Or perhaps He, too, fell into place at that moment. Strange that God chooses to live in a village named "the Fall." Śiva could not bear to leave the presence of his beloved Mohini, so he has stayed here, too, directly across from her, until today. An ancient carved Ardhanārīśvara, the Androgyne, stands to the right of the sanctum in the Śiva temple, another radical (but horizontal) blending of male into female to reveal god.

Someone has thoughtfully put up a new, gaudy Ayyappan shrine, for the god born from the union of Śiva and Mohini, just behind the *linga* temple on the edge of a lake. The rain intensifies, deepening the greens and grays. We chat for a few minutes with one of the Śaiva priests. "So you speak Telugu. Are you from here?" "No, I live in Israel. Have you heard of Israel?" "Yes, I see in the newspapers. What language do they speak in Israel—Hindi or English?"

We walk the village street near the water. A row of houses, mostly with thatched roofs, some with tiles and ancient entrance porches, hugs the edge of the lake; women are scrubbing stainless-steel pots outside in the rain. A small group of women, copper water pots on their heads, giggle as they pass us, two exotic foreigners clutching their umbrellas (Maayan is wearing her huge white hat). As always, struck by the unpremeditated beauty of such a street, the humdrum intensity of its colors and shapes, I think to myself, "This is a place where I could happily live."

* * *

Sureśvara, final lesson (for now). So what is the answer? How can the Veda's enigmatic pronouncement, the *mahāvākya—tat tvam asi*, "You are this"—bring about a change in the listener if the words themselves are necessarily displaced, mostly metaphorical, even untrue? It works, Sureśvara says, because ignorance, *avidyā*, sits as precariously as a *badarī* fruit balanced on your nose. The slightest jiggle, a breath of air, even three words in (false) human language, are enough to blow it away. It is truth that is stable, dependable, and intimately familiar, something we know intuitively from the moment we are born. We know, that is, that we are God. Though we forget it minute by minute, it is still something we know for certain. How impudent, then is this ignorance which shamelessly, brazenly tries to pass itself off as *paramârtha*, ultimate truth!

Language need not tell the truth. It can twist itself in such a way that you might see something real beyond it; it can negate itself and disappear in the course of coming into being; and under the right circumstances, it can unsettle the outer veneer of our not knowing who we are. I think it's not a bad solution to the riddle.

August 26, Rajahmundry

Second visit to the Arts College: Kanakaiah has asked me to give a lecture about translating Telugu into English. Out of loyalty to him, I agree—though I usually dread these occasions. He has promised that there will be no ritual, no fuss, no garlands or shawls, only a straight simple talk with the MA students. In my dream toward morning, I am lecturing here, the Telugu flows (pure wish fulfillment), but at some point I switch to Sanskrit; whole chunks of Sanskrit sentences are still present in my mind when I wake. (Why did I not write them down? Were they the missing key?)

Maybe the dream was a good omen. The hall is packed with students, some faces familiar from my first visit, in February, soon after my arrival in town. Bangaresvara Sarma sits close to the front, yesterday's fever abated; I am more than grateful for his friendly smile. He, too, is my teacher.

On the way in, Kanakaiah shows me the huge inscription over the doorway leading to the rooms of the Telugu Department: Telugu is the Italian of the East. Not again, I think; to Kanakaiah I protest, "Why didn't you write that Italian is the Telugu of the West?" In the staff room there are pictures of all the usual luminaries, from Nannayya to Chilakamarti Lakshmi Narasimham. C. P. Brown, the great colonial lexicographer, is tucked into the corner, and below his picture—a Wordsworthian, neurasthenic youth burning a candle over an open book—is the usual idiotic boast, in his own words, about how he singlehandedly revived Telugu just as the flame was about to flicker out. It was, says Brown, no easy task. The brutal irony is that in this room, apparently, someone once thought this statement might be true.

When I begin, somehow words come, slowly, often awkwardly, but this time—unlike at Bommur some months back—they do come. I mix the two languages, keep the English very very slow, and mostly stick to Telugu. There are other friends in the room: Venkatesh, my neighbor from downstairs, caught sight of me on my way out and, at Kanakaiah's hearty invitation, has come to hear what the odd tenant upstairs does with his time. Sri Venkatesvara Rao, as always, is finely tuned, a passionate listener; he introduces me graciously and without the usual flourishes. On the blackboard they have written my name in white chalk. In the last moments before we begin, I point to the board and whisper to Venkatesvara Rao, "Is that person supposed to be me?" He assures me that it *must* be me. He seems quite certain. In a way, today, that is good news.

But best of all, for me, is singing four Telugu verses, three from Pĕddana, one of Bhaṭṭumūrti's, and slowly explaining them in Telugu. They all know these verses well, they have nothing to learn from me; still, sitting in the dusty room overlooking the immense cricket field, I feel for a fleeting moment that even I could perhaps be part of this long, fragile song, one voice blending into the others as the melody flows backward and forward—if, that is, time still exists. A certain peace descends.

* * *

Midnight. By now the flat is silent. The street silent. The buffaloes are sleeping outside Ratnamma's home. Even the monkeys—strangely jittery and aggressive these last few days—are silent. On Nehru Road, the betel-shop lady is closing for the night. I buy a little water, I say goodbye. "You are going away to Israel?" she asks. Israel has become a place she knows. "Go and come."

In the silence, Amichai's lines, which I read last week with Venkatesvara Rao:

> "A man who comes back to Jerusalem is aware that the places
> that used to hurt don't hurt any more.
> But a light warning remains in everything,
> like the movement of a light veil: warning."[18]

In a way it could be true. There are places that don't hurt so much now, places that Rajahmundry has healed with its magic. But there are the new hurts and losses, too: the foolish war that was fought; many young people dead; C. E. dead from cancer. The papers are full of darkness, and there is much talk of another, coming war. Always, Amichai says, there are soldiers training for some new war.

I guess I'll go back.

I could, perhaps, find words for tonight's double-hitter in my flat: a celebration of Patanjali Sastry's book, and a goodbye for me. I like the way books have to be released here in Andhra, like launching a boat on the Godavari. Publishing is only the first stage; after that comes the sharing, the gift to friends, as if for this, above all, one has gone to the trouble to write and print. So we are together, again, tonight, Smile, Sri Venkatesvara Rao, Kanakaiah, Bapi Raju, Sudhakar, D. R. Indra, Sastrygaru, and me—with a huge array of curries and *pulka*s; beer, too, and Scotch for those who want it. Of course, the power goes off just as everyone arrives; I scramble for candles, but after a few minutes the current returns. This is Rajahmundry. Smile has written a new poem on the occasion of my departure; he gives us copies in his incredible miniature handwriting; after a peg or two, he recites it, brilliantly, tears in his throat, as in mine. Venkatesvara Rao sings one of his *ghazal*s: "Enter the boat of song. . . ." A pause, and then the final couplet:

prati maniṣī ŏka manase vĕḷḷi palakarincu
nuvvainā nenainā ade katha grahincu

[Every person is a single mind. Go speak to it.
Whether you, whether I, it tells the same story.]

Kanakaiah, with a softness I have never seen in him before, speaks the parting, formal blessing, naming us one by one, taking leave, giving leave to depart. I could, perhaps, find the words—exile is at home mostly, perhaps only, in language—but I think I, too, will choose silence.

August 27

Before dawn, standing on my balcony, I watch a young woman from far down the street, still in her nightdress, climb the neighbors' compound wall across from my flat to pick fresh *moduga* flowers, no doubt for her morning *pūjā*. Like tiger-clawed Vyāghrapāda at Cidambaram, she aims for the higher branches of the tree as she balances herself precariously, toes clinging to the ledge of the wall. It is Vināyaka Caturthi, the holiday of the elephant-headed Gaṇapati/Vināyaka, so today the need is great. When she has enough, she gathers them up, folds them into her dress, and heads down the street in the direction of Ratnamma's, with two or three furtive glances back to see if anyone has noticed her. In the gray-green light she doesn't see me, in my *lungi*, on the balcony above.

Something in this predawn raid on the red flowers seems all too close to home, one day before I leave, bags stuffed with stolen treasures, mostly books and papers and fresh poems.

For days now the city has been filled with orange-and-blue Vināyakas in all sizes. Every street corner, every vendor, has them stacked in rows, a chorus of pastel elephant heads and twisting trunks. The streets are a flood of incense, green leaves, vines, fruits, flowers, and Sanskrit mantras. Auto rickshaws are mostly decked in green. Here and there one sees a *pandal* canopy built around a huge terra-cotta Vināyaka, sometimes with playful variation: on Nehru Road there is one painted bright purple, riding a blue goose. These are festival days, carnival time leading up to the immersion, later in the week, of all these Gaṇapatis in the Godavari. *Gangirĕddulu*—bulls decked in festive colors—prowl the neighborhood, their gypsy owners knocking on the door of house after house, seeking gifts in exchange for blessings.

* * *

I have promised Sashi and Bobby that I will speak at the Book Release at Anakapalli today, a parting gift. Patanjali Sastry was supposed to join us, but there was a medical emergency, and he had to drive Jaya and Amalu to Guntur in the middle of the night. Sashi and I set off with Lakku for Anakapalli, alone.

Bobby, whose splendid photographs grace Sashi's book, teaches at A.M.A.L. College, a well-known professional school, and it is here that the remorseless rituals of honoring grind on and on. A huge campus, founded by the business community, stretches at the foot of a green mountain, one in the long chain of Eastern Ghats. We sit pointlessly in the staff room for an hour, drinking tea, waiting for the Minister, the inevitable and necessary Minister, to arrive; but, though he is in town, no one has thought to send someone to accompany him to the college, so—mercifully, in my view—in the end the function unrolls without him. We begin outside in a light rain: it is Mother Teresa's birthday, and we drape endless garlands around her image, a horrible plastic cast. Then, in the big hall, there are the speeches, blessings, congratulations, the lighting of lamps, the onward cascade of garlands—enough to start a large flower shop—the heavy and useless commemorative plaques, the ringing of cell phones on the dais while the speakers drone on and on. . . . In short, an exercise in emptiness. The last residue of Andhra Buddhism. Perhaps someday I will understand the Andhra delight in these hollow shows—as if something to do with power were being obscurely enacted, the power to be honored, or honored *first*. I think South Indian kings have always spent most of their time doing just this; it is the stuff of politics, not an afterthought but of the very essence.

Anakapalli in the rain is dingy, black, forlorn. But when we finally break free at five o'clock, it is still light enough to visit Bojjanakonda, 3 kilometers from town. Originally Sanghârāma, then Sankaram, this site is another Buddhist wonder, the most enticing I have seen in Andhra. Two future Buddhas, Amoghasiddhi and Ratnasambhava—perhaps fourth century AD—sit in meditation above a hewn cave halfway up the hill. Near the top there is a lovely jumble of oddly shaped red-brick *stūpa*s, faintly reminiscent of the final ascent at Borobodur in central Java. As usual, the Bodhisattvas had a splendid view: row after row of blue hills with jagged peaks; flat green paddy fields below, green within green, green upon green, with patches of black palm trees, concave trunks bent opposite the convex reality of water and field; village women winding their way along the red earthen paths, great pots on their heads. I don't know if years of meditation gave these Buddhas-to-be either peace or freedom, but I think the ravishing landscape opening out before them was fashioned out of that visionary perfection of becoming—or was it the "mad wisdom" of emptiness?—that the Mahāyāna associates with truly being free.

August 28

But I almost wrote "February 28"—finishing, I have yet to begin.

A cool, clear morning. Another low-pressure system is building up over the Bay of Bengal. More rain will fall. Janarddana Rao comes with his niece and helpers to carry off my few possessions to Dhavalesvaram, gifts to Krishnayya and his family. Still in the Bojjanakonda mode of last evening, I feel light today, lighter than before, perhaps ever before, though as always I am dragging many books and papers home to Jerusalem. A gray drizzle begins. The flat is bare. And still, householder that I am, I feel a pang when I see them load the bed, the long, solid wooden table, and that ungainly but somehow deeply comforting blue office chair onto the rickshaw truck. They cover everything in cloth and plastic, tie it all down, and then they, and the mute things, are gone.

As if a circle had come around, as if a season were coming to its end, it feels oddly right to go, though I would love to stay and see the rice grow heavy and bow.

I bring a few odds and ends, small gifts, to Nirmala and Satyanarayana. I thank her for having fed me like a maharaja for seven happy months. They won't let me go: the usually stolid Satyanarayana wipes his eyes, it is worse, Nirmala says, than saying goodbye to someone in the family. Over and over: *cālā bādhagā undi*, "It is terribly sad"—the refrain I keep hearing these days.

At around three o'clock, after I have finished packing, my suitcase stretched to the limit, Venkatesh comes up from downstairs. He is bearing gifts—a heavy diary made for Sai Baba devotees, and Sai's commentary on the *Bhagavad Gītā*. I know that, like the mitten in the Russian folktale that shelters all the animals of the forest but cracks open when, at the end, a small ant tries to squeeze its way in, my suitcase will split if I try to add these books. Besides: the Afro hairdo, the orange robe—for the hundredth time, but as if it were the first, Venkatesh points to him and says, "He is Allah, He is Jesus, He is Krishna, He is an avatar. When you come back, you must definitely, *tappanisarigā*, without fail, do his *darshan*." Yes, I say, we will do the *darshan* together. Pudupartti is perhaps the only place in South India I am not eager to see.

Kanakaiah arrives to say goodbye; his wife has a medical appointment, so he will not be able to come to the station. I offer him the sweet head of Venkaṭeśvara, gaily painted yellow and black, that I brought back from Kondapalli many months ago; this god has graced my *pūjā* room along with Maya's conch and a pounded-brass square medallion of Krishna and Rukmini from Ahmedabad and photographs of Nellaiyappar from Tirunelveli and the Ksīrârāma-linga and Sannyāseśvara from Dharmavaram—a seemingly random, beneficent collection that reflects my happy wanderings. When it is time to part, I don't see the shiny Venkaṭeśvara head, so I ask Kanakaiah where he has put it. He pats his pocket, content. It is good, I think, to carry god in one's pocket.

* * *

Like Adam at the outer edge of Eden, I stand in the dark, fragrant street, waiting for the taxi. The rain has stopped. A young moon joins us, along with a few wisps of cloud. What a beautiful street it is, I say to Sastrygaru, surely one of the loveliest in the world, rather like the Champs Elysée, only much nicer. The city is full of celebrants, the roads clogged with traffic. Under the bridge, past the photo shop, past the old bus stand, through the market: a charmed world, every inch of it alive, singing. Somehow I didn't think this day would come. At the station an immense pink Gaṇapati sits in jolly pose opposite the entrance, with Brahmin priests waving lamps before him, chanting Vedic mantras. We wait for another, fully embodied, living Gaṇapati, awkward in rubbery orange and blue, to finish walking across the street.

Venkatesvara Rao has stopped on his way to the station to photocopy for me the essay he has just finished writing, a daring attempt to imagine what the First Poet, Nannayya, was like as a man. Indragaru, my new friend, has also come to see me off. Satyanarayana and Nirmala are there before us on the platform, Nirmala in a radiant orange sari and gold earrings, as if she had been summoned to the royal court. Smile—as always—has brought me food, *chapati*s and curry for the journey. The Godavari Express is twenty minutes late.

We sit, we stand, we wait, Sastry tells some good jokes, which help. Language, language, what use is it, especially at moments like this, but how I long for it, for even one more Telugu word before leaving. Learning Telugu, I say to Venkatesvara Rao, is like what Degas said about painting: it's easy when you don't know how, but very difficult when you do.

Then suddenly it is time. In the flurry of leaving, finding my berth, trying to see them one last time through the dusty, opaque window, paying the coolie staggering under the weight of so many Telugu books, in the hubbub of the vendors' cries and then the shift into movement, wheels clacking, platform receding, I forget, I fail even to notice the Godavari as it passes beneath us. It is a good thing I had the presence of mind to say goodbye to her, to ask her permission to go, when we came through town late last night. "Go and come," she said to me.

August 29, Secunderabad

6:30 AM

Like a spring uncoiling. At daybreak I stare out the open door of the bogie. We pass Bhongir, a black torrent of stone. Telangana: goats file along a gray dirt path. The light turns white. Low clouds. The goatherd, half asleep, hides his head in folds of cloth. Bicycles. Smoke. Someone is making tea on a wood-fed flame. Stooped *tangeḍu* trees scattered over the cracked, dry plain. A lonely palm. Thorns. Eyes. Rocks.

At Secunderabad station, outside the main gate, in the crush and flow of the travelers, in light rain and a cold breeze, a man stands his ground, holding aloft packets of the short wooden sticks people used to use to brush their teeth. The crowd opens and closes around him like a river flowing over an upright stone. Barefoot, in a red shirt, stark against the early light, with astonishing regularity, in a resonant, musical voice, every twelve or thirteen seconds he sings: "*yaapulaaaa*. . . ." This is, or once was, *pannupulla*, tooth sticks. Up, down, up, a steady melody. No one seems to be buying, perhaps no one uses them anymore, and I wonder if he will stand here for hours, not giving up hope, ringing his mantra like a bell.

me-ra dar manzel-i jānān che amn-i 'aish chūn har dam
jarash faryād mīdārad ke bar bandīd meḥmalhā

[In the caravanserai of my heart,
how sure of life can I be?
At every moment the bell cries out:
"Pack up. Time to depart."][19]

Uncoiled. Heading west.

August 31, Kollapuram

Years ago I promised Vimala that one day I would come with her to her *ūru*, the village-town where she was born and grew up, and which she passionately loves. She is a proud Telangana woman, of rugged Velama stock; she has wanted to show me her native landscapes, with their phantasmagoric rocks, the ancient temples, the Krishna River flowing nearby. So I have set aside my last days in Andhra, this time around, for a visit to Kollapuram, some three- to four-hours' drive south from Hyderabad, in the heart of the Deccan plateau.

We set off early from Santoshnagar, but within minutes we are lost, trapped in a sea of mud; they are renovating the roads that connect the eastern neighborhoods of Hyderabad with the highway, and all the usual points of access and exit are blocked. For an hour or so we plunge madly through the sticky, dark swamp. Will we ever reach Kollapuram? Probably the roads used to be just like this during the monsoon months, in the old days, when the Hyderabadi Nizam ruled over his elegant, dusty domain. The driver is frustrated and irritated, but I am, as nearly always when headed for some new place, happy and at peace. There is time, a whole day ahead, either we will reach Kollapuram or we won't, I am still in Andhra, with Telugu blossoming around me.

In a heroic act of extrication, the driver manages to weave his way onto some nonexistent path that ultimately feeds into the main road. The city is expanding furiously in this direction, as in all others; after another hour on the road we approach the site of the vast new airport that is being planned. What was once a tiny city of Indo-Saracenic palaces and *madrasa*s on the bank of the Musi is now one of the fastest growing cities in Asia, a living being spreading its wings over distant rocks and streams.

We drive for an hour or two through the brown, desiccated world of rural Telangana. On either side: tamarind trees, thorny shrubs, goat tracks, and the giant boulders, burned smooth by sunlight, that are like the playing pieces left over from some game of the gods. Suddenly we notice, in the middle of a distant field, a cluster of ornate ruins. Vimala has to see them up close; I follow her through the caked clay and briars until we stand before what, clearly, is someone's elaborate tomb, with stone cupola and stucco arches and the remains of finely wrought latticework. The building is crumbling, forgotten, and there is no one near to tell us the name of the Sufi wonder-worker or, perhaps, some doomed hero who was buried here together with his wives. The interior stinks of bats and bird droppings but, all in all, this lost tomb offers us the standard romantic fantasy—Ozymandias of Avanca, the village just down the road. All that is missing is a live broadcast of Rimsky-Korsakov's *Scheherazade*, echoing over the wasteland—as once happened to me at Persepolis as I picked my way over the broken stones.

Avanca has a many-pillared temple, also neglected; and there are old carvings, some in Kākatiya style, scattered through the village streets. One—an unidentifiable goddess with broken arms—is still being worshiped, as you can see from the fresh daubs of paint and the garlands draped over it. The villagers live nonchalantly in the midst of these ancient visions. Vimala says there are stones from Avanca in the Mahbubnagar Museum; the archaeologists have been here before us. Barefoot boys emerge from their faded white school to gawk at us, two strangers from the city who have happened by, as if fallen from a distant planet. One of them, seized by a sudden intuition of our curious interests, remembers the immense stone Gaṇapati sitting peacefully in the fields a mile or two away; so we sweep the boy into our car and he directs us over a bumpy dirt path through the dry fields to the god—another ancient carving that seems to be growing organically out of the soil, like tree or crop, a ripening god-crop waiting to be harvested. The stone, with its vast elephant's head, is beige-gray-white, but there is a strange glow to it as well against the backdrop of the boulders, as if it had been delicately brushed with gold.

By early afternoon we are in Kollapuram: a sudden rush of streets radiating out from the bus station, the bazaar, and the huge old palace, in faded stucco, of the Kollapuram kings, now deserted. It is another Orientalist wonder, utterly true to type, the last relic of the days of dancing girls and Telugu poets and royal elephants (the latter used to stand, until quite recently, on the cross-street here). What magnificent poems were first performed by their local authors in the royal presence—and then forgotten? Did they celebrate the looming rocks, the old stone fort, the green-blue river, the doomed and futile heroics of generations of warring cowherds? There was a semidetached *zenana* for the king's wives and mistresses, with many windows, probably the only link to the outer world. The courtyard is overgrown with weeds. A haunting charm cloaks this desolation. I find it hard to shake the feeling that I have again arrived at the end of the world, the last stop before one falls off into empty space.

I like the city. Vimala is evidently in a kind of ecstasy of homecoming: various cousins and friends pour into the old family home, or what is left of it, with its beautiful wooden lintels and heavy wooden chairs and the inevitable massive village bed (meant to sleep how many people? Four, five, more? We will see tonight just how many human beings can be crammed into one small village bedroom). She was born in this house, where her cousin Srinu, a schoolteacher, now lives. They are still celebrating Gaṇesha's festival; the street in front of the house has been closed off by a white tent housing the god's painted image, so we have to wind our way in through a medieval alleyway, angular and narrow, leading to the back door. A steady cacophony blares from the loudspeakers outside. Some of the visitors are recovering from severe fever—Chikungunya, the mosquito-borne disease that is devastating all of Andhra. Literally half the town is sick with it. I meet the newly elected mayor, *sarpanch*—only five days in office—and can't help upbraiding him for the town's failure to deal with this plague. What, after all, would it take to rid Kollapuram of mosquitoes? A simple, collective effort, organized from above, should suffice. Suddenly, a level of frustration that I normally suppress, that hardly filters up into consciousness, breaks through my defenses, and my words carry a bitter sting. The *sarpanch* offers statistics and reminds me that he is new in the job. Give me time, he says, come back in a month; anyway, they are spraying regularly. . . . He can't quite take in the fact that I am from Israel, though I tell him three times. He speaks volubly and fails to listen, and in the end—the perfect politician—he hugs me and wishes me a safe journey home to New York.

* * *

At night we walk up the hill to the Venkaṭeśvara temple. We ring the bell to call the god to attention; we are the only pilgrims at this late hour, he may well have gone to sleep. A hot, dry breeze starts up for a few seconds, false promise of relief. For a while we stare down at the silent lights of the town. Kollapuram lies huddled at our feet; in the distance are the black, stony hills and the Krishna River, twisting southward. Sitting on the stone steps, fruitlessly fending off the endless swarms of mosquitoes—are they infected?—I remember, suddenly, that I was supposed to reinvent myself in Andhra. The absurdity of the idea suddenly breaks through the final barriers, and, cheerfully sharing the hilarity with the mosquitoes, the sliver of moon, the lonely deity inside the shrine, the lime-scented breeze, I let the laughter wash through me, cleansing the earnest remnants of hope. I will be going home as I came, heavy of tongue, light at heart, hungry still.

And yet there is that uncanny intimation of a depth that I have known nowhere else in my life, and that has infused each of these days. I push aside the impulse to analyze it, to examine its reality. Why defend myself against it? Happiness, fortunately, can't be falsified. For months I have been wandering through a fierce and gentle music, or perhaps it was wandering into me; and like the first time, decades ago, at moments

I, too, broke into words that took me far beyond myself, that shaped and colored feeling, thought, that felt like something rich and true—almost true. But then truth was not the issue. It is the depth that counts. I turn back to the shrine, I wake the god once more, hoping he won't mind; I ask permission to depart. This time, rather uncharacteristically, he is silent.

Appendix

Nala and the *Naishadhīya-carita*

The story first appears in the *Mahābhārata* (book 3) but is retold in innumerable versions, including the magnificent, complex poem (*mahākāvya*) by Śrīharsha, *Naishadhīya-carita* (twelfth century). This *Naishadhīya-carita* inspired sophisticated poetic versions in Telugu (Śrīnātha's *Śringāra-naishadhamu*) and in Tamil (Ativīrarāmapāṇṭiyan's *Naiṭatam*, sixteenth century).

Nala, king of Nishadha, learns from a golden goose of the incomparable beauty of Damayanti, daughter of the king of Vidarbha. The goose, set free by Nala, flies to Vidarbha and speaks to Damayanti of Nala's perfections; she, too, falls in love. Her father announces a *svayamvara* ceremony, at which Damayanti will choose her husband from among all the candidates who present themselves. On his way to the ceremony, Nala is intercepted by Indra, king of the gods, and three other divine regents of cosmic space: Agni, god of fire; Varuṇa, god of the ocean; and Yama, lord of the dead. They demand that Nala go to Damayanti as their love messenger and persuade her to choose one of them at the *svayamvara*. Nala has no choice but to accept this cruel mission. The gods enable him to enter Damayanti's palace unseen—but in Śrīharsha's telling, the women clearly sense his presence, and his image is reflected precisely in the mirrors of the palace and on its shiny floors. Against his own deep feelings, Nala pleads with Damayanti to marry Indra or one of the other gods; she indignantly refuses and promises to choose her mortal beloved, Nala.

On the day of the *svayamvara*, the four gods, recognizing Damayanti's passion for Nala, assume Nala's form and stand before her along with the many human kings. Damayanti thus sees five identical Nalas in the line of suitors. She prays to the gods for help in this moment of crucial choice, and suddenly four of the Nalas turn out to be a little different—their feet do not quite touch the ground, their garlands never wilt in the heat, and they neither blink nor sweat. She understands and places the garland signifying her choice around the neck of the real, human Nala.

This happy conclusion, and its sequel in the wedding and first lovemaking of the couple, is as far as Śrīharsha takes the story. In the epic, however, the *svayamvara* is only the prelude to a long story of exile, disguise, and eventual restoration. Kali, the ugly spirit of our current age, was late for the ceremony; very indignant at not having won Damayanti, he lurks in ambush for Nala. One day when Nala forgets to wash his feet before praying (or leaves a tiny spot of skin unwashed), Kali steals into his body. He also incites his brother, Pushkara, to challenge Nala to a game of dice; and Dvāpara, the spirit of the previous aeon, stacks the dice against him.

Nala, gripped by the madness of the dice, loses everything, his entire kingdom. Expelled from his city by the new king, Pushkara, Nala and Damayanti wander in the wilderness. There Nala, driven by Kali within him, abandons his sleeping wife to her fate. He is bitten by a snake, Karkoṭaka, whom he saves from a forest fire; the bite transforms Nala into a hideous dwarf, Bāhuka, a deep disguise. Damayanti makes her way to the Cedi kingdom, where she works as a hairdresser until she is recognized by a messenger sent by her father and brought home to Vidarbha.

Nala/Bahuka finds employment as cook and charioteer with Rituparṇa, king of Ayodhya. Damayanti sends messengers to scour the land in search of her husband; one of them comes to Ayodhya, speaks with Bahuka, and reports his strangely suggestive words to Damayanti. She suspects this Bahuka must be Nala. A second *svayamvara* is announced, in Ayodhya, and Rituparna asks his charioteer to drive him there in great haste. On the way, Rituparna reveals to Bahuka his superhuman skill at rapid calculation; in exchange for this useful wisdom, the *aksha-hridaya*, or "heart of the dice," Bahuka teaches Rituparna the art of controlling horses, *aśva-hridaya*. At Ayodhya, Damayanti puts Bahuka through a series of tests and concludes, correctly, that he is none other than Nala. Thus recognized by his beloved wife, Nala casts off his disguise and reverts to his natural, human form. He returns to his capital to challenge Pushkara to one last, all-or-nothing throw of the dice (even Damayanti is included in the stakes); and thanks to the new wisdom he has acquired, this time Nala wins and regains his kingdom.

Selected Dramatis Personae

Jyotirmaya Sarma · Professor of political thought at the University of Hyderabad. Former editor of the *Hindu* and the *Times of India* in Hyderabad. An authority on modern Indian (particularly nationalist) thought. Student of Isaiah Berlin and of the great Hindustani vocalist, Mallikarjuna Mansur.

Kanakaiah, M. C. · Specialist in classical Telugu literature (Government Arts College, Rajahmundry). Poet, author of a study of satire in classical Telugu.

Krishnayya, M. V. · Professor emeritus (philosophy) of Andhra University, Waltair, Visakhapatnam. An expert on Buber and Gandhi, Krishnayya is also a practicing field anthropologist, with unparalleled expertise in the village cults and rituals of northern coastal Andhra and the Godavari Delta.

Malamoud, Charles · Sanskritist, Paris. Specialist in Vedic thought and ritual. Author of *Cuire le monde: Rite et pensée dans l'inde ancienne* (1989) and three other volumes of scholarly studies on ancient India.

Narayana Rao, Velcheru · The most prominent scholar of Telugu civilization in this generation; Krishnadevaraya Professor of

Languages and Cultures of Asia at the University of Wisconsin. Author of the pathbreaking study, *The Structure of Literary Revolutions in Telugu* (*Tĕlugulo kavitā vipravāla svarūpam*, 1978), and of many volumes on the classical and modern literatures of Andhra Pradesh.

Patanjali Sastry, Tallavajjhala · Short-story writer, novelist, essayist, scholar of classical Indian art and architecture (Ph.D. dissertation on the Alampur temples), and environmental activist.

Rajamani, V. K. · Photographer (in Chennai) who has documented and photographed nearly all surviving sites of artistic production in Tamil Nadu and Kerala.

Ramakrishnan, S. · Tamil critic, editor, lexicographer, and publisher. Founder of Cre-A—one of the major Tamil publishing houses, specializing in modern literature and scholarship, and producer of the superb *Crea-A Dictionary of Contemporary Tamil.*

Sashi Sekhar, Talavajjhala · Historian, archaeologist, poet, critic. Author of *The Wheel and Its Tracks* (2006), a study and photo-documentation of nearly all known Buddhist sites in Andhra Pradesh; and of a historical and cultural study (in Telugu) of the Godavari River and the many sites that line its banks, from its source to the sea.

Smile—more formally, Mohammed Ismail (b. 1946), distinguished poet and short-story writer; author of the famous story "Khālī Sīsālu" (Empty Bottles), thus sometimes known as Sisala Ismail (to distinguish him from the well-known poet Ismail of Kakinada). Smile, formerly an officer in the government tax department, knew every Telugu writer of consequence in the second half of the twentieth century.

Sri Venkatesvara Rao, Rentala · Specialist in modern Telugu literature (Government Arts College, Rajahmundry); author of *Avagāhana*, a volume of collected critical essays; aficionado of Carnatic music.

Notes

SPRING

1 Arab-Jewish Partnership, one of the most effective of the peace organizations during the second Intifada.

2 John Greenfield Leonard, "Kandukuri Viresalingam, 1848–1919: A Biography of an Indian Social Reformer" (Ph.D. diss., University of Wisconsin, 1970).

3 Ibid., 23.

4 Ibid., 22.

5 H. Morris, *Godavary District Manual* (Madras: Government Press, 1878); cited in ibid., 23.

6 Journal of F. N. Alexander, July 11, 1860; cited in ibid., 23–24.

7 Ibid., 25.

8 Cekkiḻār, *Pĕriya purāṇam* (Koyamputtur: Kovaittamiḻcankam, 1975), 1532–34, 2476–85.

9 *Mevar poṟ kankul vara*, "Night came on like a foe": Ibid., *Tirukuṟipputtŏṇṭanāyaṉār purāṇam* 123.

10 āṉār ilaiye ayaṉum tirumālum
kāṇā aṭimuṭimuṉ kāṇpataṟku—meṉāḷ
iravu tiruvārūril ĕntai pirāṉ cĕṉṟa
paravai tiruvāyil paṭi

Cited by To. Mu Paskarat Tontaiman, *Venkaṭam mutal kumari varai: Kāvirik karaiyile* (Tirunelveli: S. R. Cuppiramaniya Pillai, 1970), 91.

HEAT

1 Smile, "Kotta samudram," in *Okhaḍe* (Vijayawada: Kavitvam Pracuranalu, 1990), 12.

2 Velcheru Narayana Rao and David Shulman, *Classical Telugu Poetry: An Anthology* (Berkeley and Los Angeles: University of California Press, 2002), 164; with thanks to R. Sri Venkatesvara Rao for a change in the final line.

3 M. V. Krishnayya collected this oral narrative in the course of fieldwork at Simhacalam.

4 Muslims.

5 K. Siva Reddy, "Padyam rāyaṭāniki," in *Varsham Varsham* (Hyderabad: Published by the author, 2004), 77.

6 G. Nagarajan, *Paṭaippukaḷ* (Nagercoil: Kalachchuvadu, 1997), 87.

RAINS

1 Preface to Oriana Fallaci, *Interview with History* (Boston: Houghton Mifflin, 1976), 13.

2 Thomas Mann, *Doktor Faustus* (Frankfurt: Fischer Verlag, 1999), 261–62.

3 *Gāthasaptasatī* 1.49; trans. Martha Ann Selby in *The Circle of Six Seasons* (New Delhi: Penguin Books, 2003), 22.

4 Cited by John Greenfield Leonard, "Kandukuri Viresalingam, 1848–1919: A Biography of an Indian Social Reformer" (Ph.D. diss., University of Wisconsin, 1970) ,79.

5 Like every beautiful woman, Damayanti has eyebrows that look (and act) like Kāma's bow—but if you focus on the gap between them, what you see is the weapon of a conquered foe.

6 *Babylonian Talmud*, tractate *Berachot* 1.2.

7 Pingaḷi Sūranna, *Prabhāvatī-pradyumnamu*; trans. V. Narayana Rao and D. Shulman as *The Demon's Daughter* (Albany: State University of New York Press, 2006).

8 Śrīnātha, *Bhīma-khaṇḍamu* 1.11; trans. V. Narayana Rao and D. Shulman in *Classical Telugu Poetry: An Anthology* (Berkeley and Los Angeles: University of California Press, 2002), 119.

9 Ismayil, *Kavitalu* (Kakinada: Twinkle Publishers, 1989), 166–67.

10 George Seferis, *A Poet's Journal: Days of 1945–1951* (Cambridge, MA: Harvard University Press, 1974), 161.

11 Pingaḷi Sūranna, *Prabhāvati-pradyumnamu* 4.116; trans. Narayana Rao and Shulman in *The Demon's Daughter*, 60.

12 Annamayya, *God on the Hill: Temple Poems from Tirupati*, trans. Velcheru Narayana Rao and David Shulman (New York: Oxford University Press, 2005), 22.

13 Ismayil, *Kavitalu*, "Ṭī kappu," 112–13.

14 Kālidāsa, *Abhijñānaśākuntala* (Varanasi: Chowkhamba Sanskrit Series, 1976), 5.2.

15 Tyāgarāja, *Tĕra tiyyaga rādā*; trans. Narayana Rao and Shulman in *Classical Telugu Poetry*, 300.

16 Luis Fernando Verissimo, *Borges and the Eternal Orangutans* (New York: New Directions, 2005), 86.

17 *Śrī-jagan-mohinī-keśava-svāmi divya caritra* (Ryali, 2006), p. 1.

18 Amichai, "Yerushalayim 1967," in *Shirei Yerushalayim*, trans. Stephen Mitchell (Jerusalem: Shocken, 1987); reprinted in *The Selected Poetry of Yehuda Amichai*, ed. Chana Bloch and Stephen Mitchell (Berkeley and Los Angeles: University of California Press, 1996).

19 Hafez, *Diwan*, 1.3.

Glossary

abhisārikā (Skt) · heroine of Sanskrit love poetry and Pahari painting, on her way to a nocturnal rendevous.

abhyudayamu (Tel) · genre of Telugu courtly poems depicting the daily routine of the king.

Advaita (Skt) · the classical philosophical school of nondualism that teaches that only God, Brahman, is real, that what is real is a single unity, and that the diversity that we perceive is the result of the fallacious splitting and projection of our minds.

agrahāram (Tel) · the Brahmin quarter of a South Indian village, often set up on lands endowed by a local king for this purpose.

ākāśa (Skt) · the subtle medium of ether through which sound passes; one of the five elements.

Āndhra bhojanam (Tel) · a rice meal.

Appanna (Tel) · see *Simhacalam*.

ārāma (Skt) · a set of five temples, formerly Buddhist shrines, spread through the Andhra Delta.

Aruna Sairam · *Carnatic* vocalist, trained in the classical tradition of T. Brinda and Veena Dhanammal.

aṭṭavīraṭṭānam (Tam) · the eight sites of Śiva's heroic feats in the Tamil country.

Bhārata-deśa (Skt) · India.

Bhartṛhari · fifth-century philosopher of language, author of the *Vākya-padīya*, a profound meditation on problems of meaning, part-whole relations, and temporality.

Bodhisattva (Skt) · a potential Buddha; see *Mahāyāna*.

Brahmā (Skt) · the creator god.

Brāhmaṇa texts · the second stratum in the canonical Vedic corpus; Sanskrit texts from the first half of the first millennium BC, dealing largely with the sacrificial cult and its esoteric meanings.

Brown, C. P. (1798–1884) · scholar, Telugu lexicographer, administrator, and judge in nineteenth-century Andhra. Brown is responsible for the publication of many classical Telugu works and the author of the indispensable *Dictionary Telugu and English*.

caitya (Skt) · Buddhist monument, often an apsidal hall with votive *stūpa*.

cakra (Skt) · the wheel or discus carried by *Vishṇu*.

camatkāra (Skt) · the smacking of the lips in wonder.

candana-yātra (Tel) · see *Candanotsavam*.

Candanotsavam (Tel) · "Sandal-peeling Festival" at *Simhacalam*, when the thick coat of sandal paste covering the god is scraped away to expose the true image, *nija-rūpa*, underneath.

Cankam poetry · the earliest surviving corpus of Tamil poetry, divided into *akam* ("inner") poems of love and *puṟam* ("outer") poems of heroism and lament; composed in the early centuries AD.

Carnatic music · the classical South Indian tradition of Indian music; among its most famous composers are *Tyāgarāja*, *Muttusvāmi Dīkshitar*, and Śyāma Śāstri, all from late eighteenth-century Tiruvarur.

cāṭu (Skt) · a free-floating oral verse.

Chalam · pen name of Gudipati Venkatachalam (1894–1974), prolific Telugu novelist and essayist, early feminist, and author of the famous novella *Maidānam* (1927), about a young Telugu married woman who flees into the wilderness with her Muslim lover.

Chalukya (Skt) · Deccan dynasties, beginning in the sixth century in the west; eastern Chalukyas ruled in the Andhra Delta during the ninth to eleventh centuries.

Chola (Tam) · dynasty of kings based in the Kaveri Delta that ruled over the Tamil land and much of South India (mid-ninth century to thirteenth century). The Chola period marks the apogee of classical Tamil civilization in state building, poetry, art, and sculpture (including the famous Chola-period bronzes).

cinna rasālu (Tel) · a type of mango.

dahara-vidyā (Skt) · secret knowledge of reality according to the Upanishads.

Dalit (Tel) · modern neologism for low-caste person/ "Untouchable."

darbar (Persian) · royal court.

darshan, darśanam (Skt) · seeing the god, the main point of pilgrimage to a temple.

devadasi (Tel) · temple dancer.

dharma-karta (Tel) · executive officer (of a temple).

dhoti (Tel) · a simple cloth worn by men to cover the lower half of their body.

dhrupad (Hindi) · a classical style of north Indian (Hindustani) music.

Dignāga · fifth-century Buddhist logician, perhaps settled in the Andhra Delta.

dora (Tel) · "master," European.

drishṭi (Skt) · the evil eye.

Gaṇapati (Skt) · elephant-headed deity; see *Vināyaka*.

gandharva (Skt) · a superhuman being, one of a class of semidivine musicians.

Gaṇeśa (Skt) · see *Gaṇapati*; *Vināyaka*.

-garu (Tel) · honorific suffix.

ghazal · major verse form in Persian and Urdu, built around end-rhyming couplets; in the final verse, the poet addresses himself by name.

gopuram (Skt) · the many-storied tower at the entrance to a temple enclosure.

griha-praveśam (Skt) · ritual entry into the new home.

Hafez · Persian poet of fourteenth-century Shiraz, master of the *ghazal* form.

hāratti (Skt) · lustration of an image in temple worship.

Hari-kathā (Skt) · a genre of performing classical mythological stories in oral song and narrative.

homa (Skt) · the offering, usually of clarified butter, into the fire.

IAS · Indian Administrative Service.

Indra (Skt) · king of the gods.

iṣṭa-devatā (Skt) · one's personal deity.

jamukulavāru (Tel) · oral bards singing epic poems.

jangiḍi (Tel) · a large wicker basket.

jīvâtma (Skt) · the individual divine self.

kacceri (Tam) · the usual word for a concert in South India (< Urdu *kacahrī*, "court," "revenue office"—where concerts were originally held).

kākara-kāya (Tel) · bitter gourd.

Kaḷāpūrṇodayamu · late sixteenth-century *Telugu prabandha*, novelesque in character, by Pingaḷi Sūranna; translated as *The Sound of the Kiss, or the Story that Must Never be Told* (Columbia University Press, 2002).

Kālidāsa · the greatest of the classical Sanskrit poets (probably early fifth century AD). Author of the *Abhijñāna-śākuntala*, among other masterpieces (see *Śākuntala*).

Kali Yuga (Skt) · our present age, fourth (and worst) in a declining series.

kāma (Skt) · desire.

Kampan · twelfth-century author of the Tamil *Rāmāyaṇa*, one of the masterpieces of Tamil poetry.

Kanyā-śulkamu · Gurajada Appa Rao's play, *Girls for Sale*, composed at Vizianagaram in the 1890s and revised in the first decade of the twentieth century; the foundational text of Telugu modernism.

kathā (Skt) · story.

kavi-goshṭhi (Skt) · assembly of poets.

kāvya (Skt) · intensified or elevated poetry.

kolam (Tam) · rice-flour threshold design; see *muggulu*.

Kolleru Lake · one of Asia's largest bodies of sweet water, situated in West Godavari district.

kriti (Skt) · a composition, usually in three parts, sung in *Carnatic music*.

Kuṟavanci (Tam) · operatic dance-drama produced in the royal courts.

laḍḍu-prasādam (Tel) · sweet balls given by the god to pilgrims.

linga (Skt) · the elongated, phallic-shaped sign of the god *Śiva*.

lingodbhava (Skt) · *Śiva*'s revelation as a *linga* of fire.

Mādhyamika (Skt) · the central philosophical stream of Buddhist *Mahāyāna*, associated with *Nāgârjuna*.

Mahābhārata · major Sanskrit epic describing the internecine conflict between two branches of a single family, the five *Pāṇḍava* brothers and their Kaurava cousins.

Mahāyāna (Skt) · the "Great Vehicle," the form of Buddhism that crystallized in the early centuries AD, perhaps along the Orissa-Andhra coast, and spread from India to China, Japan, and Tibet. Mahāyāna Buddhism is profoundly oriented toward the figure of the *Bodhisattva*, who, although standing at the very threshold of final enlightenment, chooses to stay in the world out of compassion for other living beings.

mantrin (Skt) · adviser; prime minister.

mridangam (Tam) · South Indian drum.

Mucukunda (Skt) · legendary *Chola* king with a monkey's face; said to have brought the god *Tyāgarāja* from heaven down to earth, to the temple of Tiruvarur.

muggulu (Tel) · threshold designs usually made from rice powder, traced at dawn by the women of the house; in Tamil, *kolam*.

mukti (Skt) · final liberation.

mūrcchanā (Skt) · fixed ascending and descending scales.

Muttusvāmi Dīkshitar · late eighteenth-century composer in the classical *Carnatic* tradition; lived in Tiruvarur. His "signature," always present in the final verse of his compositions, is Guruguha, a name of the god Murukan.

Nāḍi (Skt) · diagnosis by feeling the pulse; divination by random opening of a text.

Nāgârjuna · second-century AD Buddhist philosopher, perhaps from Nagarjunakonda in Andhra; the central figure in the early *Mahāyāna* school of the *Mādhyamika*, the "Middle Way." For Nāgârjuna, our native habit of distinguishing subject from object is simply wrong, a mistake that embroils us in suffering.

Nagu momu · composition by *Tyāgarāja*, late eighteenth-century *Carnatic* composer, to his personal deity, *Rāma*, in Abheri *rāga*.

Naishadhīya-carita · Sanskrit masterpiece by the twelfth-century poet *Śrīharsha*, telling the story of Nala and Damayanti.

naivedya (Skt) · an offering to a deity.

Nāngiar-kūttu (Malayalam) · solo dance style in the Kerala Kūṭiyāṭṭam tradition.

Nannayya · first Telugu poet, from the time of the Eastern Calukya king Rājarājanarendra (eleventh century).

Narasimha (Skt) · the Man-Lion avatar of *Vishṇu*.

Nasara Reddi · Telugu poet, master of the Telugu haiku; teacher of classical Telugu in Nellore.

Naṭarāja · *Śiva* as lord of the dance, from Cidambaram in the *Tamil* country.

Nāyaka · the protagonist or hero of Sanskrit drama.

nija-rūpam (Skt) · the true image or true self.

nirguṇa (Skt) · without quality or form.

Niẓam (Persian) · the title of the Asaf Jahi rulers of Hyderabad between 1720 and 1948.

padam (Tel) · short verse form intended for musical or dance performance.

Paiḍi Talli (Tel) · golden goddess of Vizianagaram city, and deity of the Vizianagaram kings. Each year in October her festival is celebrated by hundreds of thousands; her priest, in whom she resides, is seated at the edge of the fifteen-foot Sirimanu log and travels back and forth, hovering between heaven and earth, from the temple to the royal palace while the devotees pelt him with bananas.

paṇam (Tam) · small coin.

pandal (Tel) · canopy.

Pāṇḍavas · the five brothers who are the heroes of the Sanskrit *Mahābhārata*.

Pāṇini · Sanskrit grammarian of the mid-first millennium BC, author of the *Aṣṭâdhyāyī*.

pāpa (Skt) · evil, specifically the burden of past evil deeds.

paramâtma (Skt) · the supreme, divine self.

patikam (Tam) · a verse form in ten or eleven stanzas.

pāyasam (Tel) · a sweet milk pudding.

Pĕddana (Tel) · early sixteenth-century Telugu poet, author of the *Manu-caritramu*, or *Story of Man*.

Peranṭālu (pl. Peranṭāḷḷu; Tel) · an auspicious woman, object of worship, usually one who has died young or chosen to enter the fire pit (*guṇḍam tŏkkaḍam*) together with her dead husband.

prabandha (Skt) · sustained poetic text with a narrative frame.

Prabhāvatī-pradyumnamu · late sixteenth-century Telugu *prabandha* about the love of Prabhāvati, daughter of the demon Vajranābha, for Pradyumna, Krishṇa's son; translated by V. Narayana Rao and D. Shulman under the title *The Demon's Daughter*.

pradosha-pūjā (Skt) · evening service in the temple.
prasādam (Skt) · food or other gifts from a deity or teacher (following *darshan*).
pūjā (Skt) · ritual worship of a deity, usually entailing offerings of flowers, coconuts, incense, or food.
purāṇa (Skt) · literally, "old"; collections of mythological traditions and other lore, in Sanskrit and the regional languages.
Pūtanā-moksha (Skt) · ritual performance of the infant Krishna's killing of the ghoulish Pūtāna.
pyol (Anglo-Indian) · the entrance porch to a traditional village house.
rāga (Skt) · a musical "mode" established by fixed ascending and descending scales (*mūrcchanā*) and characteristic phrases and musical patterns; in north Indian Hindustani music, each *rāga* is keyed to a particular hour of the day or night and, at times, to a season of the year.
rahasya (Skt) · a secret, usually metaphysical.
Rājaśekhara · poet and poetician of the late ninth and early tenth centuries; author of the *Kāvya-Mīmāṃsā* (*Science of Poetry*), a handbook for the professional education of poets.
Rāma · hero of the Sanskrit epic, *Rāmāyaṇa*; an avatar of the great god *Vishṇu*.
Ramanujan, A. K. · poet in English and Kannada, translator from Tamil and Kannada into English, folklorist and scholar who taught for many years at the University of Chicago (d. 1993).
Rāmāyaṇa · Sanskrit lyrical epic telling the story of *Rāma*, his wife Sītā, and Rāma's battle against the ten-headed demon Rāvaṇa.
revu (Tel) · a ghat or bathing place on a river.
sabhā (Skt) · literary salon.
śakti (Skt) · literally "power," "energy," specifically that of a divinity.
śakti-pīṭha (Skt) · in a shrine, the goddess's seat; more generally, a goddess shrine.
Śākuntala · more fully, *Abhijñāna-śākuntala*, a Sanskrit play by *Kālidāsa* (early fifth century AD).
samādhi (Skt) · tomb.
Sāma Veda (Skt) · the second, musical collection of canonical Vedic hymns.
sanghālu (Tel) · literary societies.

Śankara · the systematizer of *Advaita*; said to have been born in Kerala in the eighth century AD.

sannyāsin (Skt) · a renouncer who has given up family and other social ties.

satī (Skt) · death by fire; the widow's immolation on her husband's funeral pyre.

siddhi (Skt) · a magical attainment or power.

siddhi-sthala (Skt) · a site of perfection or Yogic power.

śikhara (Skt) · spire or finial crowning a temple.

Simhacalam (Tel) · mountain shrine to *Appanna/Varāha-Narasimha*, *Vishṇu* as a combination of the Boar and the Man-Lion; in the outskirts of Visakhapatnam.

sipahi (Persian) · soldier, guard.

Śiva (Skt) · one of the two major male deities; his sign is the *linga*. A dancer with long, matted locks and the moon in his hair, Śiva shares half his body with his consort, Umā/Pārvatī.

Śivarātri (Skt) · The Night of *Śiva*, a winter festival in honor of this deity.

Śrīharsha · twelfth-century author of the Sanskrit *Naishadhīya-carita*, relating the early part of the story of Nala and Damayanti.

Śrīnātha · fifteenth-century peripatetic *Telugu* poet; author of the *Bhīma-khaṇḍamu* on Daksharama, the *Naishadhamu* (a Telugu version of *Śrīharsha*'s *Naishadhīya-carita*), the *Śivarātri-māhātmyamu*, and *Kāśī-khaṇḍamu*.

stūpa (Skt) · brick or stone mound usually built around a Buddhist relic or canonical text.

sūkshma-śarīra (Skt) · the subtle body that contains the Yogic *cakra*s.

suprabhātam (Skt) · morning wake-up prayer sung in Sanskrit to the deity.

Suraa · Sundara Ramaswamy, doyen of *Tamil* prose authors in the second half of the twentieth century; author of *The Story of a Tamarind Tree*, *JJ: Some Jottings* (translated by R. Venkatachalapathy, 2003), and many other works, including poems published under the name Pacuvaiyya.

Sureśvara · considered a direct pupil of Śankarâcārya; major *Advaita* philosopher and the author of the *Naishkarmya-siddhi*.

sūtra (Skt) · short, laconic phrase, as in an authoritative scientific text.

Svārocisha Manu (Skt) · the First Man.

svayamvara (Skt) · the ceremony in which a bride chooses her husband from among the possible suitors.

Tamil · language of the state of Tamil Nadu, in the far south of the Indian Subcontinent. A continuous literary tradition in Tamil stretches from the first century AD to the present. Tamil belongs to the Dravidian family and is sister to Telugu, Kannada, and Malayalam.

tampura (Tel) · the stringed instrument that provides background drone in a vocal or instrumental concert.

tāṇḍava (Skt) · *Śiva*'s wild dance of destruction.

taniyan (Tam) · single verse of praise, often introducing a Tamil text.

Tevâram (Tam) · the canon of *Tamil* hymns to *Śiva*, sung by three poets from the second half of the first millennium CE: Tiruñānacampantar, Appar, and Cuntaramūrtti.

Tirupati Venkaṭa Kavulu · a team of poets, Divakarla Tirupati Sastri (1872–1920) and Cellapilla Venkata Sastri (1870–1950), famous for their extempore performances in turn-of-the-century Andhra.

triśūla (Skt) · the trident carried by Lord *Śiva*.

tūtar (Tam) · love messenger.

Tyāgarāja (Skt) · the mobile festival image of *Śiva* at Tiruvarur. Named for this deity is the late eighteenth- and early nineteenth-century classical composer of *Carnatic music*, also settled in Tiruvarur.

ullekhana (Skt) · "polish," the aesthetic ideal of the medieval Sanskrit poet-craftsman.

Upanishads · the final layer of the Vedic canon; works of metaphysical exploration and riddlelike discussions among sages who seek to articulate overpowering experience.

Utprekshā (Skt) · poetic fancy.

Uttarāyaṇa (Skt) · the northern progression of the Sun, after Sankrānti in mid-January.

Veda (Skt) · the foundational canonical texts of Hinduism, from the end of the second millennium BC.

veena (Skt) · South Indian lute, usually with seven strings and a large jack-wood resonator.

Veeresalingam, Kandukuri · reformer and writer, settled in Rajahmundry (1848–1919). Veeresalingam led the reformist campaign to allow widow remarriage.

Venkaṭeśvara (Skt) · the god (*Vishṇu*) at Tirupati near the southern border of Andhra Pradesh.

veshālu (Tel) · guises, such as the goddess Gangamma takes on at Tirupati each year.

Vināyaka (Skt) · the elephant-headed deity who removes obstacles from the path of his devotees; also known as *Gaṇeśa* and *Gaṇapati*.

Virāṭa-parvan (Skt) · the section of the *Mahābhārata* epic describing the period spent by the five heroes in disguise in the kingdom of Virāṭa.

Vishṇu (Skt) · god of the middle or the center; one of the two major Hindu deities in the south of India.

yantra (Skt) · a geometric design that contains a deity or makes a deity present.

Yoga-vāsishṭha mahārāmāyaṇa · eighth-century Sanskrit text composed in Kashmir dealing with issues of perception and illusion through complex, often bewildering narratives told by the sage Vasiṣṭha to *Rāma*.

Bibliography

Amichai. *Shirei Yerushalayim*. Translated by Stephen Mitchell. Jerusalem: Shocken, 1987.

Annamayya. *God on the Hill: Temple Poems from Tirupati*. Translated by Velcheru Narayana Rao and David Shulman. New York: Oxford University Press, 2005.

Ativīrarāma Pāṇṭiyaṉ. *Naiṭatam*. Madras: K. P. Cinkaravelu Mutaliyar, [1904?].

Cekkiḻār. *Pĕriya purāṇam*. Koyamputtur: Kovaittamiḻcankam, 1975.

Cuntaramūrttināyaṉār. *Tevāram*. Translated by D. Shulman as *Songs of the Harsh Devotee*. Philadelphia: Department of South Asia Studies, University of Pennsylvania, 1990.

Cuntararāmacāmi. [Suraa]. *Je. Je.: Cila kuṟippukaḷ*. Madras: Cre-A, 1986. Translated by A. R. Venkatachalapathy. as *J. J.: Some Jottings*. New Delhi: Katha, 2003.

Fallaci, Oriana. *Interview with History*. Boston: Houghton Mifflin, 1976.

Hafez. *Diwan*. Calcutta: Urdu Guide Press, 1881.

Ismayil. *Kavitalu*. Kakinada: Twinkle Publishers, 1989.

Kālidāsa. *Abhijñānaśākuntala*. Varanasi: Chowkhamba Sanskrit Series, 1976.

Leonard, John Greenfield. "Kandukuri Viresalingam, 1848–1919: A Biography of an Indian Social Reformer." Ph.D. diss., University of Wisconsin, 1970.

Mann, Thomas. *Doktor Faustus*. Frankfurt: Fischer Verlag, 1999.

Nagarajan, Ji. *Paṭaippukaḷ*. Nagercoil: Kalaccuvadu patippakam, 1997.

Narayana Rao, Velcheru, and D. Shulman. *Classical Telugu Poetry: An Anthology*. Berkeley and Los Angeles: University of California Press, 2002.

Pāskarat Tŏṇṭaimāṉ, Tŏ. Mu. *Venkaṭam mutal kumari varai: Kāvirik karaiyile*. Tirunelveli: S. R. Cuppiramaniya Pillai, 1970.

Pĕddana, Allasāni. *Manu-caritramu*. Madras: V. Ramasvamy Sastrulu and Sons, 1969.

Seferis, George. *A Poet's Journal: Days of 1945–1951*. Cambridge, MA: Harvard University Press, 1974.

Selby, Martha Ann. *The Circle of Six Seasons*. New Delhi: Penguin Books, 2003.

Siva Reddy, K. *Varsham Varsham*. Hyderabad: Published by the author, 2004.

Smile. *Okhade*. Vijayawada: Kavitvam Pracuranalu, 1990.

Śrīharsha. *Naiṣhadhīya-carita*. New Delhi: Meharchand Lachhmandas, 1986.

Śrī-jagan-mohinī-keśava-svāmi divya caritra. Ryali: Devasthanam, 2006.

Śrīnātha. *Bhīma-khaṇḍamu*. Madras: Ananda Press, 1901.

Sūranna, Pingaḷi. Kaḷāpūrṇodayamu. Translated by V. Narayana Rao and D. Shulman as *The Sound of the Kiss, or The Story That Must Never Be Told*. New York: Columbia University Press, 2002.

———. *Prabhāvatī-pradyumnamu*. Translated by V. Narayana Rao and D. Shulman as *The Demon's Daughter*. Albany: State University of New York Press, 2006.

Verissimo, Luis Fernando. *Borges and the Eternal Orangutans*. New York: New Directions, 2005.